APPLYING SQL IN BUSINESS

APPLYING SQL IN BUSINESS

Levi Reiss

La Cité collégiale and Algonquin Côllege

Mitchell McGRAW-HILL

New York St. Louis San Francisco Auckland Bogotá Caracas Hamburg
Lisbon London Madrid Mexico Milan Montreal New Delhi Paris
San Juan São Paulo Singapore Sydney Tokyo Toronto Watsonville

Mitchell **McGraw-Hill**
55 Penny Lane
Watsonville, CA 95076

Applying SQL in Business

1 2 3 4 5 6 7 8 9 0 DOH DOH 9 0 9 8 7 6 5 4 3 2 1

ISBN 0-07-051842-4

Sponsoring editor: Erika Berg
Editorial assistant: Denise Nickeson
Production director: Betty Drury
Production services by Michael Bass & Associates
    Copyedit by Elliot Simon
    Cover and text design by Gary Head, Publishing Principals
    Composition by American Composition & Graphics, Inc.
    Project management by Michael Bass
Printer: R.R. Donnelley & Sons Company

Library of Congress Catalog No. 91-062252

Concise Contents

CHAPTER 1   **Introducing SQL**   1

CHAPTER 2   **Initial Queries**   18

CHAPTER 3   **Adding Power to Your Queries**   34

CHAPTER 4   **Arithmetic and Functions**   51

CHAPTER 5   **Querying Multiple Tables (Introduction)**   67

CHAPTER 6   **Creating and Processing Tables**   88

CHAPTER 7   **Querying Multiple Tables (Intermediate)**   108

CHAPTER 8   **Views and Indexes**   130

CHAPTER 9   **Administering the System**   151

CHAPTER 10   **Interfacing SQL with Other Systems**   172

APPENDIX A   **The Case Study Database**   193

APPENDIX B   **Modifying the Case Study Database**   200

APPENDIX C   **Getting Started with dBASE IV SQL**   212

APPENDIX D   **Getting Started with Oracle SQL**   217

APPENDIX E   **Getting Started with SQL/DS**   222

GLOSSARY   229

INDEX   235

Detailed Contents

CHAPTER 1   Introducing SQL   1

Introduction   1

Databases   3

Exercises   3

Database Management Systems (DBMS)   3

Introducing Noga's Crispy Crunch   4

Structured Query Language (SQL)   5
Types of SQL Statements   5

Data Types   6

The Company's Database—First Cut   6
Customer Table   6
Purchase Table   9

Exercises   9

Productivity Tip: MAKE BACKUPS   16

Review Questions   17

CHAPTER 2   Initial Queries   18

Writing a Query   18

Designating Columns (Field Names)   21

Try It Yourself   22

The DISTINCT Qualifier   22

Exercises 23

Designating Rows (WHERE Clause) 24

Try It Yourself 25

Exercises 27

Processing Dates 27

Exercises 28

The ORDER BY Clause 28

Exercises 30

Data Validation 30

Exercises 31

Syntax and Applications Summary 31

Productivity Tip: WATCII OUT FOR RESERVED WORDS 31

Review Questions 32

Case Study Exercises 33

CHAPTER 3 Adding Power to Your Queries 34

The OR Operator 34

Exercises 35

The AND Operator 36

Exercises 37

Combining OR and AND Operators 37

Exercises 40

The NOT Operator 40

Try It Yourself 41

The IN Operator 42

The BETWEEN Operator 44

Try It Yourself 44

Exercises 45

The LIKE Operator 45

Exercises 46

Syntax and Applications Summary 46

Productivity Tip: MAKE YOUR QUERIES EASIER TO READ   48

Review Questions   49

Case Study Exercises   50

CHAPTER 4   Arithmetic and Functions   51

Arithmetic Operations   51

Exercises   52

Aggregate Functions   53

Exercises   56

The GROUP BY Clause   57

Exercises   60

The HAVING Clause   60

Exercises   60

Combining GROUP BY, HAVING, and ORDER BY Clauses   61

Exercises   62

Arithmetic Operations on Dates   62

Try It Yourself   63

Syntax and Applications Summary   63

Productivity Tip: MAKE YOUR KEYSTROKES COUNT   64

Review Questions   64

Case Study Exercises   65

CHAPTER 5   Querying Multiple Tables (Introduction)   67

The *Join* Operation   67

Try It Yourself   71

Exercises   72

The UNION Query Operator   75

Try It Yourself   77

Exercises   77

Nested Queries   78

Exercises   80
   Nested Queries Using IN, ANY, SOME, and ALL   81

Exercises   83
   Combining a Nested Query and a *Join*   83

Exercise   84

Syntax and Applications Summary   84

Productivity Tip: NOTE DOWN YOUR ERRORS   86

Review Questions   86

Case Study Exercises   87

CHAPTER 6   Creating and Processing Tables   88

Creating Tables   88
   Creating the Customer Table   89
   Creating the Purchase Table   92
   Creating the Product Table   94

Exercises   95

Deleting Tables   95

Exercises   95

Loading Data   95

Exercises   96

Updating Table Values   97

Exercises   98

Try It Yourself   98

Deleting Rows   99

Exercises   100

Updating a Table's Structure   100

Exercises   102

Try It Yourself   103

Syntax and Applications Summary   105

Productivity Tip: LEARN YOUR IMPLEMENTATION'S COMMANDS   106

Review Questions   107

Case Study Exercises   107

CHAPTER 7 Querying Multiple Tables (Intermediate) 108

Review of the *Join* Operation 108

Exercises 111

Self-*Join*s 111

Try It Yourself 114

Exercises 114

Review of Nested Queries 114

Try It Yourself 116

Exercises 116

The EXISTS Operator 116

Using a Lookup Table 118

Exercises 119

Correlated Subquery 119

Exercises 122

Syntax and Applications Summary 125

Try It Yourself 126

Productivity Tip: TEST BY HAND 127

Review Questions 127

Case Study Exercises 128

CHAPTER 8 Views and Indexes 130

Introduction 130

Views and Their Advantages 131
    Data Security 132
    Query Simplicity 133

Exercises 134
    Flexibility 135

Exercises 137
    Data Integrity 137

Try It Yourself 139

Exercises   139
   Read-Only Views   140
   Deleting a View   141
   Modifying a View   141
   Disadvantages of Views   142

Indexes   143
   Creating Indexes   143
   Deleting an Index   146

Exercises   146

Try It Yourself   146

Syntax and Applications Summary   147

Productivity Tip: TRY IT OUT   147

Review Questions   148

Case Study Exercises   148

CHAPTER 9   Administering the System   151

Administering Multiuser Databases   151

Controlling Access   153
   The GRANT Statement   153

Exercises   157

Try It Yourself   157

Exercises   158
   The REVOKE Statement   159

Exercises   160

Transaction Processing   160

The COMMIT Statement and the ROLLBACK Statement   161

Exercises   162

Locking Tables   162

Statements for Locking Tables   163

Exercises   165

Data Integrity   165
   Referential Integrity   165

Exercises   167

System Catalog   167

Exercises 167

Syntax and Applications Summary 168

Productivity Tip: MAKE USERS IDENTIFY THEMSELVES 169

Review Questions 169

Case Study Exercises 171

CHAPTER 10 Interfacing SQL with Other Systems 172

Introduction 172

SQL-dBASE IV Interface 173

Exercises 176

SQL-R:BASE Interface 178

Exercises 180

Embedded SQL 180
  Data Entry 181
  Processing 181
  Output 182
  Embedding SQL in COBOL 182
  The Cursor Structure 186

Exercises 189

Syntax and Applications Summary 190

Productivity Tip: DON'T REINVENT THE WHEEL 190

Review Questions 191

Case Study Exercises 191

APPENDIX A The Case Study Database 193

Introduction 193

Full Version of the Database—First Cut 193
  Column Descriptions for the Cds Table and the Smlcds Table 194
  Column Descriptions for the Manufs Table 196

Small Version of the Database—First Cut 196
  Entering Data into the Tables 197

APPENDIX B   Modifying the Case Study Database   200

Introduction   200

Step I Modifying the Cds Table or the Smlcds Table   200
Modifying the Cds Table Structure   201
Modifying the Smlcds Table Structure   201

Step II Loading Data into the Cds Table or the Smlcds Table   202
Entering Data into the Cds Table   202
Entering Data into the Smlcds Table   203

Step III Creating the Works Table or the Smlworks Table   204
Creating the Works Table   204
Column Descriptions for the Works
    Table and the Smlworks Table   204
Creating the Smlworks Table   208

**Step IV Loading Data into the Works
Table or the Smlworks Table**   209
Entering Data into the Works Table   209
Entering Data into the Smlworks Table   209

APPENDIX C   Getting Started with dBASE IV SQL   212

Introduction   212

General Comments   212

Individual Chapters   213

APPENDIX D   Getting Started with Oracle SQL   217

Introduction   217

General Comments   217

Individual Chapters   218

Saving Queries   220

Reporting Formatting   220

APPENDIX E   Getting Started with SQL/DS   222

Introduction   222
General Comments   222
Individual Chapters   223
Saving Queries   225
Report Formatting   226

GLOSSARY   229

INDEX   235

Preface to the Instructor

Who Should Use This Book?

Structured Query Language (SQL) has become the standard database access language for computers of all sizes. SQL no longer is the exclusive domain of computer professionals, however. Business students with no interest in computer programming are learning SQL so that they can extract information from databases and make better business decisions. APPLYING SQL IN BUSINESS is designed for the growing number of students who need to tame their databases, whether or not they intend to become computer gurus.

Some students will use this book as a language supplement in a database management course; others, as a stand-alone text to demonstrate such principles as database administration, security, and integrity and their SQL implementation. In either case, when students master APPLYING SQL IN BUSINESS they will cross a line: They will now be able to extract information from a database by themselves, instead of relying on others.

Distinguishing Features

Applications Orientation Our central focus is on how SQL meets the expanding information needs of a new business. Most students need more than an answer to "What is SQL?" They want to apply SQL to solving business problems. Therefore we start by describing information needs in business terms, then present applicable SQL syntax as relevant to satisfying a perceived business need. This need-driven approach makes the otherwise abstract syntax easier for students to comprehend and retain.

Case Studies SQL's applications are multiple. Our ongoing case study employs SQL to organize a classical music compact disk collection. The abbreviated version of this case includes 7–10 exercises per chapter, ideal for light coverage of SQL; the in-depth version includes 10–14 exercises per chapter and supports more extensive coverage. Both versions extract data from our compact disk collection thus bridging the gap between the neat, simple data found in typical case studies and the more irregular, complex data of the real world.

Extensive Examples   Every chapter contains about 12 worked examples, fully integrated into the business application. These examples present new syntax in small increments, instead of overwhelming students. Most chapters contain figures placed side by side as a teaching tool. For example, Figure 2-3a SELECTs a single column, while Figure 2-3b repeats this command using the DISTINCT qualifier. The student sees the impact of the DISTINCT qualifier immediately. We've limited the number of examples to avoid "information overload."

Coverage of Common Errors   No matter how clearly examples are presented, students make errors. Instead of denying this reality, it's addressed in every chapter. An extensive discussion of common errors including syntax errors, logic errors, and hidden logic errors saves students (and the occasional instructor) hours of time and frustration. Addressing these errors helps students think critically instead of blindly accepting computer output.

Productivity Tips   This boxed feature found in every chapter reveals professional programmers' secrets to novices. For example, the productivity tip in Chapter 4 entitled "Make Your Keystrokes Count" describes the keystrokes that repeat previous commands. By following these practical tips students will work smarter instead of just harder—in class, and throughout their professional lives.

Most Popular Versions of SQL   Unlike most textbooks, we point out differences among popular SQL versions. The "Try It Yourself" exercises in each chapter address likely differences between the text and the SQL version actually used. They encourage students to uncover the answer themselves, an essential real-world skill. Appendices C, D, and E describe the particularities of dBASE IV SQL, Oracle SQL , and SQL/DS, thus enabling students to cope with the different versions of SQL.

Comprehensive Instructor's Manual with Transparency Masters

The Instructor's Manual that accompanies APPLYING SQL IN BUSINESS includes for each chapter a detailed lecture outline, teaching tips, a discussion of potential pitfalls, test questions and answers, and answers to review questions and solutions to exercises in the text. The solutions often are accompanied by a discussion of potential errors, and illustrated by overhead transparency masters. Other overhead transparency masters illustrate key figures in the text.

Acknowledgments

A textbook such as this one is never the product of a single individual. I would like to express my sincere appreciation to my editor Erika Berg of Mitchell Publishing, Inc., who guided me throughout the transformation of this book from our minds to your desk. I have been very happy with the production and design experts who have converted computer output virtually covered in pen and pencil comments and corrections to an attractive volume, designed for pedagogy and not sheer beauty alone. They are Betty Drury of Mitchell Publishing, Inc., and the independent consultants Michael Bass, Gary Head, and Elliot Simon.

Traces of our reviewers' comments and suggestions may be seen on every page of this text and countless more pages in landfills. They are: Len Fertuck, University of Toronto; Ranjan Kini, University of North Carolina at Greensboro; Robert Norton, San Diego Mesa College; Darleen Pigford, Western Illinois University; Tarun Sen, Virginia Polytechnic Institute and State University; and Stuart Varden, Pace University.

The final acknowledgment goes, you might have guessed, to my wife, Noga Shiloni Reiss and to Noga's Crispy Crunch, without whom this book would not have been possible.

Levi Reiss

Preface to the Student

Learning SQL is a challenge for computer users of the 1990s. Mastering SQL will enable you to create databases for all sizes of computers and to extract data that satisfies your information needs—whether you own your own business, or work for a small, medium, or large company or nonprofit organization.

You have three tools to master this material: your teacher, your computer, and this textbook. We have made every effort to produce a textbook that will maximize your learning environment. The Distinguishing Features section earlier in the Preface to the Instructor describes many of the features of this text that have been designed to help you attain your goal of applying SQL.

In addition, each chapter contains pedagogical features designed with you in mind, namely:

- Software Exercises that test your understanding of the chapter's new SQL commands, and their integration with SQL commands presented in previous chapters.

- Try It Yourself exercises that record your findings about how SQL behaves on your computer.

- Boxed features that set off and summarize key concepts within the text.

- Syntax and Applications Summary that serve as a quick reference to the chapter's SQL commands and how they are applied.

- Review Questions that complement the chapter objectives in determining your level of understanding.

- A Chapter Summary that presents a synopsis of the present chapter and introduces the next one.

A Final Word: Keep this book. The increasing popularity of SQL on computer systems of all sizes makes it likely that, sooner or later, you will be asked to generate SQL queries. And remember, if you can't, someone else can.

CHAPTER ONE

Introducing SQL

We interweave in this chapter fundamental notions about data and databases, a programming language that processes databases, and a small firm whose information needs evolve continuously. As you proceed, you meet relational database management systems, Structured Query Language (SQL), and Noga Shiloni, proud owner of Noga's Crispy Crunch. Noga is learning Structured Query Language to process her business's relational database.

OBJECTIVES

You have met this chapter's objectives when you can:

- Define in your own words the following terms: *data, information, database, database management system (DBMS), relational database management system (RDBMS), Structured Query Language (SQL), data type.*
- State the advantages of relational database management systems.
- Set up a draft table structure to meet an information problem of your choosing.
- Create the initial database for a fictitious firm (Noga's Crispy Crunch), and enter data into it (at the instructor's option).

Introduction

People and organizations need data to function. Let's say that you're rushing to your English 201 class. Getting to class requires precise answers to two questions: (1) When is the class? (2) Where is the class? Partial answers are not good enough, for unless you know the building, the room number, and the day and time of the class, you'll miss it. It is insufficient to know that English 201 is held in Thompson Hall or even in Thompson Hall, Room 217, unless you remember that it takes place on Wednesdays from 8:30 to 10:00. Students attending more than one class must carefully organize their schedule data. (In a computer context, **data** may be defined as the facts and figures that comprise the raw material supplied to a computer for processing. **Information** is the processed data available for use by an individual. One person's data may be another person's information.)

Consider the following possible schedule for a student taking five courses. (We have made several simplifications. For example, we assume that each individual course is taught in two 90-minute sessions per week, and that both sessions use the same classroom. An exercise later in the chapter examines a more realistic description.)

Course Number	Course Title	Building	Room	Day #1	Time #1	Day #2	Time #2
ENG201	Shakespeare I	Thompson	217	Wed	8:30	Fri	10:00
BIO312	Reptile Anatomy	Kirk	377	Mon	4:30	Thu	8:30
CSC211	Intro. to SQL	Debussy	909	Mon	2:00	Fri	8:30
CSC219	C Language	Debussy	808	Tue	2:00	Thu	4:30
MAT201	Computer Math I	MathAnnex	121	Mon	8:30	Wed	10:00

This schedule presents data in an organized fashion. It is a two-dimensional table composed of five rows and eight columns. Each row describes a single course. Each row contains eight data items in the same order: course number, course title, building, etc. The individual rows can be identified by either the course number or the course name.

Each column contains five associated data items. A column header such as "Course Number" describes each column's contents. The leftmost column contains the course number, for example, *ENG201* or *CSC219*. Columns may contain duplicate values; for example, the value 8:30 appears twice in the "Time #2" column. A student may have two 8:30 classes, but not scheduled for the same day.

A single table rarely contains all the data needed for a given application. A student may require a Professor table containing each professor's name, rank, classes taught, office, and office hours. Students may also find useful a Little Black Book table with the names, addresses, and telephone numbers of friends and acquaintances, and an Assignment table that includes descriptions and due dates of papers and programming assignments.

Tables are organized to meet specific information needs. The administration's version of a Professor table might contain each professor's name, rank, salary, classes taught, office, telephone number, administrative duties, and research publications. The two Professor tables, student version and administration version, include both common columns and different columns. A

Professor table designed for the faculty association would differ from these other two Professor tables. Related tables may form a *database.*

Databases

A **database** is an organized collection of associated data. Appropriately organized data may be readily accessed. The database components and their interrelationships vary according to its users and their information objectives. Limited information needs mean small, relatively simple databases. As information needs grow, the database grows larger and more complex.

> E X E R C I S E S
> 1. List the column names for a more realistic version of the Student Scheduling table. Indicate sample data for five rows in the table.
> 2. Describe an additional table that you might find useful. List the column names, and indicate sample data for five rows in the table.

Databases are not necessarily computerized. A student database containing only schedule and professor data does not warrant computerization. The student can retrieve any desired information item more rapidly by hand than by computer. In general, small databases do not require a computer. Medium and large databases are usually computerized.

A database for college administrators might encompass several hundred courses. Many courses are not offered for two 90-minute periods a week in the same room. The administrator's database should incorporate additional course-related data such as semesters offered, prerequisites, lab fees, and maximum number of students. This database should include the administrator's version of the Professor table, and a table describing classrooms. Other useful tables include Payroll tables for both academic and nonacademic staff, Library and Bookstore tables, and Equipment tables. Such large and complex databases are processed by computers equipped with software known as *database management systems.*

Database Management Systems (DBMS)

A **database management system (DBMS)** is a collection of computer software that creates, organizes, and manages databases. Such systems are commercially available for computers of all sizes, including microcomputers. Some database management systems are specifically designed to run on a series of computers ranging from microcomputers to multimillion dollar supercomputers. This text focuses on **relational database management systems (RDBMSs)**.

In 1970 Dr. E. F. Codd, then working for IBM, published a paper presenting the theoretical foundations of relational databases. Relational databases are based on a series of tables. Our previous examples could form part of a relational database. The business world, classrooms, and research laboratories have focused on relational DBMSs for the past several years. Virtually all microcomputer-based DBMSs are based on the relational model. Just by looking at the tables, even nontechnical users can obtain a fair idea of the database's contents and organization. With a little training, they can extract data from a relational database. With a little more training, they can design and modify their own relational databases. This textbook explores how an owner of a small business designs and processes a relational database to meet evolving information needs. Before presenting SQL, which is the programming language used to create and process the firm's database, we introduce Noga of Noga's Crispy Crunch, a small candy manufacturer.

Introducing Noga's Crispy Crunch

Noga Shiloni came to North America about a dozen years ago. While learning how to deal with a new language, a new job, a new culture, and new friends, she spent her little free time working with an old passion, candy making. She adapted an old-country recipe to the available ingredients and to customer tastes. Everybody loved her candy. It was crispy, it was crunchy; they called it Noga's Crispy Crunch.

First she gave the candy away, then she made small orders for friends, neighbors, and co-workers. Month by month her sales volume increased. Before long she faced a dilemma. She could completely abandon her leisure time, or she could stop making the candy and antagonize everyone she knew, or she could launch a business. A little reflection convinced her there was only one choice.

Noga was very cautious. She developed a detailed business plan. Her projected sales figures were quite conservative. She carefully selected a site and the candy-making equipment. She launched a limited advertising campaign. Everything was well thought out, well planned, and low key—everything except for the opening day (and night) celebration. It was all the candy you could eat, and she had to disappear into the kitchen three times to keep the candy coming.

When at last the invited and uninvited guests were filtering out, Noga's Uncle Mike arrived. "Noga," he said, "since I closed the pizzeria I don't need my computer. What are you doing for a computer?" "Why would I want a computer?" Noga replied. By the end of the party, Noga was the owner of a four-year-old microcomputer (an IBM-XT clone) equipped with a relational database management system, running **Structured Query Language**, abbreviated **SQL**.

Structured Query Language (SQL)

SQL, pronounced either "ess queue ell" or "sequel," is a computer language designed to process relational databases. In 1974 IBM released a prototype of SQL based on the research of Codd and other computer scientists. The present SQL was first developed in 1981 by a firm now called Oracle Corporation. Since then, numerous versions of SQL have been developed for a wide range of computers, including microcomputers. The American National Standards Institute (ANSI) has played a key role in the standardization of SQL. In 1989 it published two documents on which current versions of SQL are based: "Database Language—SQL with Integrity Enhancement" (reference number ANSI X3.135–1989) and "Database Language—Embedded SQL" (reference number ANSI X3.168–1989). However, since most software manufacturers introduce features intended to make their product special, in spite of the common name, different SQL versions boast different features. Converting one SQL application to run on another computer is usually easier than converting an application written in a traditional programming language, such as COBOL. However, converting SQL applications is not always trivial, in particular when advanced SQL features are used. Most examples in this text rely on standard SQL features, that is, those available on virtually all versions of SQL.

SQL performs activities via precise instructions known as *commands* or *statements.* SQL statements are commonly divided into four major functional groups: data definition statements, data manipulation statements, data query statements, and data control statements. The four command groups are quite similar, and the language grammar or syntax for one command group often applies to other command groups. Nontechnical users such as Noga use data query statements most often.

Types of SQL Statements

Data definition statements, such as CREATE TABLE and ALTER TABLE, operate on SQL structures called *tables.* These commands define a table's columns, add or delete columns, and delete unneeded tables. SQL enables users to create or modify *views,* which are special working versions of one or more tables. We introduce data definition commands later in this chapter.

Data manipulation statements enter, modify, or delete data within the SQL tables. These statements include INSERT INTO and UPDATE. We introduce data manipulation statements later in this chapter.

Data query statements retrieve data from one or more tables within the database. The key data query statement is the SELECT command, which is the single most widely used SQL command. Many nontechnical users restrict their knowledge of SQL to this single command. The SELECT command is covered in several chapters, starting with Chapter 2.

Data control statements, such as GRANT and REVOKE, deal with a user's right to access and process databases. The appropriate use of these statements may increase the database security. Data control statements are discussed in Chapter 9.

Data Types

Columns within the database are assigned a given **data type,** for example, CHARACTER (or CHAR), REAL, and INTEGER. The data type indicates the kind of data allowed. A column assigned the data type INTEGER may contain only whole number values such as 14 and −193. It may *not* contain such values as 14.75, Cashew, and ***. The SQL standard encompasses the SMALLINT data type, which is similar to the INTEGER data type but more efficient for small integers. The database uses a REAL data type to indicate, for instance, the number of kilos of candy ordered such as 3.5 and 15.0. Noga's Crispy Crunch database uses the CHARACTER data type for customer names such as Jones, Joe, and The Candy Kid. The SQL standard does not define a DATE data type, but most versions of SQL do. DATE-type columns contain values such as 10/28/1992 or 10/28/92. Because DATE is not part of the SQL standard, each SQL implementation handles DATE data types in its own way. See Box 1-1 for more detail.

We next apply SQL to set up a relational database for Noga's business.

The Company's Database—First Cut

Noga never seemed to have enough time to work with the computer. At her first free minute, she was on the phone to Uncle Mike to ask for help in getting her started on the computer. That evening they examined her information needs and considered how to design the data tables to meet those needs. If her candies prove as popular on the market as they are with friends and neighbors, the business will continue to grow. A growing business will require an ever larger and more complex database.

The present database consists of two tables, Customer and Purchase. Each table includes relatively few rows, letting us focus on the essential aspects of SQL. The Customer table describes ten of Noga's customers. The Purchase table describes candy purchases made on October 28 and 29, 1992. As we will see, it is easy to link data from the Customer and Purchase tables.

Customer Table

The Customer table contains basic information about Noga's Crispy Crunch customers. It contains six *columns,* or *fields:* customer name, customer number,

BOX 1-1

Data Types

Many SQL implementations allow the data types listed in the following table.

Data Type	SQL Syntax	Sample Data	Comments
Character	CHAR(length)	7 77th Ave. 231 Globe Blvd.	For nonnumeric data, including labels. Fixed length. Data with type CHAR(18) requires 18 positions.
	VARCHAR(length)		For nonnumeric data, including labels. Variable length (listed length indicates maximum). Not universally implemented.
		7 77th Ave. 231 Globe Blvd.	Requires 11 positions. Requires 15 positions.
Numeric	INTEGER	1234567893 −212589	For whole-number data, and sometimes for identifiers. A whole number between −2147483648 and +2147483647 if signed. Commas not allowed.
	SMALLINT	12 −555	For whole-number data, and sometimes for identifiers, within the following limits: A whole number between −32768 and +32767 if signed. Some implementations convert to INTEGER.
	DECIMAL(p, s) REAL(p, s) *or* NUMERIC(p, s)	3.7, −11.2	For data involving decimal points. p for precision, number of digits; s for scale, number of digits after the decimal point. Maximum p often 15. s is optional.
	FLOAT	3.1E + 12	Often for scientific applications. Very large or very small numbers.
Date	DATE	10/29/1992	For recording and processing dates. Not a standard. Implementations vary widely.

customer type, address, zip code, and phone number. Individual columns are briefly described next. Box 1-2 describes these columns in greater detail.

Custnum designates the "Customer Number" column. It is an INTEGER or SMALLINT column identifying rows or customers in the Customer table. A sample value of Custnum is *41*. This column links Customer table data with Purchase table data.

Custname designates the "Customer Name" column. It is a CHARACTER column 18 characters wide. A sample value of Custname is *Montag, Susie*.

Custtype designates the "Customer Type" column. It is a CHARACTER column whose width is 1. Legal values are *W* (for *wholesale*—selling to stores), *R* (for *retail*—selling to individuals), and *P* (for *private)*.

Custaddr designates the "Customer Address" column. It is a CHARACTER column whose width is 15. A sample value is *981 Montview*.

Zipcode designates the "Zip Code" column. It is a CHARACTER column whose width is 5. A sample Zipcode is *91213*.

Phone designates the "Telephone Number" column. It is a CHARACTER column of width 8. A sample telephone number is *456-2091*.

BOX 1-2

The Customer Table

Custnum—The customer number is a relatively small integer. Depending on your SQL implementation, Custnum is either a SMALLINT or an INTEGER data type. Note that because this column undergoes no arithmetic operations, it could be designated as a CHARACTER column.

Custname—The width of this column was chosen to simplify output. A more realistic value is 30 characters.

Custtype—Noga doesn't use *I* for *individual,* because the letter *I* might be interpreted to mean *industrial*. To reduce the chance of error, use only uppercase letters. Mike suggested that Noga include this column to help analyze the business's prospects as well as keep track of its activities. Customer rows and associated Purchase rows provide a gold mine of customer information, including purchasing habits. Noga might eventually apply this information to help build marketing campaigns and introduce new products.

Custaddr—To simplify the output, we have chosen a small value, in this case 15 characters.

Zipcode—The zip code is a key factor in organizing market research. It may help set up delivery routes if the business institutes a delivery service. Defining the zip code as a CHARACTER(5) column excludes processing seven- and nine-character American zip codes and Canadian postal codes such as *K1J 3X4*. Business expansion may require Noga to redefine this column.

Phone—Because her business is strictly local, Noga is not including the area code. Once again, Noga may have to change this column to meet future business needs.

Purchase Table

The Purchase table contains basic information about Noga's Crispy Crunch purchases. It contains six columns, or fields: purchase number, product number, customer number, purchase date, ready date, and number of kilos purchased. Individual columns are briefly described next. Box 1-3 describes these columns in greater detail.

Purchnum designates the "Purchase Number" column. It is an INTEGER or a SMALLINT column. Since a single purchase number identifies a customer's purchase of one or several types of candy, the Purchnum column is insufficient to identify uniquely a row in the Purchase table. A sample value is *1236*. (Note that two rows have this purchase number, one with product number 1 and one with product number 3.)

Prodnum designates the "Product Number" column, identifying the type of candy sold. It is an INTEGER or a SMALLINT column. Sample values are *1* and *3*.

Custnum designates the "Customer Number" column. It is an INTEGER or a SMALLINT column that appears in both the Purchase table and the Customer table. A sample value is *41*.

Purchdat designates the column indicating the purchase date. It is a DATE-type column. A sample value is *10/28/1992*, depending on the SQL implementation.

Readydat designates the column indicating when the candy is ready for pickup. The ready date should have the same format as the purchase date. A sample value is *10/28/1992*, depending on the SQL implementation.

Kilos designates the column indicating the number of kilos sold of a given product type. It is a DECIMAL or REAL column, with one digit after the decimal point. A sample value is *3.7*.

E X E R C I S E S

3. List and describe columns for a Returns table. Indicate sample data for five rows in this table.

We next comment on relational tables in general and the Customer and Purchase tables in particular.

Unlike many noncomputerized tables, relational databases treat rows and columns quite differently. Each row is identified by one or more unique fields, called the *key*. Keys are discussed in detail in Chapter 6. The customer number identifies rows in the Customer table. In combination, the purchase number and the product number identify rows in the Purchase table. Although it may not be obvious from the data in a given table, rows need not occur in any specific order. Chapter 2 shows us how to sort the table by any desired column, such as Custname or Custtype.

BOX 1-3

The Purchase Table

Purchnum—This column's data type is INTEGER or SMALLINT. The system automatically rejects the value 12.56 because of the decimal point. At a later stage Noga might want the system to reject negative purchase numbers such as −4343 and check for valid purchase numbers.

Prodnum—At present, legal product numbers are 1 to 5. A growing business will add new products and perhaps abandon some old ones. Like the Purchnum column, the Prodnum column does not uniquely identify Purchase table rows. The combination of the Purchnum column and the Prodnum column uniquely identifies rows in the Purchase table. For example, although the Purchase table contains two rows with purchase number 1236 and four rows with product number 1, it contains only one row with purchase number 1236 and product number 1.

Custnum—In the Purchase table the "Customer Number" identifies who made a given purchase; for example, customer number 41 made purchase number 1236. Custnum does not always uniquely identify a purchase. While customer number 41 made a single purchase, customer number 24 made purchases 1235 and 1239. The Customer table identifies customers by number rather than by name. Noga's business has no problem dealing with two customers named John Smith. The business will simply issue the second Mr. Smith a different customer number from the first. The Custnum column uniquely identifies customers in the Customer table. Only one customer has customer number 24. At present the Custnum column provides the only link between the Customer table and the Purchase table.

Purchdat—The benefits of the DATE data type should be fairly obvious. The system will reject illegal dates such as January 32 and 13/14/94 for DATE-type columns. Recall that each SQL implementation provides its own set of acceptable DATE formats. We choose to use the American standard format MM/DD/YYYY, for example, 12/24/1992. According to this format, dates such as 24/12/1992 are illegal; there is no 24th month. Be careful when entering dates: 06/08/1992 is not the same as 08/06/92, but both are acceptable under the American standard format.

Readydat—The "Purchase Date" and "Ready Date" columns should have the same format. (Recording one date in MM/DD/YYYY format and the other in DD/MM/YYYY or even MM/DD/YY format is asking for trouble.) However, they need not contain the same values. A customer may order candy on December 15th to be ready for a party on the 20th. Our tables do not include a ready time. Company policy states that orders may be picked up after noon on the ready date.

Kilos—Noga chooses its maximum value to be 99.9 kilos. (When Noga expects to produce Crispy Crunch by the ton, she can change this limit. By then the company will have outgrown this simple system.) SQL does not automatically ensure that this column is greater than 0.

Noga is so optimistic that she doesn't consider a Returns table. She does consider terminology presented in Box 1-4.

BOX 1 - 4

Rows, Columns, and Synonyms

A major reason for the success of relational databases is their "intuitive" presentation of data to nontechnical users. We choose to discuss relational databases in nontechnical terms: *table, row,* and *column*. Those familiar with traditional file processing may recognize the terms: *file, record,* and *field*. Relational database researchers often use the terms: *relation, tuple,* and *attribute*.

Relational DBMS	File Processing	Technical Term
Table	File	Relation
Row	Record	Tuple
Column	Field	Attribute

Column names are unique; a given table may not include two columns called *Zipcode*. There is no restriction on duplication of information within a column. For example, Noga's customers could all have the same zip code.

The two tables contain a different number of rows. The Customer table contains ten rows. Most rows in this table represent customers who purchased candy on October 28th or 29th. The table includes a few others, such as customer number 1, Jones, Joe, who did not purchase candy on these dates. The Purchase table contains 14 rows, representing purchases made on October 28th or 29th, well before the Christmas rush.

A customer may make none, one, or several purchases. In other words, a Customer table row (see customer number 1) need not correspond to any rows in the Purchase table. However, the reverse is not true. If purchase number 1235 has no customer number, Noga would not know whom to bill for the candy ordered.

Every row in the Purchase table must correspond to one and only one customer. Only one customer is billed for a given purchase. Noga issues new customers a customer number before recording their purchase. A customer may purchase more than one type of candy at the same time. In this case the Purchase table includes several rows, one for each product number. Different types of candy on a single purchase number (such as 1241) may be picked up on different days.

Some data columns may remain empty. (For example, Al Waterman never gave Noga his unlisted phone number.) On the other hand, we may expect that both retail and wholesale customers will have listed phone numbers.

Customer table data is shown in Figure 1-1. We interpret the first row of the Customer table as follows: Customer number 1 is Jones, Joe. He is a private customer whose address is 1234 Main St. with zip code 91212 and phone number 434-1231.

Custnum	Custname	Custtype	Custaddr	Zipcode	Phone
1	Jones, Joe	P	1234 Main St.	91212	434-1231
4	Armstrong, Inc.	R	231 Globe Blvd.	91212	434-7664
12	Swedish Burgers	R	1889 20th N.E.	91213	434-9090
13	Pickled Pickles	R	194 CityView	91289	324-8909
22	The Candy Kid	W	2121 Main St.	91212	563-4545
24	Waterman, Al	P	23 Yankee Blvd.	91234	-0-
37	Bobby Bon Bons	R	12 Nichi Cres.	91212	434-9045
39	Crowsh, Elias	P	7 77th Ave.	91211	434-0007
41	Montag, Susie	P	981 Montview	91213	456-2091
42	Columberg Sweets	W	239 East Falls	91209	874-9092

Figure 1-1 Customer Table Data

Purchase table data is shown in Figure 1-2. We interpret the first row of the Purchase table as follows: Purchase number 1234 is for product number 1, purchased by customer number 22. The purchase date is 10/28/1992, and the ready date is 10/28/1992. This candy order is for 3.5 kilograms.

Purchnum	Prodnum	Custnum	Purchdat	Readydat	Kilos
1234	1	22	10/28/1992	10/28/1992	3.5
1235	2	24	10/28/1992	10/30/1992	15.0
1236	1	41	10/28/1992	10/28/1992	2.0
1236	3	41	10/28/1992	10/28/1992	3.7
1237	3	4	10/28/1992	11/02/1992	3.7
1238	1	37	10/29/1992	10/29/1992	3.7
1238	2	37	10/29/1992	10/29/1992	1.2
1238	3	37	10/29/1992	10/29/1992	4.4
1239	2	24	10/29/1992	10/30/1992	3.0
1240	2	42	10/29/1992	10/31/1992	14.0
1240	5	42	10/29/1992	11/02/1992	4.8
1241	1	13	10/29/1992	10/29/1992	1.0
1241	5	13	10/29/1992	10/30/1992	7.6
1242	5	12	10/29/1992	10/29/1992	3.5

Figure 1-2 Purchase Table Data

Our next step is to create these two tables and then enter the data. Computerizing the tables involves a two-step process. First use the CREATE TABLE command to create the Customer table and the Purchase table. Then use the INSERT INTO command to enter data into these tables. The CREATE TABLE and INSERT INTO commands are explained in detail in Chapter 6.

Creating the Customer Table. To create the Customer table, enter the command shown in Figure 1-3a or the command shown in Figure 1-3b. The version in Figure 1-3a should run on all SQL implementations, perhaps with minor changes. The version in Figure 1-3b is more sophisticated but does not run on all SQL implementations.

```
a                                    b
CREATE TABLE Customer    CREATE TABLE Customer
(Custnum      INTEGER,   (Custnum      SMALLINT UNIQUE NOT NULL,
Custname     CHAR(18),   Custname     CHAR(18) NOT NULL,
Custtype     CHAR(1),    Custtype     CHAR(1),
Custaddr     CHAR(15),   Custaddr     CHAR(15),
Zipcode      CHAR(5),    Zipcode      CHAR(5),
Phone        CHAR(8) );  Phone        CHAR(8) );
```

Figure 1-3 Two Ways of CREATEing the Customer Table Structure

Check the CREATE TABLE Customer command carefully before entering it. If you notice a mistake after entering the CREATE command, enter the command

```
DROP TABLE  Customer;
```

and then reenter the CREATE TABLE Customer command. The DROP TABLE command deletes a data table. It should be used with extreme caution. It is described in Chapter 6.

Creating the Purchase Table. To create the Purchase table, enter the command shown in Figure 1-4a or the command shown in Figure 1-4b. The version in Figure 1-4a should run on all SQL implementations, perhaps with a few changes. The version in Figure 1-4b is more sophisticated but does not run on all SQL implementations.

Check the CREATE TABLE Purchase command carefully before entering it. If you notice a mistake after entering the CREATE command, enter the command

```
DROP TABLE  Purchase;
```

and then reenter the CREATE TABLE Purchase command.

Entering Data into the Customer Table. Enter data (or, technically speaking, *load* data) into the Customer table with the commands shown in Figure 1-5. *Note:* Pay particular attention when entering data for customer Waterman, Al ([6]), whose telephone number is absent (null value).

a		b	
CREATE TABLE Purchase		CREATE TABLE Purchase	
(Purchnum	INTEGER,	(Purchnum	SMALLINT NOT NULL,
Prodnum	INTEGER,	Prodnum	SMALLINT NOT NULL,
Custnum	INTEGER,	Custnum	SMALLINT NOT NULL,
Purchdat	DATE,	Purchdat	DATE,
Readydat	DATE,	Readydat	DATE,
Kilos	DECIMAL(3,1),	Kilos	DECIMAL(3,1));
UNIQUE	(Purchnum, Prodnum));		

Figure 1-4 Two Ways of CREATEing the Purchase Table Structure

```
[ 1] INSERT INTO Customer
        VALUES(1, 'Jones, Joe', 'P', '1234 Main St.', '91212',
        '434-1231');
[ 2] INSERT INTO Customer
        VALUES(4, 'Armstrong, Inc.', 'R', '231 Globe Blvd.',
        '91212', '434-7664');
[ 3] INSERT INTO Customer
        VALUES(12, 'Swedish Burgers', 'R', '1889 20th N.E.',
        '91213', '434-9090');
[ 4] INSERT INTO Customer
        VALUES(13, 'Pickled Pickles', 'R', '194 CityView',
        '91289', '324-8909');
[ 5] INSERT INTO Customer
        VALUES(22, 'The Candy Kid', 'W', '2121 Main St.',
        '91212', '563-4545');
[ 6] INSERT INTO Customer (Custnum, Custname, Custtype,
        Custaddr, Zipcode)
        VALUES(24, 'Waterman, Al', 'P', '23 Yankee Blvd.',
        '91234');
[ 7] INSERT INTO Customer
        VALUES(37, 'Bobby Bon Bons', 'R', '12 Nichi Cres.',
        '91212', '434-9045');
[ 8] INSERT INTO Customer
        VALUES(39, 'Crowsh, Elias', 'P', '7 77th Ave.', '91211',
```

```
                 '434-0007');
[ 9] INSERT INTO Customer
          VALUES(41, 'Montag, Susie', 'P', '981 Montview', '91213',
          '456-2091');
[10] INSERT INTO Customer
          VALUES(42, 'Columberg Sweets', 'W', '239 East Falls,
          '91209', '874-9092');
```

Figure 1-5 INSERTing Data into the Customer Table. The brackets [   ] and the numbers in the brackets must *not* be entered; they are included here to help you keep track of the commands.

It is necessary to verify the data entered. To do so, display your results with the following command (discussed in Chapter 2):

```
SELECT * FROM  Customer;
```

and compare the output with Figure 1-1. Note that many SQL implementations show a blank instead of -0- for Waterman's telephone number. Let's suppose that by accident you entered customer number 13's address as *194 ViewCity* instead of the correct value, *194 CityView*. Make the change by entering the following command (discussed in Chapter 6):

```
UPDATE   Customer
   SET   Custaddr = '194 CityView'
 WHERE   Custnum = 13;
```

Note that you may have to enter this command on a single line. Coding SQL statements on several lines is discussed in Chapter 2.

Entering Data into the Purchase Table. Enter data into the Purchase table with the commands shown in Figure 1-6. Display your results with the command

```
SELECT * FROM  Purchase;
```

and compare the output with Figure 1-2. Let's suppose that by accident you entered the Kilos value for purchase number 1236 and product number 3 as *4.7* instead of the correct value, *3.7*. Make the change by entering the command

```
UPDATE   Customer
   SET   Kilos = 3.7
 WHERE   Purchnum = 1236 AND Prodnum = 3;
```

```
[ 1]  INSERT INTO Purchase
      VALUES(1234, 1, 22, '10/28/1992', '10/28/1992', 3.5);
[ 2]  INSERT INTO Purchase
      VALUES(1235, 2, 24, '10/28/1992', '10/30/1992', 15.0);
[ 3]  INSERT INTO Purchase
      VALUES(1236, 1, 41, '10/28/1992', '10/28/1992', 2.0);
[ 4]  INSERT INTO Purchase
      VALUES(1236, 3, 41, '10/28/1992', '10/28/1992', 3.7);
[ 5]  INSERT INTO Purchase
      VALUES(1237, 3, 4, '10/28/1992', '11/02/1992', 3.7);
[ 6]  INSERT INTO Purchase
      VALUES(1238, 1, 37, '10/29/1992', '10/29/1992', 3.7);
[ 7]  INSERT INTO Purchase
      VALUES(1238, 2, 37, '10/29/1992', '10/29/1992', 1.2);
[ 8]  INSERT INTO Purchase
      VALUES(1238, 3, 37, '10/29/1992', '10/29/1992', 4.4);
[ 9]  INSERT INTO Purchase
      VALUES(1239, 2, 24, '10/29/1992', '10/30/1992', 3.0);
[10]  INSERT INTO Purchase
      VALUES(1240, 2, 42, '10/29/1992', '10/31/1992', 14.0);
[11]  INSERT INTO Purchase
      VALUES(1240, 5, 42, '10/29/1992', '11/02/1992', 4.8);
[12]  INSERT INTO Purchase
      VALUES(1241, 1, 13, '10/29/1992', '10/29/1992', 1.0);
[13]  INSERT INTO Purchase
      VALUES(1241, 5, 13, '10/29/1992', '10/30/1992', 7.6);
[14]  INSERT INTO Purchase
      VALUES(1242, 5, 12, '10/29/1992', '10/29/1992', 3.5);
```

Figure 1-6 INSERTing Data into the Purchase Table. The brackets [   ] and the numbers in the brackets must *not* be entered; they are included here to help you keep track of the commands.

Productivity Tip:
MAKE BACKUPS.

Every chapter contains a short suggestion on how to increase your productivity. Following these tips can help you to work smarter, rather than working harder. This chapter's tip is perhaps the most important one of all: Make backups (security copies) of your data. Store a copy of your data in a location separate from your computer. If all data is stored at a single location, a fire or a flood can be truly disastrous.

Remember, sooner or later, whether your fault or not, you will lose data. If you haven't backed up your data, you will have to reenter it. Reentering data is at best painstaking, and is sometimes virtually impossible.

This productivity tip also applies beyond your SQL course. Make sure you back up whenever you enter or process large amounts of data. The best backup policy in the world is worthless unless you apply it. A backup is like life insurance: You must have it *before* you really need it.

Chapter Summary

We introduced fundamental notions about data and databases, a programming language called Structured Query Language used to process databases, and a small firm whose information needs evolve continuously. We presented relational databases and discussed how SQL's various components interact with these databases. We concluded the chapter by creating the firm's initial database and entering data into it, in cookbook fashion. But we did not actually code any SQL queries. In Chapter 2 we begin applying the SELECT command to obtain information from the database.

Review Questions

1. Define in your own words the following terms:
   a. Data
   b. Information
   c. Database
   d. Database management system (DBMS)
   e. Relational database management system (RDBMS)
   f. Structured Query Language (SQL)
   g. Data type

2. Describe briefly the four types of SQL statements and how each interacts with the relational database.

3. Determine the legal data types for your implementation of SQL. Supply informal definitions of each data type.

4. Later chapters include a case study developing a relational database for classical compact disks. To get a head start on this project define two tables, one for compact disks and one for manufacturers. Indicate the columns comprising these two tables and include sample data for five rows in each table.

Initial Queries

In Chapter 1 we created the tables for Noga's Crispy Crunch database and entered the initial data. We next apply SQL to query or retrieve information from these tables. Such information may be invaluable in the business's daily operations. It answers questions such as "What is Swedish Burgers' phone number?" and "Which orders must be ready on 10/28/1992?" Multiple, sophisticated SQL queries may help managers and owners make crucial business decisions such as whether to set up a delivery service.

SQL queries are composed with the SELECT command, also called the SELECT statement. This chapter presents elementary forms of the SELECT statement. Later chapters apply more complex forms of this statement to meet more sophisticated information needs.

OBJECTIVES

You have met this chapter's objectives when you can:

- Code elementary SQL queries, including comparisons.
- Define in your own terms the following SQL reserved words: *SELECT, FROM, DISTINCT, WHERE, ORDER BY.*
- Apply these reserved words to help meet business and other information-processing needs.

Writing a Query

A SELECT statement chooses (selects) rows from one or more tables according to specified criteria. It produces output containing one or more columns for each row selected. Our first SELECT statement is short but powerful:

```
SELECT   *

FROM   Customer;
```

The asterisk (*) specifies that all columns are selected; the FROM specifies that columns are selected from the Customer table. This same command could have been written:

```
SELECT   Custnum, Custname, Custtype, Custaddr, Zipcode, Phone

FROM   Customer;
```

Those familiar with DOS may note the similarity between SQL's * and DOS's *, used as a wild card. See Box 2-1 and Box 2-2 for important aspects of coding SQL statements.

This query generates the following results:

Custnum	Custname	Custtype	Custaddr	Zipcode	Phone
1	Jones, Joe	P	1234 Main St.	91212	434-1231
4	Armstrong, Inc.	R	231 Globe Blvd.	91212	434-7664
12	Swedish Burgers	R	1889 20th N.E.	91213	434-9090
13	Pickled Pickles	R	194 CityView	91289	324-8909
22	The Candy Kid	W	2121 Main St.	91212	563-4545
24	Waterman, Al	P	23 Yankee Blvd.	91234	-0-
37	Bobby Bon Bons	R	12 Nichi Cres.	91212	434-9045
39	Crowsh, Elias	P	7 77th Ave.	91211	434-0007
41	Montag, Susie	P	981 Montview	91213	456-2091
42	Columberg Sweets	W	239 East Falls	91209	874-9092

BOX 2-1

Reserved Words and User-Defined Words

Reserved words compose SQL's technical vocabulary. These words are reserved for the SQL system and should be used only as SQL intends. For example, a table or a column should not be named SELECT. In accordance with common practice, this text capitalizes SQL's reserved words.

User-defined words are those chosen by individuals to refer to objects, such as column names and table names. Exact rules for user-defined words vary from one SQL implementation to another. These rules are discussed in detail in Chapter 6. We limit user-defined words to eight characters in length. Although the computer does not distinguish capitalization, we do here: We capitalize only the first letter in our user-defined words. This practice enables us to distinguish immediately between reserved words and user-defined words. Check with your supervisor or teacher to determine rules to follow when creating table and column names.

Coding SQL Statements on Several Lines

The query

```
SELECT   *
    FROM   Customer;
```

could have been written on a single line:

```
SELECT * FROM   Customer;
```

However, this is rarely done. Although both queries generate the same results, the first one is easier to read and to modify because different parts appear separately. A word of advice: Get in the habit of writing simple queries in an organized fashion. You'll be glad you did when you're working with complex queries.

Coding SQL statements on several lines requires special "tricks" for some SQL implementations. For example, consider the microcomputer database software R:BASE. With this product, a carriage return entered after the * in

```
SELECT * FROM   Customer;
```

"cuts off" the command, causing an error. The problem is solved by coding a special character, the +, after the *, as follows:

```
SELECT   * +
    FROM   Customer;
```

This special character is called a *continuation character*. Our examples present SQL statements coded on separate lines without any continuation character. If necessary, check with your teacher or a technical manual to determine your SQL implementation's use of continuation characters, or other procedures for coding SQL statements on several lines.

The command

```
SELECT   *
    FROM   Purchase;
```

produces the following results:

Purchnum	Prodnum	Custnum	Purchdat	Readydat	Kilos
1234	1	22	10/28/1992	10/28/1992	3.5
1235	2	24	10/28/1992	10/30/1992	15.0

1236	1	41	10/28/1992	10/28/1992	2.0
1236	3	41	10/28/1992	10/28/1992	3.7
1237	3	4	10/28/1992	11/02/1992	3.7
1238	1	37	10/29/1992	10/29/1992	3.7
1238	2	37	10/29/1992	10/29/1992	1.2
1238	3	37	10/29/1992	10/29/1992	4.4
1239	2	24	10/29/1992	10/30/1992	3.0
1240	2	42	10/29/1992	10/31/1992	14.0
1240	5	42	10/29/1992	11/02/1992	4.8
1241	1	13	10/29/1992	10/29/1992	1.0
1241	5	13	10/29/1992	10/30/1992	7.6
1242	5	12	10/29/1992	10/29/1992	3.5

These two SELECT statements display all data contained in the Customer and Purchase tables. This data is used throughout the book.

The semicolon is the standard way of terminating SQL statements. While your system may not require a semicolon, you should get in the habit of entering it.

We next examine how to select individual columns.

Designating Columns (Field Names)

Noga felt submerged in paper. The previous SQL statements produced information overload. All she wanted was a simple list of customer numbers and customer names. For the time being, any extraneous columns would distract or mislead her. SQL can limit the columns appearing in the output. To output only the customer number and the customer name from the Customer table, code the query shown in Figure 2-1.

```
SELECT   Custnum, Custname
  FROM   Customer;

Custnum        Custname
      1        Jones, Joe
      4        Armstrong, Inc.
     12        Swedish Burgers
     13        Pickled Pickles
     22        The Candy Kid
     24        Waterman, Al
     37        Bobby Bon Bons
     39        Crowsh, Elias
     41        Montag, Susie
     42        Columberg Sweets
```

Figure 2-1 Elementary Query Designating Columns

TRY IT YOURSELF

1. Test your SQL implementation to determine whether commas are required to separate column names in the SELECT statement. Even if commas are not required to separate column names, why should you enter them?

2. Test your SQL implementation to determine whether a given column name may be repeated within a single query, as in the following example:

```
SELECT   Custname, Custnum, Custname
   FROM   Customer;
```

If it is legal to repeat a column name in a SELECT statement, when might this feature be useful?

Most SQL implementations require that commas (,) separate listed columns. Columns may appear in any order; they are not limited to the order in which they occur in the table. To output the customer name *before* the customer number, code the query shown in Figure 2-2.

```
SELECT   Custname, Custnum
   FROM   Customer;
```

```
Custname              Custnum

Jones, Joe                  1

Armstrong, Inc.             4
```
(Remaining output suppressed to save space.)

Figure 2-2 Changing the Order of Columns Output

The DISTINCT Qualifier

To concentrate her marketing effort, Noga wanted to know the zip codes of customers purchasing candy. She coded the query shown in Figure 2-3a. The zip codes appear in the order in which they occurred in the Customer table, not in any useful order. Furthermore, duplicates occur. To determine the number of different zip codes, Noga might tally them manually. Or she could use the reserved word DISTINCT, as shown in Figure 2-3b. Adding the DISTINCT qualifier to the SELECT statement provides two benefits: (1) Individual zip codes are listed only once, and (2) the zip codes are sorted.

a

```
SELECT   Zipcode
   FROM   Customer;
```

```
Zipcode
91212
91212
91213
91289
91212
91234
91212
91211
91213
91209
```

b

```
SELECT   DISTINCT Zipcode
   FROM   Customer;
```

```
Zipcode
91209
91211
91212
91213
91234
91289
```

Figure 2-3 The DISTINCT Qualifier

The DISTINCT qualifier suppresses only those rows that are exactly the same, as shown in Figure 2-4. In this case, nine of the ten rows in the Customer table are displayed. Which Customer table row is absent from the output? Why doesn't it appear?

```
SELECT   DISTINCT Custtype, Zipcode
   FROM   Customer;
```

Custtype	Zipcode
P	91211
P	91212
P	91213
P	91234
R	91212
R	91213
R	91289
W	91209
W	91212

Figure 2-4 DISTINCT Qualifier Operating on Two Columns

Note, some implementations generate output in a different order.

EXERCISES

1. Write an SQL query to generate a list of DISTINCT customers who have purchased candy. Show the output.
2. Write an SQL query to generate a list of DISTINCT customers who have

purchased candy and the types of candy they have purchased. Show the output. Explain the difference in the number of rows selected by these two SQL statements, if any.

Designating Rows (WHERE Clause)

Noga had to review purchase order 1238. She wasn't at all interested in wading through the entire Purchase table. She used the WHERE clause to display only those rows meeting the selection criteria, as shown in Figure 2-5.

```
SELECT   *
   FROM   Purchase
   WHERE   Purchnum = 1238;
```

Purchnum	Prodnum	Custnum	Purchdat	Readydat	Kilos
1238	1	37	10/29/1992	10/29/1992	3.7
1238	2	37	10/29/1992	10/29/1992	1.2
1238	3	37	10/29/1992	10/29/1992	4.4

Figure 2-5 Elementary Query Designating Rows

There was no time to sit back and relax. She next required a list of customers whose zip code is 91212. Because the Zipcode column is defined as a CHARACTER column, this query is a bit more complicated than the previous one. The WHERE clause compares only objects of a similar type. For example, it compares CHARACTER columns to other CHARACTER columns or to character values. Standard SQL uses the single quote mark (') to indicate the beginning and the end of a series of characters. In technical terms this process is known as *delimiting a character string*. She coded the query shown in Figure 2-6.

```
SELECT   *
   FROM   Customer
   WHERE   Zipcode = '91212';
```

Custnum	Custname	Custtype	Custaddr	Zipcode	Phone
1	Jones, Joe	P	1234 Main St.	91212	434-1231
4	Armstrong, Inc.	R	231 Globe Blvd.	91212	434-7664
22	The Candy Kid	W	2121 Main St.	91212	563-4545
37	Bobby Bon Bons	R	12 Nichi Cres.	91212	434-9045

Figure 2-6 Use of a Character String

The WHERE clause generates output only for those rows meeting the specified condition, such as equality (see Box 2-3). The tested condition is either

> *TRY IT YOURSELF*
>
> **3.** Determine what happens on your SQL implementation if no quotes are used to delimit the character string 91212 in the query shown in Figure 2-6.
>
> **4.** Determine what happens on your SQL implementation if double quotes (") are used to delimit the character string 91212 in the query shown in Figure 2-6.
>
> **5.** Determine what happens on your SQL implementation if two single quote marks (' ') are used to delimit the character string 91212 in the query shown in Figure 2-6.

True or False. The row is output only if the condition is True. Rows whose zip code is equal to the characters 91212 (Zipcode = '91212') are output; the other rows are not. Any or all columns may be displayed in the output. Noga need not display the zip code. After all, she knows that it is 91212. However, the output is less subject to misinterpretation if she includes the zip code.

Sometimes the use of quotes can be a bit complicated. For example, if Bob Ferreta changed the name of his company to Bob's Bon Bons, Noga could use the following query to display information related to his business:

```
SELECT   *
  FROM   Customer
 WHERE   Custname = 'Bob''s Bon Bons';
```

In this case, two single quotes (not a double quote) are used so the computer does not divide the customer name in the middle. Some SQL implementations interpret the second single quote in the condition

```
Custname = 'Bob''s Bon Bons'
```

to mean the end of the tested name. In this case, the condition is effectively shortened to

```
Custname = 'Bob'
```

and the rest of the statement,

```
s Bon Bons
```

is ignored.

BOX 2-3

SQL Comparisons

SQL provides the following comparison operators:

English	SQL
less than	<
less than or equal to	<=
equal to	=
not equal to	<>
greater than	>
greater than or equal to	>=

Numeric columns such as INTEGER, SMALLINT, REAL, and DECIMAL columns may be compared only to numeric values, such as 1238 and 1.2, or to other numeric columns. DATE columns may be compared only to other DATE columns or to dates. A greater value of a DATE column means a date found later in the calendar. CHARACTER columns may be compared only to other CHARACTER columns or to character strings, such as '91212'. A greater value of a CHARACTER column can be interpreted as a name found further back in an alphabetical listing such as a telephone book; for example, JONES is greater than BARNETT. Sometimes it is not obvious which of two character strings is greater; for example, *111 Incorporated* or *ABC Cleaners.* The order of characters is known as the *collating sequence,* and depends on the specific SQL implementation.

Common Errors

Proper spelling is a must when applying SQL. People may interchange the two column names *Custnum* and *Custno.* SQL considers these two names to be completely different. The query

```
SELECT   Custno
   FROM   Customer;
```

generates an error message such as the following:

```
-ERROR-   Column Custno not found
```

To avoid spelling errors, it's a good idea to keep a copy of the column names at hand when querying a table.

If we eliminate the quotes surrounding the customer type and run the following query:

```
SELECT   Custnum, Phone
  FROM   Customer
 WHERE   Custtype = R;
```

an error message such as the following is generated:

```
-ERROR- Column R not found
```

This is an example of a **syntax error**, which means SQL's syntax or grammar rules have not been followed.

E X E R C I S E S

3. Write an SQL query to generate purchases made on October 28th. Show the output.

4. Write an SQL query to generate purchases of exactly 14.0 kilos of any type of candy. Show the output.

The equals operator (=) is too specific for many purposes. Rather than determining who bought an exact amount of one type of candy, Noga wanted to know who bought a lot of a given type of candy. In this case, *a lot of* means more than 9 kilos at one time. She entered the query shown in Figure 2-7.

```
SELECT   *
  FROM   Purchase
 WHERE   Kilos > 9;
```

Purchnum	Prodnum	Custnum	Purchdat	Readydat	Kilos
1235	2	24	10/28/1992	10/30/1992	15.0
1240	2	42	10/29/1992	10/31/1992	14.0

Figure 2-7 Use of a Comparison Operator

E X E R C I S E S

5. Write an SQL query to generate all small, single-candy purchases, where *small* is defined as 3.5 kilos or less. Show the output.

6. Write an SQL query to generate all purchases whose ready date and purchase date are the same. Show the output.

Processing Dates

SQL implementations vary widely in their date processing. The following examples were coded using R:BASE, which handles dates more simply than most other SQL implementations. If you are using another SQL implementation, you may have to rewrite queries involving DATE data types to avoid errors. Check the appendices to see if your system is discussed. If not, check your system manual.

Noga wanted information on all purchases to be ready on October 29, 1992, or in R:BASE terms on 10/29/1992. She obtained this information with the query shown in Figure 2-8.

```
SELECT   *
   FROM   Purchase
  WHERE   Readydat  =  '10/29/1992';
```

Purchnum	Prodnum	Custnum	Purchdat	Readydat	Kilos
1238	1	37	10/29/1992	10/29/1992	3.7
1238	2	37	10/29/1992	10/29/1992	1.2
1238	3	37	10/29/1992	10/29/1992	4.4
1241	1	13	10/29/1992	10/29/1992	1.0
1242	5	12	10/29/1992	10/29/1992	3.5

Figure 2-8 Selecting Purchases Ready on a Given Date

E X E R C I S E S

7. Write an SQL query to generate all purchases whose ready date is October 29, 1992. Show the output.

8. Write an SQL query to generate all purchases whose ready date is after October 28, 1992. Show the output.

The ORDER BY Clause

Recall from Chapter 1 that data in a table is not in any particular order. The ORDER BY clause arranges rows in a table; it sorts data to meet user needs.

Noga wanted a list of customer names in alphabetical order, accompanied by their customer type and phone number. To do so she coded the query shown in Figure 2-9.

```
SELECT   Custname, Custtype, Phone
   FROM   Customer
  ORDER   BY Custname;
```

Custname	Custtype	Phone
Armstrong, Inc.	R	434-7664
Bobby Bon Bons	R	434-9045
Columberg Sweets	W	874-9092

```
Crowsh, Elias              P      434-0007
Jones, Joe                 P      434-1231
Montag, Susie              P      456-2091
Pickled Pickles            R      324-8909
Swedish Burgers            R      434-9090
The Candy Kid              W      563-4545
Waterman, Al               P      -0-
```

Figure 2-9 Use of the ORDER BY Clause

Then Noga decided she wanted the customer list sorted by customer type, and within each customer type, sorted by customer name, in alphabetical order. She wanted the customer type in descending order (from the letter *Z* to the letter *A*, or from the largest value to the smallest one), so she coded the query shown in Figure 2-10a. Note the use of the reserved word DESC. The same query can be repeated using position numbers; in this case Custname is in position 1, Custtype is in position 2, and Phone is in position 3. The resultant query is shown in Figure 2-10b. The use of position numbers does not change the output.

a

```
SELECT    Custname,Custtype,Phone
   FROM   Customer
  ORDER   BY Custtype DESC Custname;
```

b

```
(Position   1          2     3)
SELECT    Custname,Custtype,Phone
   FROM   Customer
  ORDER   BY 2 DESC 1;
```

```
Custname                Custtype      Phone
Columberg Sweets             W        874-9092
The Candy Kid                W        563-4545
Armstrong, Inc.              R        434-7664
Bobby Bon Bons               R        434-9045
Pickled Pickles              R        324-8909
Swedish Burgers              R        434-9090
Crowsh, Elias                P        434-0007
Jones, Joe                   P        434-1231
Montag, Susie                P        456-2091
Waterman, Al                 P        -0-
```

Figure 2-10 Use of the ORDER BY Clause—Descending Order. Both query **a** and query **b** produce the same output. In the query shown in Figure 2-10b, do not code the line in parentheses.

E X E R C I S E S

9. Write an SQL query to generate all purchases whose purchase date is October 28, 1992, in order of the number of kilos purchased. Show the output.

10. Write an SQL query to generate all purchases, in descending order of the number of kilos purchased. Use position numbers. Show the output.

Data Validation

We may use comparisons to check for invalid data. Consider the following Errorpur table, which has exactly the same structure as the Purchase table, the only difference being that each row contains at least one error:

Purchnum	Prodnum	Custnum	Purchdat	Readydat	Kilos
2234	18	22	10/28/1992	10/29/1992	3.5
2235	4	23	10/28/1992	10/30/1992	-15.0
2236	2	14	10/28/1992	10/24/1992	2.0
7937	7	11	10/28/2002	11/02/1992	0.0

We stated in Chapter 1 that current product numbers in the Purchase table range from 1 to 5. The query shown in Figure 2-11 tests for product numbers exceeding the designated maximum.

```
SELECT  *
   FROM  Errorpur
  WHERE  Prodnum > 5;
```

Purchnum	Prodnum	Custnum	Purchdat	Readydat	Kilos
2234	18	22	10/28/1992	10/29/1992	3.5
7937	7	11	10/28/2002	11/02/1992	0.0

Figure 2-11 Validating Product Numbers

Noga's Crispy Crunch is only made to order. Thus, for any purchase the purchase date must not exceed the ready date. A query to detect such problems is shown in Figure 2-12.

```
SELECT  *
   FROM  Errorpur
  WHERE  Purchdat > Readydat;
```

Purchnum	Prodnum	Custnum	Purchdat	Readydat	Kilos
2236	2	14	10/28/1992	10/24/1992	2.0
7937	7	11	10/28/2002	11/02/1992	0.0

Figure 2-12 Validating Date Columns

E X E R C I S E S

(All the following exercises may be coded using syntax or language rules that you have already learned. You may have to reformulate the English-language query before expressing it in SQL terms.)

11. Write an SQL query to generate error rows from the Errorpur table given the requirement that the purchase date be prior to the year 2000. Show the output.

12. Write an SQL query to generate error rows from the Errorpur table given the requirement that the kilos purchased be greater than zero. Show the output.

Syntax and Applications Summary

```
SELECT   * or one or more column names
   FROM   table name
  WHERE   expression   comparison operator   expression
  ORDER   BY one or more column names
```

Notes.

1. The DISTINCT qualifier is used to eliminate duplicates and to place rows in order. Column names are separated by commas.

2. The WHERE clause is used to limit the rows output. Presently, expressions are column names or values. Comparison operators include

$$< , <=, =, <>, >, >=$$

Comparisons are limited to objects of the same type. For example, DATE-type columns must be compared with other such columns or with dates.

3. The ORDER BY clause is used to sort the output by one or more columns. Sort columns may be either listed as such or indicated by position number. Results are sorted from lowest to highest values unless DESC is coded.

Productivity Tip:

WATCH OUT FOR RESERVED WORDS.

Photocopy the list of your SQL implementation's reserved words. Keep this list for reference. *Never* employ these words as user-defined words, even if the computer does not indicate an error. It is pointless to get away with a rule infraction today only to have your statement blow up in your face tomorrow. And even if it is legal, a statement such as

```
SELECT   *
   FROM   FROM;
```

is confusing, to say the least. Such statements should be avoided at all costs.

Chapter Summary

We have learned how to select columns and rows for output according to a single condition. For example, a single SELECT statement can output purchases greater than 10 kilos; or another SELECT statement can output purchases made on October 28th. In the next chapter we will learn how to combine two or more conditions. For example, to output purchases greater than 10 kilos made on October 28th.

Review Questions

1. Define in your own terms the following SQL reserved words, and describe their use:
   a. SELECT
   b. FROM
   c. DISTINCT
   d. WHERE
   e. ORDER BY

2. What is the difference between a row and a column? May they be interchanged?

3. What is meant by a *comparison?* How are comparisons expressed in SQL? Why are they useful?

4. What is a syntax error? How can you correct it?

Case Study. Appendix A describes two versions of a database for classical music compact disks, consisting of the following two tables.

1. Cds table or Smlcds table, with information describing each of the seven compact disks (rows) in the database. These two tables are similar. The Cds table contains 11 columns; the Smlcds table contains eight columns.

2. Manufs table, with information describing each of the nine manufacturer's series (rows) in the database. This table is the same for both versions of the

database. The Manufs table contains six columns.

Each chapter from here on contains case study exercises that apply SQL commands to process these databases. In this and subsequent chapters, unstarred questions can be answered using either the full database (presently, tables Cds and Manufs) or the smaller database (presently, tables Smlcds and Manufs). Starred questions require the use of the full database.

Case Study Exercises

1. Write an SQL query to select 'DDD' recordings. Show the output displaying only the CD ID, the manufacturer code, the industry standard code, the title, and the year first recorded.

2. Write an SQL query to display the manufacturer code and the series for manufacturer P9.

3. Write an SQL query to display the distinct manufacturer code and city for manufacturer P9.

4. Write an SQL query to select manufacturers offering a discount of 30% or better. Show the output.

5. Write an SQL query to select CDs whose price is $12.00 or less. Show selected columns in the output.

6. Write an SQL query to select CDs first recorded before 1970. Show selected columns in the output, sorted by date first recorded.

7. Write an SQL query to select CDs first recorded before 1970. Show selected columns in the output, sorted by price, in descending order.

* 8. Write an SQL query to select CDs with more than three works. Show selected columns in the output.

* 9. Write an SQL query to select CDs longer than 60 minutes. Show selected columns in the output, sorted by length, in descending order.

*10. Write an SQL query to select CDs recorded by the Virtuosi Di Roma. (Watch your spelling.) Show selected columns in the output.

CHAPTER THREE

Adding Power to Your Queries

In Chapter 2 we began querying tables. Almost as soon as we got an answer to one query, we thought of another. Before long we thought of queries that we could not yet express in SQL. For example, we could list all purchases greater than 10 kilos, we could list all purchases made on October 28th, but our knowledge of SQL was insufficient to combine these two queries. That is, we were unable to generate a list of all purchases greater than 10 kilos made on October 28th. We will shortly learn how to code this and related queries. Such queries require reserved words such as OR and AND, whose significance in SQL resembles their English-language meaning. We will learn how to determine whether a column's value is IN a series of values and whether it is BETWEEN one value and another.

Our processing of character data has been limited to checking a column for exact values such as a zip code of 91212 or a customer type of 'W'. We will extend this character processing with the LIKE operator. This powerful feature lets us process items such as street addresses and telephone exchanges even if the details are incomplete.

OBJECTIVES

You have met this chapter's objectives when you can:

- Code SQL queries using the following operators: *OR, AND, NOT, IN, BETWEEN, LIKE.*
- Apply these operators to help meet business and other information-processing needs.

The OR Operator

Often a single condition is insufficient to describe specific processing requirements. Noga wanted a list of all customers who are either wholesale (Custtype = 'W') or retail (Custtype = 'R'). She obtained this list by coding the

query shown in Figure 3-1a. This single SELECT statement uses the OR operator to combine two conditions, creating a *compound condition*. A compound
condition connected by the OR operator is True if at least one condition is
True. Let's now "play computer" to see how these results were obtained.

The computer examines the "Custtype" column of each row, one by one, to
determine whether the row should be included in the output.

a   b

```
SELECT    *                    SELECT    *
   FROM   Customer                FROM   Customer
  WHERE   Custtype = 'W'          WHERE  Custtype = 'R'
     OR   Custtype = 'R';            OR  Custtype = 'W';
```

Custnum	Custname	Custtype	Custaddr	Zipcode	Phone
4	Armstrong, Inc.	R	231 Globe Blvd.	91212	434-7664
12	Swedish Burgers	R	1889 20th N.E.	91213	434-9090
13	Pickled Pickles	R	194 CityView	91289	324-8909
22	The Candy Kid	W	2121 Main St.	91212	563-4545
37	Bobby Bon Bons	R	12 Nichi Cres.	91212	434-9045
42	Columberg Sweets	W	239 East Falls	91209	874-9092

Figure 3-1 The OR Operator

First Row (Custnum 1, Custtype 'P'). The Custtype is not equal to 'W'; the row
is not yet output, but another test remains. The Custtype is not equal to 'R'.
This row is not output.

Second Row (Custnum 4, Custtype 'R'). The Custtype is not equal to 'W'; the
row is not yet output, but another test remains. The Custtype is equal to 'R'.
This row is output.

Test the remaining rows for yourself. You should get the same results as the
computer. Note, this query processes wholesale and retail customers equivalently, which is exactly what Noga wanted.

The query in Figure 3-1a could also be written as shown in Figure 3-1b, generating the same output. If you are unsure about the OR operator, test the
query by hand.

E X E R C I S E S

1. Write an SQL query generating customers whose zip code is either 91212
   or 91213. Show the output.

2. Write an SQL query generating purchases of less than 2 kilos or purchases greater than 10 kilos. Show the output.

The OR operator may combine tests on different columns, as in the query in Figure 3-2.

```
SELECT   Purchnum, Prodnum, Custnum, Purchdat, Kilos
  FROM   Purchase
 WHERE   Purchdat = '10/28/1992' OR Kilos > 10;
```

Purchnum	Prodnum	Custnum	Purchdat	Kilos
1234	1	22	10/28/1992	3.5
1235	2	24	10/28/1992	15.0
1236	1	41	10/28/1992	2.0
1236	3	41	10/28/1992	3.7
1237	3	4	10/28/1992	3.7
1240	2	42	10/29/1992	14.0

Figure 3-2 OR Operating on Different Columns

SQL's OR operator differs slightly from the common English-language use of *or*. When we say, "We are going to the movies or to a restaurant tonight," we mean that we are going *either* to the movies *or* to a restaurant but not to both. SQL's OR carries no such implication. For instance, in the output row for purchase number 1235 in Figure 3-2, Purchnum 1235 has a Purchdat equal to 10/28/1992 and a Kilos value greater than 10. This row is included in the output. We interpret the OR as follows: The row is selected if the purchase date equals 10/28/1992 or the kilos purchased is greater than 10 or both these conditions hold.

Common Error

SQL does not allow the following query:

```
SELECT   *
  FROM   Customer
 WHERE   Custtype = 'W' OR 'R';
```

Later in this chapter we will see a legal shortcut to test for two or more values of the same field.

The AND Operator

Noga wanted information about purchases of more than 10 kilos made on October 28th. The OR operator does not apply here, since both conditions must hold. The AND operator is more restrictive than the OR operator. A compound condition connected by the AND operator is True only if both conditions are True.

Consider the query shown in Figure 3-3. Only rows whose purchase date is 10/28/1992 *and* whose "Kilos" column contains a value greater than 10 are selected. Examining the rows in Figure 3-2 one by one we see that only purchase number 1235 was selected. Purchase number 1234 has the requested purchase date but too few kilos. The same holds for purchase numbers 1236 and 1237. Why wasn't the row with purchase number 1239 selected? Why weren't the remaining rows selected?

```
SELECT  Purchnum, Prodnum, Custnum, Purchdat, Kilos
  FROM  Purchase
 WHERE  Purchdat = '10/28/1992' AND Kilos > 10;
```

Purchnum	Prodnum	Custnum	Purchdat	Kilos
1235	2	24	10/28/1992	15.0

Figure 3-3 The AND Operator

Box 3-1 summarizes the OR and AND operators.

EXERCISES

3. Write an SQL query for retail customers whose zip code is 91212. Show the output.

4. Write an SQL query for purchases whose purchase date and whose ready date are both 10/29/1992. Show the output.

Combining OR and AND Operators

Sometimes we require information that depends on more than two conditions. We may combine OR operators, AND operators, or both AND and OR operators. If only OR operators are used, the query is straightforward and normally will not be misinterpreted. The same holds when only AND operators are used.

When the OR operator and the AND operator are combined, however, errors are likely to occur. People may readily interpret the following query in two different ways, which we will call A and B.

BOX 3-1

Summary of OR and AND Operators

When the OR operator connects two conditions, the resultant condition is True unless both conditions are False.

Condition 1	Condition 2	Result of Condition 1 or Condition 2
True	True	True
True	False	True
False	True	True
False	False	False

When the AND operator connects two conditions, the resultant condition is False unless both conditions are True.

Condition 1	Condition 2	Result of Condition 1 and Condition 2
True	True	True
True	False	False
False	True	False
False	False	False

```
SELECT   Custnum
  FROM   Customer
 WHERE   Zipcode = '91212'
    OR   Zipcode = '91213'
   AND   Custtype = 'P';
```

A. *Processing the AND before processing the OR:* Correct
   i. First combine Zipcode = '91213' AND Custtype = 'P' to generate customer number 41.
   ii. Then combine this customer (OR) customers with Zipcode = '91212'. Because customer numbers 1, 4, 22, and 37 have a zip code of 91212, such a query would generate customer numbers 1, 4, 22, 37, and 41.

B. *Processing from left to right:* Incorrect
   i. First combine Zipcode = '91212' OR Zipcode = '91213' to generate customer numbers 1, 4, 12, 22, 37, and 41.

ii. Then combine these customers (AND) those with Custtype = 'P'. Because customer numbers 1, 24, 39, and 41 are private customers, such a query would generate customer numbers 1 and 41.

Analysis A and analysis B lead to two different conclusions. Of course, the computer must always interpret a given query the same way. This query generates the following results:

```
Custnum
      1
      4
     22
     37
     41
```

The computer applies interpretation A. It executes the AND operator before executing the OR operator. In technical terms we say that the AND operator is higher on the *hierarchy of operations* than the OR operator. (See Box 3-2.)

In this particular case the computer's actions do not correspond to most people's needs. What if you want the computer to combine the zip codes first and then perform the AND operation? The answer is simple: Use parentheses to regroup conditions, as shown in Figure 3-4. Parentheses are higher on the hierarchy of operations than the AND operator. (See Box 3-2.)

BOX 3-2

Hierarchy of Operations

The ANSI SQL reference (p. 44) states, "Expressions within parentheses are evaluated first and when the order of evaluation is not specified by parentheses, NOT is applied before AND, AND is applied before OR, and operators at the same precedence level are applied from left to right."

The hierarchy of operations is as follows:

( )

NOT

AND

OR

Remember, the computer will execute operations in the order that you specify. It's up to you to specify the order that you want.

```
SELECT   Custnum
  FROM   Customer
 WHERE   (Zipcode = '91212' OR Zipcode = '91213')
   AND   Custtype = 'P';

Custnum
      1
     41
```

Figure 3-4 Combining OR and AND Operators

E X E R C I S E S

5. Write an SQL query selecting purchases greater than 10 kilos and whose ready date equals October 28, 1992 or whose purchase date equals October 28, 1992. Show the output.

6. A stickler might argue that we have not proved that the computer executes an AND before an OR. Perhaps it executes the query from right to left. Write an SQL query to prove that the computer does not execute a command from right to left. Show the output.

The NOT Operator

We may want to select rows that do not meet one or more conditions. For example, Noga could obtain information about customers whose customer number was not less than 37 with the query shown in Figure 3-5a.

a
```
SELECT   Purchnum, Custnum, Prodnum
  FROM   Purchase
 WHERE   NOT (Custnum < 37);
```

b
```
SELECT   Purchnum, Custnum, Prodnum
  FROM   Purchase
 WHERE   Custnum >= 37;
```

Purchnum	Custnum	Prodnum
1236	41	1
1236	41	3
1238	37	1
1238	37	2

```
1238              37              3
1240              42              2
1240              42              5
```

Figure 3-5 Using the NOT Operator and Its Equivalent

TRY IT YOURSELF

1. Are the parentheses necessary in the query in Figure 3-5a?

This query could have also been written as in Figure 3-5b. Most experienced SQL users find the second version of the query easier to code and less subject to misinterpretion.

Be very careful with the NOT. The query shown in Figure 3-6a gives results that may be surprising. It is equivalent to the query in Figure 3-6b and generates the entire table. Let's analyze how this output is generated (Box 3-3 shows a similar error.)

a

```
SELECT   *
   FROM   Customer
  WHERE   NOT (Custtype = 'P')
     OR   NOT (Custtype = 'R')
     OR   NOT (Custtype = 'W');
```

b

```
SELECT   *
   FROM   Customer
  WHERE   Custtype <> 'P'
     OR   Custtype <> 'R'
     OR   Custtype <> 'W';
```

Figure 3-6 Equivalent Queries. Either query generates the entire table.

The first row has a customer type of 'P', so the condition

```
Custtype <>   'P'
```

is False, whereas the condition

```
Custtype <> 'R'
```

is True. The condition

```
Custtype <> 'W'
```

is also True. Because at least one condition connected by OR operators is True, the row is selected. The remaining rows also generate output. (If you are not sure, test them yourself.)

BOX 3-3

Logic Errors

As we have already seen, not all errors result in SQL's rejecting a query. In many cases the system will generate a wrong answer or, perhaps more precisely, the right answer to the wrong question. This is known as a *logic error;* the query was understandable but did not correctly express the user's information need.

Complex queries involving the NOT operator may produce logic errors. For example, suppose that Noga wanted information on purchases not ready on 10/28/1992 or on 10/29/1992. Either of the following two queries generates the entire table:

```
SELECT   *                              SELECT   *
   FROM   Purchase                         FROM   Purchase
  WHERE   NOT Readydat = '10/28/1992'      WHERE   Readydat <> '10/28/1992'
OR NOT         Readydat = '10/29/1992';       OR   Readydat <> '10/29/1992';
```

While this query may be correctly coded using either the NOT operator or the <> comparison operator, it may also be coded as follows:

```
SELECT   *
   FROM   Purchase
  WHERE   Readydat < '10/28/1992'
     OR   Readydat > '10/29/1992';
```

This generates the correct output consisting of six rows. Note that overuse of the NOT operator is confusing. But not using the NOT does not mean you will avoid a logic error. In other words, logic errors may still occur even if the NOT operator is avoided.

The IN operator

Noga wanted a list of customers whose zip code is 91212, 91213, or 91214. Applying OR operators leads to a rather clumsy query, as shown in Figure 3-7a. This query may be recoded as in Figure 3-7b.

Note, because the IN operator specifically designates acceptable values of the "Zipcode" column, many implementations do not require the single quote mark ('). Besides being shorter to code, the IN operator offers other advantages over a series of OR operators. Modifying the IN operator is extremely easy; for example, to select zip code 91211 instead of 91214. Furthermore, the IN operator is quite visual; you don't need much SQL training to see which zip codes are included in the query in Figure 3-7b.

a

```
SELECT    Custnum,Custtype,Zipcode
  FROM    Customer
 WHERE    Zipcode  =  '91212'
    OR    Zipcode  =  '91213'
    OR    Zipcode  =  '91214';
```

b

```
SELECT    Custnum,Custtype,Zipcode
  FROM    Customer
 WHERE    Zipcode IN (91212,91213,91214);
```

Custnum	Custtype	Zipcode
1	P	91212
4	R	91212
12	R	91213
22	W	91212
37	R	91212
41	P	91213

Figure 3-7 Replacing OR Operators by the IN Operator

The IN and NOT operators may be combined. Two queries validating the Customer table for illegal customer types are shown in Figure 3-8a and 3-8b. Neither query generates any rows, but query b is easier to code and understand. Both the IN and the NOT IN operators require an explicit list of values. If the desired values are not specifically stated, we must use a different SQL operator.

a

```
SELECT    *
  FROM    Customer
 WHERE    NOT (Custtype  =  'P')
   AND    NOT (Custtype  =  'R')
   AND    NOT (Custtype  =  'W');
```

b

```
SELECT    *
  FROM    Customer
 WHERE    Custtype NOT IN('P','R','W');
```

Figure 3-8 Replacing AND NOT Operators by the NOT IN Operator

The BETWEEN Operator

The BETWEEN operator checks a column for values within a given range. For example, to find medium-sized purchases of a single type of candy, Noga coded the query applying the BETWEEN operator shown in Figure 3-9a. She could have coded an equivalent query without the BETWEEN operator, as in Figure 3-9b. Note that the BETWEEN operator is inclusive. Thus, the clause

```
WHERE Kilos BETWEEN 3.5 AND 10.0
```

selects rows whose Kilos are equal to 3.5, 10.0, or any intermediate value.

```
a
SELECT   *
    FROM   Purchase
    WHERE   Kilos BETWEEN 3.5 AND 10.0;
```

```
b
SELECT   *
    FROM   Purchase
    WHERE   Kilos >= 3.5
       AND   Kilos <= 10.0;
```

Purchnum	Prodnum	Custnum	Purchdat	Readydat	Kilos
1234	1	22	10/28/1992	10/28/1992	3.5
1236	3	41	10/28/1992	10/28/1992	3.7
1237	3	4	10/28/1992	11/02/1992	3.7
1238	1	37	10/29/1992	10/29/1992	3.7
1238	3	37	10/29/1992	10/29/1992	4.4
1240	5	42	10/29/1992	11/02/1992	4.8
1241	5	13	10/29/1992	10/30/1992	7.6
1242	5	12	10/29/1992	10/29/1992	3.5

Figure 3-9 The BETWEEN Operator and Its Equivalent

TRY IT YOURSELF

2. What happens if you reverse the order of the fields in a BETWEEN operator? For example,

```
Zipcode BETWEEN 91213 AND 91209
```

3. Will the BETWEEN operator work with dates in different months?

EXERCISES

7. Using the NOT BETWEEN operator, write an SQL query that selects large and small but not medium-sized purchases. Rewrite this query without using the NOT BETWEEN operator. Show the output for both queries.

8. Write an SQL query that selects purchases whose ready date is between 10/29/1992 and 10/31/1992. Show the output.

The LIKE Operator

Noga had a problem. She needed to call a customer on Main Street but couldn't remember either the customer name or the full street address. She didn't want to scan the entire Customer table to find this information. How could she select customers by address without knowing the exact address? The answer is, by using the LIKE operator, which searches groups of characters known as *character strings* according to a user-supplied pattern. A special *character string* is discussed in Box 3-4.

The LIKE operator employs two special characters, the percent sign (%) and the underscore (_). The percent sign instructs the system to ignore any number of characters (including zero characters) when comparing a column's data with the given character string. The underscore instructs the system to ignore a single character when comparing a column's data with the given character string. To see how the LIKE operator works, let's look at a few examples.

The condition

```
Custaddr LIKE '%Main%'
```

is True for the customer addresses 1234 Main St. and 2121 Main St. The first percent sign ignores any number of characters prior to the M in Main. The second percent sign ignores any characters following the n in Main. This condition is also True for customer addresses Main Avenue and 1234 Main, in which case the second percent sign ignores zero characters.

The condition

```
Custaddr LIKE '_ _3_ Main%'
```

is True for the customer address 1234 Main St. It is False for the customer address 2121 Main St., which contains no 3.

The condition

```
Custaddr LIKE '%3_Main%'
```

is False for the customer address 1234 Main St., because the underscore after the 3 allows for only a single character, not both the 4 and the space. This condition is True for the customer address 723 Main St. The LIKE operator is illustrated in the query shown in Figure 3-10.

```
SELECT   *
  FROM   Customer
 WHERE   Custaddr LIKE '%Main%';
```

Custnum	Custname	Custtype	Custaddr	Zipcode	Phone
1	Jones, Joe	P	1234 Main St.	91212	434-1231
22	The Candy Kid	W	2121 Main St.	91212	563-4545

Figure 3-10 The LIKE Operator

Common Error

People familiar with MS-DOS may be tempted to replace SQL's percent sign with MS-DOS's asterisk (*), both of which designate any number of characters. They may be tempted to replace SQL's underscore with MS-DOS's question mark (?), both of which designate a single character. Neither of these substitutions will work. For example, the query

```
SELECT   *
  FROM   Customer
 WHERE   Custaddr LIKE '*Main*';
```

generates an error message such as the following:

```
-WARNING- No rows exist or satisfy the specified clause.
```

> E X E R C I S E S
>
> **9.** Write an SQL query to find all customers living on a street that begins with an M. Show the output.
>
> **10.** Write an SQL query to find all private customers in telephone exchange 434. Show the output.

Syntax and Applications Summary

The WHERE clause in the SELECT statement is extended to meet more complicated selection criteria. The notion of expression is extended to include the comparison of a column to another column or value. We consider five new examples of the WHERE clause.

BOX 3 - 4

NULLs

Sometimes we are faced with incomplete data. For example, customer number 24, Al Waterman, has an unlisted telephone number. Noga may record a new customer in the Customer table before assigning it a customer type. SQL provides a special value known as the *NULL value* for such cases. SQL implementations differ in how they display the NULL value. One possibility is

```
-0-
```

Another possibility is blanks. However, the NULL value is different from a blank value.

When we created the Customer table, we designated columns "Custnum" and "Custname" as NOT NULL. NOT NULL and PRIMARY KEY columns may not contain null values. If we don't know the customer name or the customer number, we shouldn't introduce the customer data into the database. When a column is not forbidden from assuming NULL values, we may enter a NULL value in several ways. Each of the following three INSERT INTO statements creates Al Waterman's row in the Customer table:

```
INSERT INTO Customer (Custnum, Custname, Custtype, Custaddr, Zipcode)
VALUES(24, 'Waterman, Al', 'P', '23 Yankee Blvd.', '91234',);

INSERT INTO Customer
VALUES(24, 'Waterman, Al', 'P', '23 Yankee Blvd.', '91234',);

INSERT INTO Customer
VALUES(24, 'Waterman, Al', 'P', '23 Yankee Blvd.', '91234', NULL);
```

Note that in the last option the reserved word NULL is *not* enclosed in quotation marks.

The following SELECT statement obtains all customers with NULL telephone numbers:

```
SELECT   Custnum, Custname
  FROM   Customer
 WHERE   Phone IS NULL;
```

It generates the following output:

```
Custnum   Custname
     24   Waterman, Al
```

```
WHERE expression OR/AND expression
```

OR means the resultant condition is True if either or both expressions are True. AND means the resultant condition is True only if both expressions are True.

```
WHERE NOT expression
```

NOT means the resultant condition is True if the expression is False, and vice versa.

```
WHERE expression IN (one or more values)
```

IN means the resultant condition is True if the expression is equal to one or more values within the parentheses. These values are separated by commas.

```
WHERE expression BETWEEN (smaller value AND greater value)
```

BETWEEN means the resultant condition is True if the expression is greater or equal to the smaller value and less than or equal to the greater value.

```
WHERE character value LIKE 'pattern'
```

LIKE means the resultant condition is True if the character value is equal to pattern. A percent sign in the pattern means ignore zero or more characters when making the comparison. An underscore in the pattern means ignore exactly one character when making the comparison. The LIKE clause allows users to find information even if they are unsure of the exact spelling.

Many of these reserved words may be combined, as shown in this chapter's examples and exercises.

Productivity Tip:

MAKE YOUR QUERIES EASIER TO READ.

The liberal use of parentheses makes your queries easier to read and understand. For example, although each of the following two SQL queries generates exactly the same computer output (try them), people are less likely to make an error when interpreting the right-hand query.

```
SELECT   Custnum                SELECT   Custnum
  FROM   Customer                  FROM   Customer
 WHERE   Zipcode = '91212'        WHERE   Zipcode = '91212'
```

```
OR    Zipcode = '91213'        OR    (Zipcode = '91213' AND
AND   Custtype = 'P';                Custtype = 'P');
```

Careful presentation involving coding statements on several lines is very important. Sloppy spacing makes even the right-hand query hard to understand. For example, the following may take a few seconds less to code than the suggested format.

```
SELECT Custnum FROM Customer WHERE Zipcode = '91212' OR
(Zipcode = '91213' AND Custtype = 'P');
```

But the query's poor format can lead to serious errors that may take hours or even days to correct.

Chapter Summary

This chapter illustrated how to code queries corresponding to two or more conditions. It also showed how to select rows given incomplete information such as a partial street address. The next chapter extends SQL queries into the realm of arithmetic, for both single rows and groups of related rows.

Review Questions

1. Define in your own terms the following SQL reserved words, and describe their use:
   a. OR
   b. AND
   c. NOT
   d. IN
   e. BETWEEN
   f. LIKE

2. What is meant by *the hierarchy of operations?* Why is it important?

3. Give an example of a query involving a combination of OR/AND/NOT that is unchanged when parentheses are added.

4. Give an example of a query involving a combination of OR/AND/NOT that is changed when parentheses are added.

5. Using the LIKE operator, recode two additional versions of the query shown in Figure 3-10.

Case Study Exercises

Remember, unstarred questions may be answered using either the full database or the smaller database, consisting of tables Smlcds and Manufs. Starred questions require the full database, consisting of tables Cds and Manufs. Given the large number of columns in the tables, output only essential columns.

1. Write an SQL query to select CDs that are either 'DDD' or first recorded after 1980. Show the output.

2. Write an SQL query to display information for the manufacturer P9 when the discount is at least 30%. Show the output.

3. Write an SQL query to select CDs whose title includes the word *Piano*. Show the output.

4. Write an SQL query to select CDs with the word *Classics* in the "Series" column that cost more than $12.00. Show the output.

5. Using the IN operator, write an SQL query to select European manufacturers (Rome or Paris). Show the output.

6. Write an SQL query to select manufacturers offering a discount of 30% or better or a quality rating of not less than 8. Show the output.

7. Write an SQL query using the BETWEEN operator to select CDs first recorded in the 1960s. Show the output.

*8. Write an SQL query to select CDs longer than 60 minutes recorded by a chamber orchestra. Use the IN operator. Show the output.

*9. Write an SQL query to select CDs longer than 60 minutes recorded by a chamber orchestra. Use the LIKE operator. Show the output.

*10. Write an SQL query to select CDs with three to five works. Show the output.

CHAPTER FOUR

Arithmetic and Functions

Previous chapters demonstrated a wide variety of queries for retrieving data from the Purchase and Customer tables. Our simplest query generated the list of all rows and columns in a given table. More complicated queries displayed selected columns from a table based on complex conditions such as private customers in telephone exchange 434. Chapter 4 begins with a query applying an arithmetic operation to convert kilograms to pounds. We apply more advanced SQL features to perform more complex calculations such as determining the total amount of candy sold and the amount sold by product type. We learn several SQL clauses that regroup and display output to meet diverse information needs. We conclude this chapter with arithmetic operations on the DATE data type.

OBJECTIVES

You have met this chapter's objectives when you can:

- Code SQL queries using the following arithmetic operations: * (multiplication), / (division), + (addition), − (subtraction).
- Code SQL queries using the following aggregate functions: SUM, AVG, MAX, MIN, COUNT.
- Code SQL queries using the GROUP BY and HAVING clauses.
- Apply all of these arithmetic operations, aggregate functions, and clauses to meet business and other information-processing needs.

Arithmetic Operations

Noga was worried. She had grown up with the metric system. Only when she opened the store did she learn that 1 kilogram equals 2.2 pounds. The kid helping in the kitchen, who wasn't familiar with the metric system, couldn't tell a kilogram from a kilometer. With all her other activities, where would

Noga find the time to teach him the metric system? Why should she have to teach him? She could teach him SQL arithmetic operations. (See Box 4-1.)

SQL can teach him metric while furnishing him with purchase information. Noga executed the SQL query showing kilograms and pounds side by side as illustrated in Figure 4-1. Note, a SELECT statement does not change the data. In other words, SQL does not save the number of pounds (Kilos*2.2). To keep these values, she could define a new column in the Purchase table. (This process is discussed in Chapter 6.) Usually, however, this is not necessary; if Noga needs this information, she can code a query such as the one in Figure 4-1.

Check your SQL implementation to see how many digits are displayed after the decimal point. Some implementations do not align (line up) the decimal points in the output rows. Such output is as unattractive as it is hard to read.

```
SELECT   Purchnum, Prodnum, Custnum, Kilos, Kilos*2.2, '(pounds)'
   FROM  Purchase;
```

Purchnum	Prodnum	Custnum	Kilos	Kilos*2.2	'(pounds)'
1234	1	22	3.5	7.7	(pounds)
1235	2	24	15.0	33.0	(pounds)
1236	1	41	2.0	4.4	(pounds)
1236	3	41	3.7	8.14	(pounds)
1237	3	4	3.7	8.14	(pounds)
1238	1	37	3.7	8.14	(pounds)
1238	2	37	1.2	2.64	(pounds)
1238	3	37	4.4	9.68	(pounds)
1239	2	24	3.0	6.6	(pounds)
1240	2	42	14.0	30.8	(pounds)
1240	5	42	4.8	10.56	(pounds)
1241	1	13	1.0	2.2	(pounds)
1241	5	13	7.6	16.72	(pounds)
1242	5	12	3.5	7.7	(pounds)

Figure 4-1 Converting Kilos to Pounds

Right after Noga finished running the query in Figure 4-1, she received an emergency phone call from the exclusive supplier of a secret ingredient found only in product number 5: The shipment would be several days late. Such a delay might force her to ration the product, so, Noga thought of a 50% across-the-board reduction of all affected purchases. To get this information she wrote the query (calculating both kilograms and pounds) illustrated in Figure 4-2.

E X E R C I S E S

1. Write an SQL query charging $10 a kilo for all candy purchases. Show the output.

2. Write an SQL query charging $10 a kilo plus a $2 packing fee for all candy purchases. Show the output.

```
SELECT    Purchnum, Prodnum, Custnum, Kilos, Kilos / 2, Kilos * 2.2 / 2
FROM      Purchase
WHERE     Produm = 5;
```

Purchnum	Prodnum	Custnum	Kilos	Kilos / 2	Kilos * 2.2 / 2
1240	5	42	4.8	2.4	5.28
1241	5	13	7.6	3.8	8.36
1242	5	12	3.5	1.75	3.85

Figure 4-2 Arithmetic Calculations for One Product

BOX 4-1

SQL's Five Arithmetic Operations

SQL provides five arithmetic operators:

**, ^	Exponentiation
*	Multiplication
/	Division
+	Addition
−	Subtraction

An example of exponentiation is 3 ** 2, or 3 * 3 (the number 3 multiplied by itself), for a value of 9. Not all SQL implementations use ** or ^ as the symbol for exponentiation. However, most SQL business users rarely require exponentiation.

SQL arithmetic operators process numeric columns, such as REAL, INTEGER, and SMALL-INT. They do not work on nonnumeric data types, such as CHARACTER. This chapter ends with examples of arithmetic operations on DATE data types.

Noga checked the back cupboards one last time and found enough of the secret ingredient to produce 20 kilograms of candy number 5. Would she still have to ration the product? Instead of using pencil and paper or electronic calculator, let's see how Noga used an SQL feature called *aggregate functions* to obtain the answer.

Aggregate Functions

SQL provides five special functions called *aggregate functions*: SUM, AVG, MAX, MIN, and COUNT. These functions generate elementary statistics, summarizing data for an entire table or for selected rows within the table. The five aggregate functions obey similar language restrictions.

SUM. SUM(*column*) calculates the sum of all selected values for a given column. SUM(Kilos) generates the total of the "Kilos" column. Rows containing NULL values in the "Kilos" column do not affect this sum. (See Box 3-4 to review NULL values.)

AVG. AVG(*column*) calculates the average, or mean, of all selected values for a given column. AVG(Kilos) generates the average of the "Kilos" column. Rows containing NULL values in the "Kilos" column do not affect this average.

MAX. MAX(*column*) calculates the maximum of all selected values of a given column. MAX(Kilos) generates the largest value in the "Kilos" column. Rows containing NULL values in the "Kilos" column do not affect this maximum.

MIN. MIN(*column*) calculates the minimum of all selected values of a given column. MIN(Kilos) generates the smallest value in the "Kilos" column. Rows containing NULL values in the "Kilos" column do not affect this minimum.

COUNT. COUNT is unique among the aggregate functions because it comes in two versions:

1. COUNT(*column*) calculates the number of all selected values of a given column. COUNT(Kilos) counts the non-NULL values in the "Kilos" column. This is similar to the other four aggregate functions. To count the number of distinct values, use COUNT(DISTINCT *column*).

2. COUNT(*) calculates the total number of rows in a table. This result is independent of the presence of duplicates and NULL values in the rows. COUNT is the only aggregate function that may process complete rows and individual columns. Incorrect use of the count function is shown in Box 4-2.

Noga wanted to know how many kilos of candy she sold. She obtained this value with the query illustrated in Figure 4-3.

```
SELECT   SUM(Kilos)
   FROM   Purchase;

   SUM (Kilos)
           71.1
```

Figure 4-3 The Aggregate Function SUM

The query in Figure 4-3 did not meet Noga's precise information need. It calculated *all* candy sales rather than sales for product number 5. The appropriate query is illustrated in Figure 4-4. Because she had enough of the secret ingredient to produce 20 kilograms of product number 5, she was able to fill all orders without rationing the product.

```
SELECT   SUM(Kilos)
  FROM   Purchase
 WHERE   Prodnum = 5;


SUM (Kilos)
       15.9
```

Figure 4-4 The Aggregate Function SUM for One Product

The COUNT function may be used differently from the other aggregate functions. COUNT (*) indicates that all columns are processed. For example, to determine the number of purchases involving product number 5, Noga coded the query shown in Figure 4-5a. This information could also be generated with the query in Figure 4-5b.

a

```
SELECT   COUNT (*)
  FROM   Purchase
 WHERE   Prodnum = 5;


COUNT (*)
       3
```

b

```
SELECT   COUNT(Purchnum)
  FROM   Purchase
 WHERE   Prodnum = 5;


COUNT (Purchnum)
                3
```

Figure 4-5 Two Ways of Using the Aggregate Function COUNT for One Product

Noga wanted to know how many product numbers were in the Purchase table. She determined this with the query shown in Figure 4-6a. Here, the logic error was not hidden. She needed the DISTINCT quantifier discussed in Chapter 2. Noga then coded the query shown in Figure 4-6b.

a

```
SELECT   COUNT(Prodnum)
  FROM   Purchase;


COUNT(Prodnum)
           14
```

b

```
SELECT   COUNT(DISTINCT Prodnum)
  FROM   Purchase;


COUNT(Prodnum)
           4
```

Figure 4-6 Two Ways to COUNT Products in the Purchase Table

EXERCISES

3. Write an SQL query to find the maximum number of kilos of a single type of candy. Show the output.

4. Write an SQL query to find the maximum number of kilos of a single type of candy, provided that the ready date is October 28th or October 29th. Show the output.

BOX 4-2

Hidden Logic Errors

Chapter 3 presented queries containing logic errors (see Box 3-3) that generated obviously incorrect results. Sometimes queries contain hidden logic errors. Although such queries are in error, they generate seemingly correct results. For instance, each of the two following queries,

```
SELECT   COUNT (*)          SELECT   COUNT (*)
   FROM  Purchase              FROM  Purchase
  WHERE  Prodnum = 5;         WHERE  Prodnum > 4;
```

generates the following output:

```
COUNT (*)
        3
```

However, these queries are not equivalent. If we want to know how many purchases involved product number 5 we should use the left-hand query. The right-hand query gives the right answer until someone purchases candy whose product number is 6 or more. Then the output will be incorrect.

When a query that "always worked" no longer generates correct output, suspect a hidden logic error. The query was really always wrong, but incomplete testing made it seem correct. A similar phenomenon often occurs in computer programming.

Common Error

Inspired by Chapter 2's examples, Noga wanted the number of distinct combinations of customer types and zip codes. She attempted to output this count with the following query:

```
SELECT   COUNT(DISTINCT Custtype, Zipcode)
   FROM  Customer;
```

which generates an error message such as:

```
COUNT   is an unknown field.
```

Her query attempted to count two columns. But aggregate functions operate only on a single column or, for the COUNT (*) function only, all columns. In technical terms, we say that aggregate functions take only a single argument.

The GROUP BY Clause

When referring to the Purchase table, we must distinguish between purchases of a single type of candy and a customer's complete purchase. Each row in the Purchase table corresponds to the purchase of a single type of candy. A complete purchase may include several rows, all with the same purchase number. Noga applied SQL's GROUP BY clause to process rows sharing a purchase number, which generates information by complete purchase. A query that calculates the sum of candy bought for each purchase number is shown in Figure 4-7.

```
SELECT   Purchnum, SUM(Kilos)
  FROM   Purchase
 GROUP   BY Purchnum;


Purchnum        SUM(Kilos)
    1234              3.5
    1235             15.0
    1236              5.7
    1237              3.7
    1238              9.3
    1239              3.0
    1240             18.8
    1241              8.6
    1242              3.5
```

Figure 4-7 GROUPing Purchase Numbers

After reviewing the results in Figure 4-7, Noga realized she needed the candy data broken down by date as well as by product number. Furthermore, she wanted to know how many individual candy purchases composed each output row. So she coded the query shown in Figure 4-8.

```
SELECT   Prodnum, Purchdat, SUM(Kilos), COUNT(*)
  FROM   Purchase
 GROUP   BY Prodnum, Purchdat;
```

Prodnum	Purchdat	SUM(Kilos)	COUNT(*)
1	10/28/1992	5.5	2
1	10/29/1992	4.7	2
2	10/28/1992	15.0	3
2	10/29/1992	18.2	1
3	10/28/1992	7.4	2
3	10/29/1992	4.4	1
5	10/29/1992	15.9	3

Figure 4-8 GROUPing Product Numbers by Purchase Date

Noga then wanted to extract the same information for purchases made on 10/29/1992. Manually selecting one of two possible dates might not be too bad. Manually selecting one of two dozen possible dates is onerous and error-prone. Besides, couldn't she use the computer and SQL to do the selection for her? To select the purchase date 10/29/1992 she added the WHERE clause to the earlier query. Let's see how this works.

The computer first selects the purchase date and then groups the selected rows. Therefore the WHERE clause should precede the GROUP BY clause. (Note, some SQL implementations insist that the WHERE clause precede the GROUP BY clause, others do not. But no matter what your particular SQL implementation allows, *you* should code your queries correctly.) The query is shown in Figure 4-9.

```
SELECT   Prodnum, Purchdat, SUM(Kilos), COUNT(*)
  FROM   Purchase
 WHERE   Purchdat = '10/29/1992'
 GROUP   BY Prodnum, Purchdat;
```

Prodnum	Purchdat	SUM(Kilos)	COUNT(*)
1	10/29/1992	4.7	2
2	10/29/1992	18.2	3
3	10/29/1992	4.4	1
5	10/29/1992	15.9	3

Figure 4-9 GROUPing Product Numbers for One Purchase Date

The GROUP BY clause extends the power of aggregate functions to calculate statistics for selected rows. Although this clause is a powerful tool for processing instead of merely extracting data, it is easy to make errors using it.

Common Errors

It is easy to make errors when working with the GROUP BY clause and aggregate functions.

Misuse of WHERE Clause. Suppose we want to rerun the query shown in Figure 4-9 to process only for products whose SUM(Kilos) is greater than 10, independent of the purchase date. A simple but incorrect solution is replacing the clause

```
WHERE   Purchdat = '10/29/1992'
```

with the clause

```
WHERE   SUM(Kilos) > 10.0
```

forming the following query:

```
SELECT  Prodnum, Purchdat, SUM(Kilos), COUNT(*)
  FROM  Purchase
  WHERE  SUM(Kilos) > 10.0
  GROUP  BY Prodnum, Purchdat;
```

This query generates an error message such as the following:

```
illegal  SELECT  function
```

The query is illegal because the WHERE clause evaluates rows one at a time, while aggregate functions such as SUM evaluate groups of rows. We will see shortly how to code such queries. But first we examine another common error and solve some exercises using the GROUP BY clause.

Misuse of SELECTed Columns. When coding a query with one or more aggregate functions, all SELECTed columns must appear in an aggregate function or in a GROUP BY clause. Noga wanted the purchase number and the total number of kilos sold for each product number. She coded the following query:

```
SELECT  Purchnum, SUM(Kilos)
   FROM  Purchase
  GROUP  BY Prodnum;
```

It generates an error message such as the following:

```
- ERROR - Illegal column specification
```

This query attempts to select individual purchase numbers from groups of rows sharing a product number.

5. Write an SQL query to find the count of customers for each zip code. Show the output.

6. Write an SQL query to find the maximum customer number for each type of customer. Show the output.

7. Write an SQL query to find the maximum number of kilos of a single type of candy for every purchase number. Show the output.

The HAVING Clause

Noga wanted to know the amount of candy sold and the number of individual candy purchases that make up complete purchases of more than 10 kilos. She knew that the WHERE clause wouldn't work because it evaluates rows one at a time, while aggregate functions such as SUM evaluate groups of rows. The **HAVING clause** applies a condition to a group of rows. She coded the query with the HAVING clause shown in Figure 4-10. The HAVING and WHERE clauses are compared in Box 4-3.

```
SELECT   Prodnum, Purchdat, SUM(Kilos), COUNT(*)
  FROM   Purchase
 GROUP   BY Prodnum, Purchdat
HAVING   SUM(Kilos) > 10.0;
```

Prodnum	Purchdat	SUM(Kilos)	COUNT(*)
2	10/28/1992	15.0	1
2	10/29/1992	18.2	3
5	10/29/1992	15.9	3

Figure 4-10 The HAVING Clause

8. Write an SQL query to find the maximum number of kilos of a single type of candy for every purchase number provided that the ready date is October 28th or October 29th. Show the output.

9. Write an SQL query to find the customer count for each customer type for each zip code. Show the output.

10. Write an SQL query to find the customer count for each customer type for each zip code, selecting only those zip codes with more than one customer. Show the output.

```
BOX 4-3
```

The HAVING Clause versus the WHERE Clause

Many people get confused between the HAVING clause and the WHERE clause. Both are used to specify rows within one or more tables.

WHERE clause   applies to single rows.

HAVING clause   applies to groups of rows, as formed by the GROUP BY clause.

Combining GROUP BY, HAVING, and ORDER BY Clauses

Noga's philosophy was to solve potential problems before they became real problems. She really wasn't sure about combining the various clauses available for the SELECT statement. Why not try simple examples on the computer? That way, when she truly needed such queries, she would know how to code them. She returned to the query shown in Figure 4-9, which already contained the WHERE clause and the GROUP BY clause. First she added the HAVING clause, as shown in Figure 4-11a. Then she added the ORDER BY clause (presented in Chapter 2), as shown in Figure 4-11b. While these sample queries may not be practical, they are important in showing the result of combining various clauses.

a

```
SELECT   Prodnum, SUM(Kilos), COUNT(*)
  FROM   Purchase
 WHERE   Purchdat = '10/29/1992'
 GROUP   BY Prodnum, Purchdat;
HAVING   SUM(Kilos) > 15
```

Prodnum	SUM(Kilos)	COUNT(*)
2	18.2	3
5	15.9	3

b

```
SELECT   Prodnum, SUM(Kilos), COUNT(*)
  FROM   Purchase
 WHERE   Purchdat = '10/29/1992'
 GROUP   BY Prodnum, Purchdat
```

```
HAVING   SUM(Kilos) > 15
 ORDER   BY Prodnum DESC;
```

Prodnum	SUM(Kilos)	COUNT(*)
5	15.9	3
2	18.2	3

Figure 4-11 Two Ways of Combining Several Clauses in the SELECT Statement

E X E R C I S E S

11. Write an SQL query to find the count of customers of each customer type for each zip code, in zip code order. Show the output.

12. Write a new query of your choice using the WHERE, HAVING, GROUP BY, and ORDER BY clauses and AND or OR operator. Present two versions of this query, explaining the output generated.

Arithmetic Operations on Dates

Simple arithmetic operations may be done on columns defined as SQL DATE data type. Noga wanted to know the number of days between a candy purchase and its ready date. She simply subtracted the "Purchdat" column from the "Readydat" column, as shown in Figure 4-12. She reduced the output by selecting only rows for which the difference between the ready date and the purchase date was not zero. In other words, she selected rows whose ready date does not equal its purchase date.

```
SELECT   Purchnum, Prodnum, Custnum, Readydat — Purchdat
  FROM   Purchase
 WHERE   (Readydat — Purchdat) <> 0;
```

Purchnum	Prodnum	Custnum	Readydat — Purchdat
1235	2	24	2
1237	3	4	5
1239	2	24	1
1240	2	42	2
1240	5	42	4
1241	5	13	1

Figure 4-12 Subtracting Dates

Noga wanted to keep track of candy that customers didn't pick up. Her policy was that any candy not picked up within a week of the purchase date should no longer be sold because it was no longer fresh (she refused to use preservatives in her candies). Rather than flip pages in her calendar, Noga coded the query shown in Figure 4-13.

```
SELECT   Purchnam, Prodnum, Custnum, Readydat, Readydat + 7
  FROM   Purchase;
```

Purchnum	Prodnum	Custnum	Readydat	Readydat + 7
1234	1	22	10/28/1992	11/04/1992
1235	2	24	10/30/1992	11/06/1992
1236	1	41	10/28/1992	11/04/1992
1236	3	41	10/28/1992	11/04/1992
1237	3	4	11/02/1992	11/09/1992
1238	1	37	10/29/1992	11/05/1992
1238	2	37	10/29/1992	11/05/1992
1238	3	37	10/29/1992	11/05/1992
1239	2	24	10/30/1992	11/06/1992
1240	2	42	10/31/1992	11/07/1992
1240	5	42	11/02/1992	11/09/1992
1241	1	13	10/29/1992	11/05/1992
1241	5	13	10/30/1992	11/06/1992
1242	5	12	10/29/1992	11/05/1992

Figure 4-13 Adding a Week to the Ready Date

As mentioned in Chapter 1, each SQL implementation provides its own way to process dates. For example, some SQL versions include a date function *@DAY*, which selects the day of the month from DATE-type columns. Other SQL versions express this function as *DAY*.

TRY IT YOURSELF

1. Determine whether your SQL implementation includes a DAY-type function. If so, write an SQL query using this function. Show the output. How might this function be applied?

2. Determine whether your SQL implementation includes a MONTH-type and a YEAR-type function. If so, write SQL queries using these functions. Show the output. How might these functions be applied?

Syntax and Applications Summary

SQL allows five arithmetic operators, + (addition), − (subtraction), * (multiplication), / (division), and ** or ^ (exponentiation). Addition and subtraction may be performed on DATE-type columns.

SQL calculates elementary statistics with five aggregate functions, SUM, AVG, MAX, MIN, and COUNT, that operate on an entire table or selected rows. NULL values do not affect the values generated by these functions. The COUNT (*) function calculates the total number of rows in a table. This result is independent of the presence of duplicates and NULL values in the rows.

The GROUP BY clause, ordinarily used with the aggregate functions, gathers rows according to shared values of one or more columns. Conditions applying to groups are handled by the HAVING clause rather than the WHERE clause.

Productivity Tip:

MAKE YOUR KEYSTROKES COUNT.

Learn how to repeat commands from the keyboard. Most SQL implementations come with a user interface that allows you to repeat all or part of your keyboard entry, without having to retype everything. For example, in dBASE the Up arrow key recalls the previous command, so pressing this key twice recalls the command entered before the previous command. Among dBASE's other navigation keys, the Home key moves the cursor to the beginning of the command line. By using your implementation's special keystrokes judiciously, you can save extra keystrokes and valuable time.

Chapter Summary

In this chapter we learned the SQL commands required to convert kilograms to pounds. We applied SQL's aggregate functions to determine the total amount of candy sold by purchase and by product type. We examined SQL clauses that regroup and display output to meet diverse needs. We concluded with the arithmetic processing of dates. We queried either the Customer table or the Purchase table, but never the two together. In the next chapter we will link these two tables, for example, to obtain the phone number of customers who purchased candy to be ready on October 29th. Then we examine nested queries, that is, queries within queries, that let us obtain information even when key details are missing.

Review Questions

1. Define in your own terms the following SQL aggregate functions, and describe their use:

a. SUM
b. AVG
c. MAX
d. MIN
e. COUNT

2. Define in your own terms the following SQL clauses, and describe their use:
   a. GROUP BY
   b. HAVING

3. What is a *hidden logic error?* How can you tell if you have made such an error? Do you prefer that your logic errors be hidden or not? Justify your answer.

4. Describe in your own words the difference between the WHERE clause and the HAVING clause. When should each clause be used?

5. What arithmetic operations are available for DATE data types on your SQL implementation? Name an application of each of these functions.

Case Study Exercises

Recall that unstarred questions may be answered using either the full database (tables Cds and Manufs) or the smaller database (tables Smlcds and Manufs). Starred questions require the full database. Given the large number of columns in the tables, output only essential columns.

1. Write an SQL query to determine the total price (Price times Copies) of each CD. Show the output in alphabetical order by title.

2. Write an SQL query to determine the total price of each CD. Show the output in descending order by total price.

3. Write an SQL query to determine the total price and the average price of CDs. Show the output.

4. Write an SQL query to count the number of CDs in each Cdcode ('ADD', etc.). Calculate the average price of these CDs. Show the output.

5. Write an SQL query to count the number of CDs with the word *Classics* in the "Series" column. Group the results by Cdcode. Show the output.

6. Write an SQL query to determine the average discount for manufacturers grouped by city. Show the output.

7. Write an SQL query to determine the earliest year recorded and the latest year recorded for each Cdcode.

*8. Write an SQL query to determine the minimum price per work and the maximum price per work. Show the output.

*9. Write an SQL query to determine the minimum price per minute and the maximum price per minute. Show the output.

*10. Write SQL queries to compare the minimum price, the average price, and the maximum price of CDs for chamber orchestras and nonchamber orchestras. Show the output.

CHAPTER FIVE

Querying Multiple Tables (Introduction)

Chapter 4 showed us how to apply SQL's arithmetic processing features, both simple commands and aggregate functions. We mastered several SQL clauses that regroup and display output to meet diverse information needs. We extended arithmetic processing to include dates. But all our queries accessed only a single table at once, either the Customer table or the Purchase table. This chapter begins with the important join *operation, which links two or more tables. This operation can obtain phone numbers of customers who purchased candy with an October 29th ready date. We examine the UNION command that strings together two or more SQL statements, and its restrictions. We conclude the chapter by coding nested queries, that is, queries inside queries, that let us obtain information even when key details are missing.*

OBJECTIVES

You have met this chapter's objectives when you can:

- Code SQL *joins* with or without aliases.
- Code SQL queries using the UNION operator.
- Code SQL nested queries.
- Code SQL queries using the ANY, SOME, and ALL operators.
- Apply all of these SQL operations to meet business and other information-processing needs.

The *Join* Operation

Noga was unhappy that the data she needed always seemed to be spread over both the Purchase table and the Customer table. For example, the Purchase table didn't contain enough customer information. While it did include customer number, important data such as customer type and phone number were absent. On the other hand, the Customer table provided no information whatsoever about candy purchases. Noga questioned the point of having data in two tables if you can't easily mix and match the data when you need to. Fortunately, even nontechnical users can apply SQL to process data contained in two or more tables.

A key aspect of relational databases is the ease of linking data contained in two or more tables in response to selection and presentation criteria. SQL's *join* operation is one way to combine data from two or more tables. Note, in spite of its name, this SQL operation does not contain the word *join*. In fact, *join* is not even a reserved word in SQL.

Noga wanted to combine rows from the Purchase table with associated rows from the Customer table, linking each purchase with the customer who made it. The connection is established via the customer number, which is common to both tables. To simplify the output generated, Noga displayed only three columns. She coded the SQL command shown in Figure 5-1 to obtain the customer name, the customer number, and the purchase number associated with each purchase. Let's look at this *join* operation line by line.

```
SELECT   Custname, Customer.Custnum, Purchnum
  FROM   Customer, Purchase
 WHERE   Customer.Custnum = Purchase.Custnum;
```

Custname	Customer.Custnum	Purchnum
Armstrong, Inc.	4	1237
Swedish Burgers	12	1242
Pickled Pickles	13	1241
Pickled Pickles	13	1241
The Candy Kid	22	1234
Waterman, Al	24	1235
Waterman, Al	24	1239
Bobby Bon Bons	37	1238
Bobby Bon Bons	37	1238
Bobby Bon Bons	37	1238
Montag, Susie	41	1236
Montag, Susie	41	1236
Columberg Sweets	42	1240
Columberg Sweets	42	1240

Figure 5-1 A *Join* Operation

Line 1. The first line,

```
SELECT Custname, Customer.Custnum, Purchnum
```

limits the output to three columns. Because the "Custnum" column exists in two tables (Customer and Purchase), most SQL implementations require that the query specify which table's "Custnum" column is desired. The expression

```
Customer.Custnum
```

refers to the "Custnum" column in the Customer table. The technical term for this specification is *qualifying the column name.*

Line 2. The second line,

```
FROM Customer, Purchase
```

joins the two tables. The number of rows generated depends on the WHERE clause.

Line 3. The third line,

```
WHERE Customer.Custnum = Purchase.Custnum;
```

restricts output to rows whose customer number in the Customer table equals the customer number in the Purchase table. Each "Custnum" column is qualified by its table name.

When the computer executes this query, it compares the first row in the Customer table to each of the 14 rows in the Purchase table, looking for a match between the two customer numbers. The initial value of

```
Customer.Custnum
```

is 1. The WHERE clause commands the computer to generate output only for Purchase table rows whose customer number is 1, that is, where

```
Purchase.Custnum
```

equals 1. It finds no such row, and so customer number 1 does not appear in the output. Next the computer compares the Customer table's second row, where

```
Customer.Custnum
```

equals 4, to each of the 14 rows in the Purchase table. The computer first generates output when processing the Purchase table's fifth row, purchase number 1237, whose customer number is equal to 4. The first output row contains a customer name of *Armstrong, Inc.,* a customer number of 4, and a purchase number of *1237*. This customer made no other purchases. Next comes customer number 12. The computer scans each of the 14 rows in the Purchase table for customer number 12 (purchase number 1242). Verify by hand this query's remaining output.

Noga thought that qualifying column names rendered the *join* operation tedious. The use of an *alias* reduces this work. An **alias** is a temporary table name that obeys the SQL table-naming conventions. One alias for Customer is X. To use an alias: Type the table name, then a space, and then the alias. Figure 5-2a shows a query composed of a *join* operation with the DISTINCT qualifier (see Chapter 2) that suppresses duplicate rows and places the output in alphabetical order by customer name. Figure 5-2b presents the same query except that the alias *X* replaces the table name Customer. The two queries generate identical output except for column headers.

a

```
SELECT   DISTINCT Custname, Customer.Custnum, Purchnum
  FROM   Customer, Purchase
 WHERE   Customer.Custnum = Purchase.Custnum;
```

Custname	Customer.Custnum	Purchnum
Armstrong, Inc.	4	1237
Bobby Bon Bons	37	1238
Columberg Sweets	42	1240
Montag, Susie	41	1236
Pickled Pickles	13	1241
Swedish Burgers	12	1242
The Candy Kid	22	1234
Waterman, Al	24	1235
Waterman, Al	24	1239

b

```
SELECT   DISTINCT Custname, X.Custnum, Purchnum
  FROM   Customer X, Purchase
 WHERE   X.Custnum = Purchase.Custnum;
```

Custname	X.Custnum	Purchnum
Armstrong, Inc.	4	1237
Bobby Bon Bons	37	1238
Columberg Sweets	42	1240
Montag, Susie	41	1236
Pickled Pickles	13	1241
Swedish Burgers	12	1242
The Candy Kid	22	1234

```
Waterman, Al                    24              1235
Waterman, Al                    24              1239
```

Figure 5-2 DISTINCT *Join* Operation—**a,** without an Alias, **b,** with an Alias

---

TRY IT YOURSELF

1. Play computer to generate output for the following query:

   ```
   SELECT   Custname, Customer.Custnum, Purchnum
     FROM   Purchase, Customer
    WHERE   Customer.Custnum = Purchase.Custnum;
   ```

   How does this query's output compare with the output for the query in Figure 5-1?

2. Does your SQL implementation require that you qualify the "Custnum" column in the query in Figure 5-1? Does it make a difference which table name is used when identifying the customer number?

3. What happens if we reverse the order of the columns tested for equality in the WHERE clause?

4. The alias *X* does not readily stand for Customer. Does your SQL implementation allow the alias *C* for Customer?

The *join* operation we have been examining is known as an **equijoin,** because rows are generated whenever the contents of the relevant columns are equal. SQL allows *join*s other than equijoins. Their utility depends on the application. For example, it is legal to *join* rows whose customer number in the Customer table is twice the customer number in the Purchase table. Such a query would link Al Waterman, customer number 24, with purchase number 1242 made by customer number 12 (Swedish Burgers). It has no practical application. But remember, SQL itself cannot determine whether a given query is meaningful or not; SQL can only determine the query's legality. It's up to you to determine the query's validity. Blind acceptance of computer-generated output inevitably leads to trouble. The more complicated the query, the greater the likelihood of generating false output.

Business is always full of surprises. The Queen of England was coming to visit Noga's town on October 29th. Noga was pleased when the city council asked her to supply candy for the high tea honoring the Queen. But the

Queen's motorcade was scheduled to pass within two blocks of the store. The police would cordon off her store between 12 noon and 2 p.m., eliminating candy pickups. Noga had to call affected customers. The candy's ready date and the customer's phone number were on different tables. But Noga now knew how to *join* the tables. Note, in the following query the column that *join*s the tables does not appear in the output. The query is shown in Figure 5-3.

```
SELECT   DISTINCT Custname, Phone
  FROM   Customer, Purchase
 WHERE   Customer.Custnum = Purchase.Custnum
   AND   Readydat = '10/29/1992';
```

Custname	Phone
Swedish Burgers	434-9090
Pickled Pickles	324-8909
Bobby Bon Bons	434-9045

Figure 5-3 Combining a *Join* Operation with the AND Operator

E X E R C I S E S

1. Write an SQL query to find the customer name and number for all customers purchasing more than 7 kilos of a single type of candy. Show the output.
2. Write an SQL query to find the customer name and number for all customers buying candy whose purchase date is different from the ready date. Show the output.

Common Errors

While the *join* operation is fairly easy to carry out, it is subject to several errors.

Omitting the WHERE Clause. Omitting the WHERE clause in a *join* operation is a serious error. It doesn't keep the *join* operation from taking place. On the contrary, it generates all possible combinations of rows in the *join*ed tables. The query

```
SELECT   *
  FROM   Customer, Purchase;
```

generates 140 (10 × 14) rows, most of which are meaningless. For example, the first output row combines the first row in the Customer table, customer number 1, whose name is Jones, Joe, with the first row in the Purchase table, purchase number 1234. This row is incorrect. In fact, customer number 22 made purchase number 1234. Furthermore, because this query did not specify which columns to select, all 12 columns from the two tables would be displayed.

Omitting the Comma Separating the Table Names. Omitting the comma separating the table names causes an error. The query

```
SELECT   Custname, Phone
  FROM   Customer Purchase
 WHERE   Customer.Custnum = Purchase.Custnum
   AND   Readydat = '10/29/1992';
```

generates an error message such as the following:

```
-ERROR-   Correlation Customer not found
```

Clearly, the computer has misunderstood the query. (We will study correlations in Chapter 7.)

Misspecifying Output Columns. Recall from Chapter 4 the use of aggregate functions as in the following query, which adds all purchases for a given customer, irrespective of purchase number or product type:

```
SELECT   Custnum, SUM(Kilos)
  FROM   Purchase
 GROUP   BY Custnum;
```

It generates the following results:

Custnum	SUM(Kilos)
4	3.7
12	3.5
13	8.6

(Remaining output suppressed.)

Noga applied the *join* operation to add the customer name and telephone number to this information as follows:

```
SELECT   X.Custnum, Custname, Phone, SUM(Kilos)
  FROM   Purchase, Customer X
 WHERE   X.Custnum = Purchase.Custnum
 GROUP   BY X.Custnum;
```

This command generates an error message such as the following:

```
-ERROR-   Illegal column specification
```

This query is rejected because output columns must appear either within a GROUP BY clause or in an aggregate function such as SUM. While this restriction applies to the GROUP BY clause, in effect it eliminates a *join* operation.

Misidentifying Columns. As with any query, identifying columns correctly is essential. Because *join*s may involve many columns, the possibility of error is increased. Consider the following query:

```
SELECT  Custname, X.Custnum
  FROM  Customer X, Purchase
 WHERE  X.Custnum = Purchase.Purchnum;
```

which generates an error message such as the following:

```
-WARNING- No rows exist or satisfy the specified clause
```

The *join* operation is not restricted to linking two tables. Noga's expanding business is at the point of requiring a third table to store additional data. Chapter 7 applies more sophisticated *join* operations, such as SELECTing data from three tables. The *join* is summarized in Box 5-1. Our next subject is the UNION operator, which permits us to string together the results of two or more queries.

BOX 5-1

The *Join* Operation Summarized

The *join* operation combines two or more tables to generate a single table, based on a common column to link each pair of tables. Most SQL implementations require that common columns be qualified by the name of the table in which they appear, for example,

```
Customer.Custnum
```

Data from the linked tables is specified by the familiar WHERE clause. Aliases may be used to abbreviate table names.

The UNION Query Operator

The **UNION query operator** combines the output of two or more separate SELECT statements. Noga applied the UNION query operator to obtain the customer number of all private customers and the customer number associated with purchases whose ready date is 10/28/1992, as shown in Figure 5-4a.

a

```
SELECT   Custnum
  FROM   Customer
 WHERE   Custtype = 'P'
 UNION
SELECT   Custnum
  FROM   Purchase
 WHERE   Readydat = '10/28/1992';
```

```
Custnum
       1
      22
      24
      39
      41
```

b

```
SELECT   Custnum
  FROM   Customer
 WHERE   Custtype = 'P'
 UNION   ALL  (Shows Duplicates)
SELECT   Custnum
  FROM   Purchase
 WHERE   Readydat = '10/28/1992';
```

```
Custnum
       1
      24
      39
      41
      22
      41
      41
```

Figure 5-4 a, The UNION Query Operator, and **b,** the UNION ALL Query Operator

Unlike most SQL commands, which automatically generate duplicates, the UNION command suppresses duplicates.

Customer number 41 appears only once even though she is private (see the Customer table) and purchased candy whose ready date is 10/28/1992 (see the Purchase table). To generate duplicates, specify UNION ALL, as shown in Figure 5-4b.

In a sense UNION corresponds to DISTINCT (no duplicates) and UNION ALL corresponds to the bare-bones command (duplicates.)

Because they process distinct tables, the two SELECT statements in either part of Figure 5-4 may not be combined into a single SELECT statement with an OR operator.

Common Error

The output in Figure 5-4a or 5-4b is not very useful, because the customer numbers are not further identified. The following command attempts to identify further the two sets of customer numbers:

```
SELECT   Custnum, Custtype
   FROM   Customer
  WHERE   Custtype = 'P'
  UNION
SELECT   Custnum, Readydat
   FROM   Purchase
  WHERE   Readydat = '10/28/1992';
```

This command generates an error message such as the following:

```
-ERROR- Column type mismatch in UNION
```

The UNION query operator requires that each SELECT statement contain an equal number of columns, and each corresponding column have the same data type and length. (Some SQL implementations ease the length restriction.) "Custtype" and "Readydat" are not even the same data type.

The UNION query operator is relatively inflexible, for it requires that corresponding columns be of the same data type and length. In spite of this limitation, it is important to learn the UNION query operator so you can apply it when appropriate.

The ORDER BY clause may be used with the UNION query operator but only following the final SELECT statement. The ORDER BY clause sorts all the results. The position number is required because the output results may be untitled. Figure 5-5 illustrates the composite query and its output.

```
SELECT   Custnum, Custnum
   FROM   Customer
  WHERE   Custtype = 'P'
  UNION
SELECT   Custnum, Purchnum
   FROM   Purchase
  WHERE   Readydat = '10/28/1992'
  ORDER   BY 2;
```

Custnum	UNNAMED
1	1
24	24
39	39
41	41
22	1234
41	1236

Figure 5-5 ORDERing the Results of a UNION

TRY IT YOURSELF

5. The "Custnum" column appears twice in the initial query of Figure 5-5. What happens if the second occurrence is replaced by another column of the Customer table?

6. See what happens when you try to sort results for the query in Figure 5-5 by the "Custnum" column.

7. See what happens when you try to sort results for the query in Figure 5-5 by the "UNNAMED" column or a similar column name as supplied by your SQL implementation.

EXERCISES

3. Apply the UNION query operator to combine two previous SQL queries using columns of your choice, provided they are compatible, as discussed earlier. Show the output.

4. Write two separate SQL queries using the ORDER BY clause to sort the results of Exercise 3 in two different ways. Show the output of each query.

Nested Queries

A **nested query** is a query within another query. Many SQL implementations permit up to 16 levels of queries. For simplicity, we restrict our examination of nested queries to two levels. While nested queries several levels deep may be confusing, many people find two-level nested queries easier than *join* operations.

Noga wanted information on Al Waterman's purchases. Because she didn't remember his customer number, she couldn't use the *join* operation. She could code two separate queries: the first one to find Al's customer number in the Customer table, and the second one to obtain information from the Purchase table, once she knew his customer number. This process has two drawbacks:

1. It is clumsy to code two queries.
2. She would have to write down Al's customer number or take a chance on memorizing it, so she might make a mistake entering the customer number in the second query.

One reason Noga used a computer was to avoid having to jot down such bits of information. So she used a nested query to meet her information needs, as shown in Figure 5-6. The statement there works as follows: First the computer analyzes the query within parentheses, called the **inner query** or **subquery.** The inner query evaluates a single column, in this case, the "Customer Number" (24). The inner query automatically supplies the selected value to the query outside the parentheses, also called the **outer query,** which completes the selection process. Thus a nested query enabled Noga to obtain information from the tables even when she forgot such details as Al Waterman's customer number. Box 5-2 summarizes nested queries.

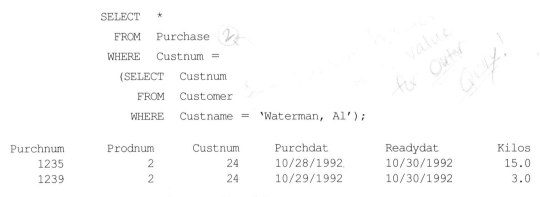

```
SELECT    *
    FROM    Purchase
    WHERE    Custnum =
        (SELECT    Custnum
            FROM    Customer
            WHERE    Custname =    'Waterman, Al');
```

Purchnum	Prodnum	Custnum	Purchdat	Readydat	Kilos
1235	2	24	10/28/1992	10/30/1992	15.0
1239	2	24	10/29/1992	10/30/1992	3.0

Figure 5-6 An Elementary Nested Query

Next, Noga discovered the following message scribbled on a napkin: "Somebody on Globe called about her order." Without SQL, such an incomplete message might be useless. However, even this message is enough to generate a useful SQL query. Noga modified the query in Figure 5-6 to obtain purchase information without knowing the customer number, the customer name, or the exact customer address. Figure 5-7 presents the modified query. (On the back of the napkin Noga found the phone number, so she didn't have to code a *join* to get this information. Later in the chapter we will see how to combine a nested query and a *join.*)

```
SELECT   *
   FROM   Purchase
  WHERE   Custnum =
     (SELECT   Custnum
         FROM   Customer
        WHERE   Custaddr LIKE '%Globe%');
```

Purchnum	Prodnum	Custnum	Purchdat	Readydat	Kilos
1237	3	4	10/28/1992	11/02/1992	3.7

Figure 5-7 A More Sophisticated Nested Query

Bob Ferreta from Bobby Bon Bons called about his order. Though he was one of Noga's best customers, he was always bugging her about setting up a delivery service. He never could find the time to pick up his candy. Noga was considering his request seriously. She wondered how many customers lived close to Bob. What does *close* mean in computer terms? Noga decided to list customers who shared his zip code. She coded the query shown in Figure 5-8.

```
SELECT   *
   FROM   Customer
  WHERE   Zipcode =
     (SELECT   Zipcode
         FROM   Customer
        WHERE   Custname = 'Bobby Bon Bons');
```

Custnum	Custname	Custtype	Custaddr	Zipcode	Phone
1	Jones, Joe	P	1234 Main St.	91212	434-1231
4	Armstrong, Inc.	R	231 Globe Blvd.	91212	434-7664
22	The Candy Kid	W	2121 Main St.	91212	563-4545
37	Bobby Bon Bons	R	12 Nichi Cres.	91212	434-9045

Figure 5-8 A Nested Query Selecting a Given Zip Code

Nested Queries Summarized

A nested query is one query within another. First the inner query or subquery (the one within parentheses) supplies a selected value or values to the outer query. Then the outer query tests these values to generate final output. If the inner query is known to generate only a single value, comparison operators such as = and > may be used. If the inner query might generate several values, the IN, ANY, SOME, or ALL operator must be used (see Box 5-3).

   These two sets of queries are equivalent:

```
SELECT   *                              SELECT   Custnum
   FROM   Purchase                         FROM   Customer
  WHERE   Custnum =                        WHERE   Custname = 'Waterman, Al';
(SELECT   Custnum                                  followed by
   FROM   Customer                       SELECT   *
  WHERE   Custname = 'Waterman, Al');       FROM   Purchase
                                           WHERE   Custnum = 24;
```

It is usually easier to code a nested query than to code one query, and then copy a value (such as customer number 24) into a second query.

E X E R C I S E S

5. Write an SQL nested query to find information about the customer who ordered 14 kilos of candy. Show the output.

6. Write an SQL nested query to find information about purchases whose ready date is the same as customer number 4's. Show the output.

Common Errors

Forgetting a Parenthesis. When coding nested queries it is very easy to forget a parenthesis. For example, the nested query:

```
SELECT   *
   FROM   Customer
  WHERE   Zipcode =
    (SELECT   Zipcode
       FROM   Customer
      WHERE   Custname = 'Bobby Bon Bons';
```

generates an error message such as the following:

```
-ERROR- Parentheses required around the list of items for the
IN clause.
```

Inner Query Incorrectly Specifies Too Many Values. Until now all our successful nested queries contained an inner query generating a single value. Consider an alternative example:

```
SELECT   *
   FROM   Purchase
  WHERE   Custnum =
    (SELECT   Custnum
       FROM   Customer
      WHERE   Zipcode = '91213');
```

The subquery generates customer numbers 12 and 41. As written, the outer query cannot process two separate customers. The nested query produces an error message such as the following:

```
-ERROR- Too many rows returned
```

The next section illustrates nested queries whose subqueries generate several values or rows.

Nested Queries Using IN, ANY, SOME, and ALL

Noga had been seriously thinking about setting up a delivery service. To do so she needed all the information she could get. For example, she wanted purchase information by zip code. But her previous query seemed to indicate it was impossible to use a nested query for zip codes with more than one customer. This restriction is not strictly true.

To resolve this dilemma, Noga used the *IN* operator. Recall from Chapter 3 that the IN operator indicates whether a proposed item is equal to any value among a series of values. Figure 5-9 illustrates a nested query applying the IN operator.

The *ANY* operator and the *SOME* operator are completely equivalent. In the following discussion and examples you may replace ANY by SOME and obtain exactly the same results.

Common Error

Columberg Sweets was on the warpath. As a wholesale customer it expected discounts. Noga wanted to examine Columberg's purchases before making

```
SELECT *
  FROM   Customer
  WHERE   Custnum IN
     (SELECT   Custnum
         FROM   Customer
       WHERE   Zipcode = '91213');
```

Custnum	Custname	Custtype	Custaddr	Zipcode	Phone
12	Swedish Burgers	R	1889 20th N.E.	91213	434-9090
41	Montag, Susie	P	981 Montview	91213	456-2091

Figure 5-9 A Nested Query Applying the IN Operator

any commitment. She knew their customer number was 42, and wrote a nested query comparing their purchases with those of other customers.

```
SELECT    *
   FROM   Purchase
  WHERE   Kilos >
     (SELECT   Kilos
         FROM   Purchase
       WHERE   Custnum = 42);
```

This generated an error message:

```
-ERROR- Too many rows returned
```

Earlier, Noga had corrected such an error by using the IN operator. This time she corrected it by using the ANY operator, as shown in Figure 5-10a. The results may be interpreted as follows: Each output row contains more kilos than the number of kilos in at least one of customer number 42's rows. An equivalent query is shown in Figure 5-10b.

Both of these nested queries have a problem. One output row is for customer number 42. This is because 14.0 kilos (product number 2 on purchase number 1240) is greater than 4.8 kilos (product number 5 on purchase number 1240). To correct this problem, Noga used the ALL operator to compare the maximum purchase by customer 42 to the other purchases, as shown in Figure 5-11a. This generated less output. The results may be interpreted as follows: Each output row contains a number of kilos greater than all of the rows for customer number 42. An equivalent query is shown in Figure 5-11b.

a

```
SELECT   *
   FROM   Purchase
   WHERE  Kilos >
      ANY  (SELECT Kilos
      FROM   Purchase
      WHERE  Custnum = 42);
```

b

```
SELECT   *
   FROM   Purchase
   WHERE  Kilos >
      (SELECT  MIN(Kilos)
      FROM   Purchase
      WHERE  Custnum = 42);
```

Purchnum	Prodnum	Custnum	Purchdat	Readydat	Kilos
1235	2	24	10/28/1992	10/30/1992	15.0
1240	2	42	10/29/1992	10/31/1992	14.0
1241	5	13	10/29/1992	10/30/1992	7.6

Figure 5-10 Two Equivalent Nested Queries

a

```
SELECT   *
   FROM   Purchase
   WHERE  Kilos >
      ALL  (SELECT Kilos
      FROM   Purchase
      WHERE  Custnum = 42);
```

b

```
SELECT   *
   FROM   Purchase
   WHERE  Kilos >
      (SELECT  MAX(Kilos)
      FROM   Purchase
      WHERE  Custnum = 42);
```

Purchnum	Prodnum	Custnum	Purchdat	Readydat	Kilos
1235	2	24	10/28/1992	10/30/1992	15.0

Figure 5-11 Two Additional Equivalent Nested Queries

E X E R C I S E S

7. Write an SQL nested query to generate information for all customers on Main Street. Show the output.

8. Write two different SQL nested queries to generate information for all purchases ready after Pickled Pickles' *earliest* ready date. You may identify this customer by customer number 13. Show the output.

9. Write two different SQL nested queries to generate information for all purchases ready after Pickled Pickles' *latest* ready date. You may identify this customer by customer number 13. Show the output.

Combining a Nested Query and a *Join*

Noga was ready to call it quits for this round of *join*s and nested queries. She knew she'd have to reexamine both *join*s and nested queries if her database grew to service her expanded business. She needed an answer to one short question now: Could she combine the *join* operation with a nested query? She wanted to go back to the Al Waterman query and generate both customer information and purchase information, even if she could not remember his customer number. The answer to her question is yes. She obtained this information with the query shown in Figure 5-12. (She had one further question: When was Al Waterman going to give her his unlisted phone number?)

```
SELECT    Customer.Custnum, Custname, Phone, Purchnum, Prodnum, Kilos
  FROM    Purchase, Customer
 WHERE    Customer.Custnum =
   (SELECT   Custnum
      FROM   Customer
     WHERE   Custname = 'Waterman, Al'
       AND   Purchase.Custnum = Customer.Custnum);
```

Customer.Custnum	Custname	Phone	Purchnum	Prodnum	Kilos
24	Waterman, Al	-0-	1235	2	15.0
24	Waterman, Al	-0-	1239	2	3.0

Figure 5-12 Combining a *Join* Operation with a Nested Query

E X E R C I S E S

10. Add a *join* operator to one of the previous nested query exercises. The combined query should display columns from each of the tables. Show your output.

Syntax and Applications Summary

The *join* operation allows data to be combined from two or more tables. Columns in the SELECT clause that appear in more than one table are identified by *table-name.column-name,* a process known as *qualifying the column name.*
    The FROM clause indicates the joined tables as follows:

```
FROM table-name1, table-name2, etc.
```

The WHERE clause indicates how the tables are joined, for example,

```
WHERE table-name1.columna = table-name2.columna
```

Output rows are generated only when this condition is met.
    Nested queries are queries within queries. They take the following form:

BOX 5-3

Summary of the Use of the IN, ANY, SOME, and ALL Operators in Nested Queries

The IN, ANY, SOME, and ALL operators may be used when coding nested queries. Recall that the value or values generated by the inner query are processed by the outer query. Consider an inner query processing customers with a given zip code: If several customers share this zip code, however, the outer query cannot use comparison operators such as = and > to compare directly the "Custnum" column to all such customers. But it can determine if the "Custnum" column's value is among (IN) those customers.

The ANY and SOME operators are totally equivalent, and may be used only with nested queries. In our example, the ANY and SOME operator may replace the IN operator. But the ANY and SOME may also be used with comparison operators such as >. The expression

```
Kilos > ANY (inner query)
```

evaluates as True if the Kilos value in the outer query is greater than that generated by at least one row in the inner query (see Figure 5-10a). The expression

```
Kilos > ALL (inner query)
```

evaluates as True if the Kilos value in the outer query is greater than that generated by every single row in the inner query (see Figure 5-11a).

```
SELECT   output-column-name1, output-column-name2, etc.
  FROM   table-name1
 WHERE   column-name1 operator
    (SELECT   column-name2
       FROM   table-name2
      WHERE   expression);
```

If the inner query, the one within parentheses, is known to generate only one value, the operator may be a comparison operator. When the inner query might generate more than one value, the operator must be one of the following: IN, ANY, SOME, or ALL. The IN operator tests whether any *column-name1* is contained in the values selected for *column-name2*. The ANY and SOME operators are used with comparison operators, such as =. They test whether a *column-name1* value meets the specified condition for any value generated by the inner query. The ALL operator is used with comparison operators, such as =. It tests whether a *column-name1* value meets the specified condition for all values generated by the inner query.

Productivity Tip:
NOTE DOWN YOUR ERRORS.

Undoubtedly you have made errors coding SQL queries. There is absolutely nothing wrong in making an error—once. But making the same error twice is a waste of time. Never go to the computer without your error notebook. Whenever something goes wrong, describe the error in your notebook, including the query, the expected results, the results actually obtained or the error message, and the reason for the error. If you can't explain the error yourself, find someone who can. Check your list of errors before coding a similar query. Review your notebook before tests.

Chapter Summary

This chapter introduced queries involving two tables. We explored alternate ways of processing such queries, the *join* operation and nested queries. We added to our toolbox several new aspects of the SELECT statement. We have not yet finished examining this very powerful statement. But first we will examine the statements for table creation and for loading them with data. We will show how to modify existing tables and add a new table to handle a business's increased processing needs.

Review Questions

1. Define in your own words the following SQL terms, and describe their use:
   a. *join* operation
   b. equijoin
   c. alias
   d. UNION query operator
   e. nested query
   f. inner query
   g. subquery
   h. outer query
   i. ANY operator
   j. SOME operator
   k. ALL operator

2. What is the similarity between the *join* operation and a nested query?

3. What is the difference between the *join* operation and a nested query? When is each one useful?

4. When may a comparison operator be used in a nested query?

Case Study Exercises

Recall that unstarred questions may be answered using either the full database (tables Cds and Manufs) or the smaller database (tables Smlcds and Manufs). Starred questions require the full database. Because of the large number of columns in the tables, output only essential columns.

1. Write an SQL query to select CDs available at a 27.5% or more discount. Show the output.

2. Write an SQL query to select CDs with at least four copies in stock. Show the output.

3. Write an SQL query to show the quality, discount, and year first recorded of all 'ADD' CDs. Show the output.

4. Write an SQL query to select CDs in a Classics series whose quality rating is eight or more. Show the output.

5. Use the UNION query operator to combine two SQL queries, one selecting CDs first recorded in 1970 or before and another with five or more copies in stock. Use the ORDER BY clause to sort the results as desired. Show the output.

6. Modify the query for Case Study Exercise 5 so as to sort the results in a different order. Show the output.

7. Write an SQL nested query selecting CDs for manufacturers located in Chicago. Show the output.

8. Write an SQL nested query to select manufacturers whose quality rating is better than any quality ratings for LM. Show the output.

9. Write an SQL nested query with a *join* to select CDs for manufacturers whose quality rating is better than all quality ratings for LM. Show the output.

*10. Write an SQL query to show the discount and quality rating of CDs recorded by a chamber orchestra. Show the output.

*11. Use the UNION query operator to combine two SQL queries, one whose title includes the word *Symphony*, another whose orchestra name includes the word *Symphony*. Show the output. Recode the query without the UNION query operator.

*12. Modify the queries for Case Study Exercise 11 using the character string *Symph* to account for spelling variations. Show the output.

Creating and Processing Tables

Previous chapters examined multiple facets of the SELECT statement, the single most important Data Manipulation Language (DML) command. The SELECT statement is used to query tables. Until now you used teacher-supplied tables or you built the tables by blindly entering the commands described at the end of Chapter 1 and in Appendix A. We focused on the queries, not on the tables. Although our study of queries is far from complete, we now change the focus to the tables themselves. We start by examining Data Definition Language (DDL) commands to create and delete tables. We create the additional tables required for Noga's candy business and for the case study. We next learn the associated DML commands for inserting data into these tables. We conclude the chapter by examining the DDL commands required to modify presently existing tables.

OBJECTIVES

You have met this chapter's objectives when you can:

- Apply the SQL Data Definition Language commands for: naming tables, naming columns, creating tables, deleting tables, modifying tables.
- Code the SQL Data Manipulation Language statements for loading, modifying, and deleting data.
- Apply all of these Data Definition Language commands and Data Manipulation Language commands to meet business and other information-processing needs.

Creating Tables

Noga was determined to make changes in the way she did business and, consequently, to make changes in her tables.

First was the delivery question. Bob Ferreta wasn't the only customer who wanted her to deliver candy. Personnel was no problem. (Her assistant had been a deliverer for Uncle Mike's pizzeria before Mike's retirement, and Uncle Mike had sent him with the highest recommendations.) So the Purchase table required a new column indicating pickup or delivery.

Her pricing system had been too simple. Noga charged the same amount for each product, independent of its ingredients. She probably lost money on some products and barely broke even on others. Noga needed to bring her prices in line with production costs. This meant creating a new table containing product information, the Product table (discussed later in the chapter).

The present pricing system had another drawback: It charged all customers the same price, independent of customer type or purchase amount. Several customers let Noga know that they expected discounts. Adding a discount column would modify the Customer table.

Before changing the database, Noga decided to review how the present tables were organized and loaded with data. (This information appeared at the end of Chapter 1. You may have already blindly entered these commands into the computer.) We next join Noga in examining these operations.

Creating the Customer Table

The Customer table contains basic information about customers who have ordered Noga's Crispy Crunch. To create the Customer table, enter either of the following commands. The left-hand version should run on all SQL implementations, perhaps with minor changes. The right-hand version is more sophisticated but does not run on all SQL implementations.

```
CREATE TABLE Customer        CREATE TABLE Customer

(Custnum    INTEGER,         (Custnum     SMALLINT UNIQUE NOT NULL,

Custname    CHAR(18),        Custname     CHAR(18) NOT NULL,

Custtype    CHAR(1),         Custtype     CHAR(1),

Custaddr    CHAR(15),        Custaddr     CHAR(15),

Zipcode     CHAR(5),         Zipcode      CHAR(5),

Phone       CHAR(8) );       Phone        CHAR(8) );
```

The CREATE TABLE statement creates a new table and defines columns within the table. Both the table name and the column names must obey SQL naming conventions (see Box 6-1). Note: this command does *not* enter (load) any data into the table. To load data into the table, we use the INSERT command, discussed later in the chapter.

Like other SQL commands, the CREATE TABLE command may be coded on several lines, for clarity. The first line names the new table; successive lines identify each column in the table. All lines except the first and the last terminate with a comma. We examine these lines one by one. If you are unsure about data types, review Box 1-1.

Naming Conventions

Naming conventions are the rules for assigning names to objects such as tables and columns. Since, as you might assume, the exact details of these conventions depend on the SQL implementation, it is best to choose names conservatively, to avoid difficulties when transferring data from one SQL implementation to another.

Column and table names often may contain up to 18 characters. The initial character must be a letter. Succeeding characters may be letters, numbers, or an underscore. For legibility, we start names with an uppercase letter and use lowercase letters for succeeding characters. Remember, we never use a reserved word for table or column names. Some SQL implementations distinguish only the first eight characters in a name. Such systems consider the table names Customer and Customers to be identical. A final point: Although your fingers may tire when typing long names, working with names abbreviated beyond recognition tires the mind.

Line 1.

```
CREATE   TABLE Customer
```

This line assigns the name "Customer" to the new table. If a table named Customer already exists, an error message is issued, and no new table is created.

Line 2.

```
(Custnum   INTEGER,
```

or

```
(Custnum   SMALLINT UNIQUE NOT NULL,
```

An opening parenthesis announces the beginning of a group of statements. "Custnum" is the name of the table's first column. Depending on the SQL implementation, this line takes different forms. Both INTEGER and SMALLINT columns contain only whole numbers, ones without a decimal point. SMALLINT values range from −32768 to +32767.

The reserved word UNIQUE ensures that the "Custnum" column contains unique values. In other words, no two customers may have the same customer number. The reserved words NOT NULL ensure that the "Custnum" column contains a value; that is, it may not remain blank. Columns used as keys (see Box 6-2), such as the "Custname" column in the Customer table, must be both UNIQUE and NOT NULL. Otherwise, they would not adequately identify individual records. If your SQL implementation does not include UNIQUE and NOT NULL, you must reject duplications and null values yourself.

B O X   6 - 2

Keys

A **key,** also known as a **primary key,** is one or more columns that uniquely identify rows within a table. For example, the "Custnum" column is the primary key for the Customer table. While there may be two customers named Jones, Joe, there may not be two customers with customer number 1. (If there were, billing would become a major problem.) The key column or columns may not contain NULLs. In the case of the Purchase table, neither the "Purchnum" nor the "Prodnum" column may contain NULLs. Obviously, it is easier to maintain system integrity if SQL itself enforces rules on the key columns.

Line 3.

```
Custname   CHAR(18),
```

or

```
Custname   CHAR(18) NOT NULL,
```

The "Custname" column contains a maximum of 18 characters.

Line 4.

```
Custtype   CHAR(1),
```

The customer type column contains a single character. Because we have not coded the NOT NULL option, this column may remain blank.

Line 5.

```
Custaddr   CHAR(15),
```

The customer address column is 15 characters wide.

Line 6.

```
Zipcode   CHAR(5),
```

The zip code column is five characters wide.

Line 7.

```
Phone   CHAR(8) );
```

The phone number column is eight characters wide.

    The second closing parenthesis indicates the end of the column list. The semicolon indicates the end of the command. In summary: The CREATE TABLE statement names a table, lists its columns and their data types, and may indicate restrictions on the columns, in particular, the key column or columns.

Creating the Purchase Table

The Purchase table contains basic information about orders for Noga's Crispy Crunch. To create the Purchase table, enter either of the following commands. The left-hand version should run on all SQL implementations, perhaps with minor changes. The right-hand version is more sophisticated but does not run on all SQL implementations.

```
CREATE TABLE Purchase              CREATE TABLE Purchase
 (Purchnum    INTEGER,              (Purchnum    SMALLINT NOT NULL,
  Prodnum     INTEGER,              Prodnum      SMALLINT NOT NULL,
  Custnum     INTEGER,              Custnum      SMALLINT NOT NULL,
  Purchdat    DATE,                 Purchdat     DATE,
  Readydat    DATE,                 Readydat     DATE,
  Kilos       DECIMAL(3,1),         Kilos        DECIMAL(3,1) );
  UNIQUE      (Purchnum, Prodnum) );
```

We examine the SQL statement creating the Purchase table line by line.

Line 1.

```
CREATE   TABLE Purchase
```

This table name must be unique.

Line 2.

```
(Purchnum   INTEGER,
```

or

```
(Purchnum   SMALLINT NOT NULL,
```

The purchase number is not unique. A single purchase number may identify a purchase composed of several types of candy.

Line 3.

```
Prodnum   INTEGER,
```

or

```
Prodnum   SMALLINT NOT NULL,
```

The product number is not unique. There may be several purchase orders for a given product number.

Line 4.

```
Custnum   INTEGER,
```

or

```
Custnum   SMALLINT NOT NULL,
```

The customer number appears in the Purchase table and in the Customer table, with a major difference. In the Customer table it is unique, whereas in the Purchase table it is not unique. Why this difference? The customer number is the primary key in the Customer table. It uniquely identifies rows in the Customer table. For example, the Customer table contains only one row with customer number 24. But the customer number is not the primary key in the Purchase table. The Purchase table contains several rows with customer number 24.

Line 5.

```
Purchdat   DATE,
```

The purchase date column is defined with the DATE data type, allowed in most SQL implementations. For DATE-type columns, SQL automatically rejects impossible dates, such as the 31st of June and any day in the 13th month.

Line 6.

```
Readydat   DATE,
```

The ready date column also is defined with the data type DATE. Though these two columns are of the same type, they do not necessarily contain the same values. For instance, a client may purchase candy one day and pick it up three days later.

Line 7.

```
Kilos   DECIMAL(3,1),
```

The "Kilos" column is defined as a decimal number, three digits long, with a single decimal point. This gives a maximum value of 99.9 kilos, approximately 220 pounds. Some systems express this statement as

```
Kilos   REAL(3,1)
```

or

```
Kilos   NUMERIC (3,1)
```

Line 8.

```
UNIQUE   (Purchnum, Prodnum) );
```

(*Note:* This line is not allowed on all implementations.) Neither the "Purchnum" column nor the "Prodnum" column is unique. But the combination of purchase number and product number is unique, forming a primary key. The Purchase table contains several rows with purchase number 1236 and several rows with product number 1. Only one row has both purchase number 1236 and product number 1. Some SQL implementations use the line

```
PRIMARY KEY (Purchnum, Prodnum) );
```

instead of the line

```
UNIQUE   (Purchnum, Prodnum) );
```

Creating the Product Table

Prodnum. This INTEGER or SMALLINT column is the primary key of the Product table.

Description. This CHAR(30) column associates a description such as Celestial Cashew Crunch with the product. Noga felt her products' popularity would improve with distinctive product names to supplement the product numbers.

Unitcost. This DECIMAL(4,2) column indicates Noga's cost per kilo.

Unitprice. This DECIMAL(4,2) column indicates the product's selling price per kilo. If the Unitprice is less than the Unitcost, Noga is selling at a loss.

E X E R C I S E S

1. Create the Product table using the column definitions just described. Load this table with data in Exercise 5. If your system allows it, use the PRIMARY KEY constraint or its equivalent.

Deleting Tables

What do you do if you make a mistake when creating a table? While it is possible to modify a table, sometimes the simplest procedure is to delete it. The DROP TABLE command deletes a table (permanently). It has the following syntax:

```
DROP TABLE   table-name
```

Note: This command should be used with extreme caution. There is no undelete command. So unless you have made backups, as recommended in Chapter 1's Productivity Tip, once a table is deleted it is lost and gone forever. Some SQL implementations request you to confirm table deletion. Do *not* automatically confirm. If you haven't been careful with your table names, you may find yourself deleting the wrong table.

E X E R C I S E S

2. Create a table called Test containing columns of your choice. Delete the table called Test.

(*Note:* When testing SQL language rules, we often employ a table name such as Test, only to delete such a table later without fear.)

Loading Data

Figure 1-5 listed commands necessary to load data into the Customer table. We examine the first of these commands,

```
INSERT  INTO Customer
VALUES(1, 'Jones, Joe', 'P', '1234 Main St.', '91212', '434-1231');
```

The INSERT INTO command loads one or more rows into the named table. It is a data manipulation command. VALUES lists data to be added, in order of the columns within the table. Recall that the Customer table contains the following columns: Custnum, Custname, Custtype, Custaddr, Zipcode, and Phone. This INSERT INTO command creates a row whose columns contain the following values:

```
Column   Custnum  Custname      Custtype  Custaddr       Zipcode  Phone
  Data         1  Jones, Joe           P  1234 Main St.  91212    434-1231
```

Note the use of the single quotes for CHAR data in the INSERT INTO statement. They are mandatory for many SQL implementations.

We could have explicitly listed column names in the INSERT INTO command as follows:

```
INSERT INTO Customer(Custnum, Custname, Custtype, Custaddr, Zipcode, Phone)
        VALUES(1, 'Jones,Joe', 'P', '1234 Main St.', '91212', '434-1231');
```

It is not necessary to list columns if their order is the same as in the table. However, if Noga had paper files whose data appeared in a different order (for example, customer name, customer number, customer address, customer type, zip code, and telephone number), she could enter the data with the following command:

```
INSERT INTO Customer(Custname, Custnum, Custaddr, Custtype, Zipcode, Phone)
        VALUES('Jones, Joe', 1, '1234 Main St.', 'P', '91212', '434-1231');
```

EXERCISES

3. If you have not already done so, create the Customer table and load it with data, as shown in Figure 1-5. Note, if a Customer table already exists, name the new table "Newcust."

4. If you have not already done so, create the Purchase table and load it with data, as shown in Figure 1-6. Note, if a Purchase table already exists, name the new table "Newpurch."

5. Load the Product table with the following data:

Prodnum	Description	Unitcost	Unitprice
1	Celestial Cashew Crunch	7.45	10.00
2	Unbrittle Peanut Paradise	5.75	9.00
3	Mystery Melange	7.75	10.50
4	Millionaire's Macadamia Mix	12.50	16.00
5	Nuts Not Nachos	6.25	9.50

Be very careful entering the data. This table will be used repeatedly in the rest of the book. (If you make a mistake entering the data, correct it with the UPDATE command covered in the next section.)

Updating Table Values

The UPDATE command changes values in a table. For example, if you enter customer number 41's (Susie Montag's) phone number as 456-9021 instead of the correct value, 456-2091, then you could update her row with the command

```
UPDATE    Customer
   SET    Phone = '456-2091'
 WHERE    Custnum = 41;
```

This UPDATE command resembles the SELECT command. Many rows may be updated at one time.

Noga received some bad news: The Post Office was going to change all 91212 zip codes to 99989. So she coded an SQL UPDATE command to make the requested changes, as shown in Figure 6-1. The postal change turned out to be a mistake. So when Noga received official notification of the error, she coded the UPDATE statement shown in Figure 6-2 to reverse the changes.

```
UPDATE    Customer
   SET    Zipcode = '99989'
 WHERE    Zipcode = '91212';
```

To check the results Noga coded the following query:

```
SELECT    *
  FROM    Customer
 WHERE    Zipcode = '99989'
```

Custnum	Custname	Custtype	Custaddr	Zipcode	Phone
1	Jones, Joe	P	1234 Main St.	99989	434-1231
4	Armstrong, Inc.	R	231 Globe Blvd.	99989	434-7664
22	The Candy Kid	W	2121 Main St.	99989	563-4545
37	Bobby Bon Bons	R	12 Nichi Cres.	99989	434-9045

Figure 6-1 An UPDATE Command

Not all changes may be reversed so easily. For example, suppose the Post Office directive required changing zip code 91212 to 91289. After the update,

five rows would have a zip code of 91289. A simple UPDATE changing all
91289 zip codes to 91212 would be incorrect, because Pickled Pickles' true zip
code is 91289, not 91212.

```
UPDATE   Customer
   SET   Zipcode = '91212'
 WHERE   Zipcode = '99989';
```

Figure 6-2 Returning the Customer Table to Its Previous State

Be very careful before updating tables, in particular, when using statements
that affect several rows. Powerful commands enable you to make more errors,
faster. Don't avoid employing powerful commands, but use them carefully.

E X E R C I S E S

6. Create the Custtest table using the same columns as in the Customer
table. Use this table when testing the query in Figure 6-4 and doing
Exercises 7 and 8.

The INSERT INTO command also may be used to copy tables. Copy
Customer table data into the Custtest table with the command shown in
Figure 6-3. The INSERT statement includes a SELECT statement coded accord-
ing to previously learned SQL syntax rules:

TRY IT YOURSELF

1. Create a copy of the Customer table containing only wholesale and
retail customers.

2. Create a copy of the Product table containing only candies that have a
nut (cashew, etc.) in their description.

```
INSERT   INTO Custtest
SELECT   *
  FROM   Customer;
```

Check the results by entering the following query:

```
SELECT   *
  FROM   Custtest;
```

Custnum	Custname	Custtype	Custaddr	Zipcode	Phone
1	Jones, Joe	P	1234 Main St.	91212	434-1231
4	Armstrong, Inc.	R	231 Globe Blvd.	91212	434-7664
12	Swedish Burgers	R	1889 20th N.E.	91213	434-9090
13	Pickled Pickles	R	194 CityView	91289	324-8909
22	The Candy Kid	W	2121 Main St.	91212	563-4545
24	Waterman, Al	P	23 Yankee Blvd.	91234	-0-
37	Bobby Bon Bons	R	12 Nichi Cres.	91212	434-9045
39	Crowsh, Elias	P	7 77th Ave.	91211	434-0007
41	Montag, Susie	P	981 Montview	91213	456-2091
42	Columberg Sweets	W	239 East Falls	91209	874-9092

Figure 6-3 Copying the Customer Table

Deleting Rows

Important: Use the Custtest table when trying any of the following commands. The DELETE statement's syntax is similar to that for SELECT and INSERT statements. To delete rows for customers whose zip code is 91212, code the query shown in Figure 6-4. After execution of this query, the Custtest table will no longer contain customers with a 91212 zip code. Note that the DELETE command does *not* refer to individual columns; it deletes complete rows.

```
DELETE
    FROM    Custtest
    WHERE   Zipcode = '91212';
```

Check its effect with the following query:

```
SELECT   *
    FROM    Custtest;
```

Custnum	Custname	Custtype	Custaddr	Zipcode	Phone
12	Swedish Burgers	R	1889 20th N.E.	91213	434-9090
13	Pickled Pickles	R	194 CityView	91289	324-8909
24	Waterman, Al	P	23 Yankee Blvd.	91234	-0-
39	Crowsh, Elias	P	7 77th Ave.	91211	434-0007
41	Montag, Susie	P	981 Montview	91213	456-2091
42	Columberg Sweets	W	239 East Falls	91209	874-9092

Figure 6-4 Deleting Rows from the Custtest Table

EXERCISES

7. Code the DELETE command to remove all private customers from the Custtest table. Code a SELECT command to show the remaining data on this table. Show the output.

8. Code the DELETE command to remove all remaining customers from the Custtest table. Code a SELECT command to show that no data remains on this table. Delete the Custtest table.

Common Errors

This chapter's syntax is not complicated, so most errors are likely to arise from simple inattention rather than misunderstanding. Check your statements carefully by hand before trying them on the computer.

SELECT statements present all data contained in the tables. In contrast, INSERT, UPDATE, and DELETE statements don't present data, they *change* it. Take care in coding these statements, because errors often lead to difficult-to-reverse data changes.

The most common error in table creation is attempting to create a table that already exists. A similar error occurs when attempting to delete (DROP) a nonexistent table. This chapter's Productivity Tip recommends learning your SQL implementation's commands to obtain a directory of SQL tables. Using such a directory should reduce the likelihood of these errors.

A common error associated with the INSERT INTO command is inserting data in the wrong column. The more columns in the table, the more likely this error is to occur. When you attempt to insert character data in a numeric field, the system signals an error. But when you attempt to insert numeric data in a character field, the system does not signal an error. Obviously, the second case is more dangerous. (You're better off learning that your brakes are shot when your car is at the mechanic's than when it's winding down a mountain road.)

Be very careful of the SELECT statements used to choose rows to UPDATE or to DELETE. A seemingly minor error can have disastrous results.

Perhaps the worst error to be made is deleting (DROPping) the wrong table. As recommended previously, backups are essential.

Updating a Table's Structure

Creating or deleting tables and creating, deleting, or modifying data within tables is fairly easy. Changing a table's structure may be more difficult.

Noga realized it wasn't enough to create the Product table. She had to change the other tables' structure. The Purchase table needed another column to indicate whether the purchase would be picked up or delivered. The

Customer table needed another column to indicate the percent discount allowed. She used the ALTER TABLE command to add a column to the Purchase table:

```
ALTER TABLE Purchase ADD Pickdel CHAR(1);
```

This command adds the "Pickdel" column at the end of the Purchase table. Its exact syntax varies somewhat from one SQL implementation to another. The ALTER TABLE command, just like the CREATE TABLE command, only affects table structure; it does not add data to the table. So Noga needed to load data into the "Pickdel" column. She had neither the time nor the energy to code 14 separate UPDATE Purchase statements, but this wasn't necessary. For the time being, only Bobby Bon Bons and the two wholesale customers wanted delivery. All other customers picked up their purchases.

She had to code two UPDATE statements, one to set most "Pickdel" columns to *P* and another to set a few remaining "Pickdel" columns to *D*. Noga used a trick to ease the job. First she set every "Pickdel" column to *P* with the command shown in Figure 6-5. Then she coded a more complicated statement using a nested query to set the "Pickdel" column to *D* for the three customers, as shown in Figure 6-6.

```
UPDATE    Purchase
   SET    Pickdel = 'P';
```

Figure 6-5 Step 1 in a Two-Step UPDATE Process

```
UPDATE    Purchase
   SET    Pickdel = 'D'
 WHERE    Custnum IN
    (SELECT    Custnum
       FROM    Customer
      WHERE    (Custname = 'Bobby Bon Bons' OR Custtype ='W') );
```

Figure 6-6 Step 2 in a Two-Step UPDATE Process. No output is shown because this query is immediately followed by the query in Figure 6-7.

Just as Noga was about to check the contents of this new "Pickdel" column, Pat Patterson of Pickled Pickles called.

"I heard you're doing deliveries. About time. I'll pick up my candy on the 29th, but I want you to deliver on the 30th."

Before Noga had a chance to answer, Pat hung up. Now she had a choice. She could call Pat back to say she doesn't deliver partial orders, or she could change the delivery policy. Noga was already preparing partial orders to be ready on different days, so why not deliver partial orders at customer request?

It made sense to save Pat a second trip. So Noga coded the SQL statement shown in Figure 6-7.

```
UPDATE   Purchase
   SET   Pickdel = 'D'
 WHERE   Readydat = '10/30/1992'
   AND   Custnum IN
     (SELECT   Custnum
         FROM   Customer
        WHERE   Custname = 'Pickled Pickles');
```

Selected output is shown below:

Purchnum	Prodnum	Custnum	Pickdel
1234	1	22	D
1235	2	24	P
1236	1	41	P
1236	3	41	P
1237	3	4	P
1238	1	37	D
1238	2	37	D
1238	3	37	D
1239	2	24	P
1240	2	42	D
1240	5	42	D
1241	1	13	P
1241	5	13	D
1242	5	12	P

Figure 6-7 Revised Step 2 in a Two-Step UPDATE Process

Next came the discounts. First Noga thought she would base the discount on customer type. The following two exercises create a new, modifed table and then load it with data.

E X E R C I S E S

Important: Do **not** use the Customer table in Exercise 9 or Exercise 10.

9. Create a table called *Custtst2*. This statement is similar to the

```
CREATE   TABLE Customer
```

statement presented near the beginning of the chapter. Include a DECI-MAL(3,2) column called "Discount" in the Custtst2 table.

10. Load the "Discount" column of the Custtst2 table created in Exercise 9 with a value calculated as follows: Wholesale customers get a 10% discount, retail customers get a 5% discount, and private customers get a 2% discount. Code a SELECT command to show the data on this table.

Noga was concerned about this discount policy. She felt the discount should depend on the amount of candy bought, not on the customer type. This meant handling discounts in a separate table, not in a "Discount" column of the Customer table. (If you have followed directions, there is no problem. You have added a "Discount" column to the Custtst2 table, not the Customer table.) Let's help Noga create a separate Discount table.

E X E R C I S E S

11. Create a Discount table with three columns, "Reduction" defined as DECIMAL (3,2); "Lowerlim," a small integer; and "Upperlim," defined as DECIMAL(4,2). Load this table with values calculated as follows: Customers who purchase less than 5 kilos of a given type of candy get a 2% discount on that candy purchase. Enter .02 for this value. Customers who purchase between 5 and 15 kilos of a given type of candy get a 5% discount on that candy purchase. Customers who purchase more than 15 kilos of a given type of candy get a 10% discount on that candy purchase. Code a SELECT command to show the data on this table.

The ALTER TABLE command may be used to add a column to the end of a table. Noga applied it to add the "Pickdel" column of the Purchase table. We used it in Exercise 9 to add the "Discount" column to the Custtst2 table. In many SQL implementations you may not use this command to add a column to the middle of the table, change the order of columns in the table, or change the size of a column. Other SQL implementations include an ALTER TABLE MODIFY command to perform some or all of these activities.

Noga needed to redefine the "Kilos" column of the Purchase table to accommodate purchases of 100 kilos or more. While she had not yet made such a large sale, she wanted to plan ahead.

TRY IT YOURSELF

3. See if your SQL implementation allows you to change the "Kilos" column in the Purchase table from DECIMAL(3,1) to DECIMAL(4,1). Even if it does, continue with the method in Box 6-3.

BOX 6-3

How to Modify a Table's Structure

Modifying a table's structure is fairly complicated with most SQL implementations. Before trying this on your computer, back up your tables.

Step 1. Create an Oldpurch table as follows (either series of commands, depending on your SQL implementation):

```
CREATE TABLE Oldpurch                    CREATE TABLE Oldpurch
   (Purchnum    INTEGER,                    (Purchnum    SMALLINT NOT NULL,
    Prodnum     INTEGER,                     Prodnum     SMALLINT NOT NULL,
    Custnum     INTEGER,                     Custnum     SMALLINT NOT NULL,
    Purchdat    DATE,                        Purchdat    DATE,
    Readydat    DATE,                        Readydat    DATE,
    Kilos       DECIMAL(3,1),                Kilos       DECIMAL(3,1) );
    UNIQUE      (Purchnum, Prodnum) );
```

This structure is the same as that of the Purchase table. The Oldpurch table is a backup of the Purchase table.

Step 2.   Load data from the Purchase table into the Oldpurch table.

```
INSERT   INTO Oldpurch
   SELECT   *
      FROM   Purchase;
```

Step 3.   Delete the Purchase table.

```
DROP   TABLE Purchase;
```

Note, if we don't carry out this step, the next step will not work. (Why not?)

Step 4.   Create a modified Purchase table as follows:

```
CREATE TABLE Purchase                    CREATE TABLE Purchase
   (Purchnum    INTEGER,                    (Purchnum    SMALLINT NOT NULL,
    Prodnum     INTEGER,                     Prodnum     SMALLINT NOT NULL,
```

```
    Custnum      INTEGER,              Custnum      SMALLINT NOT NULL,

    Purchdat     DATE,                 Purchdat     DATE,

    Readydat     DATE,                 Readydat     DATE,

    Kilos        DECIMAL(4,1),         Kilos        DECIMAL(4,1) );

    UNIQUE       (Purchnum, Prodnum) );
```

Step 5.   Load data from the Oldpurch table into the Purchase table.

```
INSERT   INTO Purchase
   SELECT   *
     FROM   Oldpurch;
```

The Purchase table is now ready to accommodate purchases of more than 100 kilos.

   This modification procedure is fairly tedious. Take your time analyzing modifications before making them. If you have several table modifications, do them together. And don't forget to back up all affected tables before modifying table structures.

Syntax and Applications Summary

Table creation is accomplished with the command

```
CREATE TABLE table-name (column-name1 data-type1, column-name2,
data-type2, etc.);
```

The table name must be unique. Some SQL implementations allow column names to be designated as UNIQUE and NOT NULL. These requirements must be respected for primary keys.

   Table deletion is performed with the command

```
DROP TABLE table-name;
```

Data is loaded with the command

```
INSERT INTO table-name (list of column names, optional if all
columns are used) VALUES(     )
```

Values for each column, separated by commas, are placed within the parentheses. Character values are placed within single quotes.

Data is changed with the command

```
UPDATE   table-name
   SET   column-name1 = expression1,
         column-name2 = expression2, etc.
 WHERE   clause; (optional)
```

One or more *rows may be deleted* with the command

```
DELETE
  FROM   table-name
 WHERE   clause;
```

A *column may be added* to the table structure with the command

```
ALTER TABLE table-name ADD column-name data type;
```

Restrictions on the ALTER TABLE command may require a procedure such as that shown in Box 6-3 to make changes to a table's structure.

Productivity Tip:

LEARN YOUR IMPLEMENTATION'S COMMANDS.

We have already pointed out how easy it is to make a mistake in your table names when creating and deleting tables. Fortunately, many SQL implementations include a user interface to execute DOS-like functions, such as DIR (maybe with another name such as LIST). Learn these commands. If you're lucky, your implementation includes commands to rename and copy tables. The better you master your implementation's user interface, the more time you can spend working with SQL, and the less time you'll spend correcting your errors.

Chapter Summary

Until this chapter, our knowledge of SQL was limited to a group of data manipulation commands known as queries. Such commands do not modify any data but only serve to display it. This chapter introduced Data Definition Language statements used to create, modify, and delete tables. We also introduced Data Manipulation Language statements to load, modify, and delete data within the tables. After a short review, Chapter 7 starts where Chapter 5 left off. In Chapter 5 both Noga's candy business and the compact disk case study were limited to two tables. Now each of these applications has three tables. In consequence, the *join* operations and nested queries will become more complicated, and more informative.

Review Questions

1. Define in your own words the following SQL activities, and describe their use:
   a. creating tables
   b. modifying tables
   c. deleting tables
   d. loading data
   e. modifying data
   f. deleting data
2. Discuss the conventions for naming tables and columns.
3. Describe the data types available in your SQL implementation.
4. Describe in your own words the use of the following SQL commands:
   a. CREATE
   b. UPDATE
   c. SET
   d. INSERT

Case Study Exercises

Because of length, changes to the case study are discussed in Appendix B rather than here. There are several activities to carry out.

1. Modify either the Cds or the Smlcds table by adding new columns that enable the vendor to record data for CD boxes in addition to individual CDs. Also, modify the Cds table to include a column indicating if the CD or box contains a descriptive booklet.

2. Load the modified Cds table or Smlcds table with data for the new columns.

3. Create a new table to record data for individual works in the compact disks. Depending on the database version used, create either the Works table or the Smlworks table.

4. Load the Works table or Smlworks table with data.

CHAPTER SEVEN

Querying Multiple Tables (Intermediate)

Chapter 5 introduced important SQL features for querying two tables simultaneously, the join *operation and nested queries. Chapter 6 left off our study of these operations in order to show how to create and modify tables. We will apply the* join *operation and nested queries to such new and modified tables to meet the expanded information needs.*

First we review this join *operation. Then we apply the* join *to the new Product table and to the modified Customer and Purchase tables. We present a three-table* join *operation, and introduce a new type of* join *operation, the self-*join. *Then we review the nested query and combine the nested query with a* join. *We examine two useful SQL features, the EXISTS operator and lookup tables. We close the chapter with a series of examples involving a new type of nested query, the correlated subquery.*

OBJECTIVES

You have met this chapter's objectives when you can:

- Code SQL statements to perform *join* operations on two or three tables.
- Code SQL statements to perform self-*join*s.
- Code SQL statements using the EXISTS operator.
- Code SQL statements using a lookup table.
- Code SQL statements to perform correlated subqueries.
- Apply these SQL statements to meet business and other information-processing needs.

Review of the *Join* Operation

After working so hard to create the Product table and to modify the Customer and Purchase tables, Noga couldn't remember exactly how the *join* operation worked, except that it connects two or more tables. She reviewed the query in Figure 5-2a, which applies a *join* operation and is repeated in Figure 7-1.

```
SELECT   DISTINCT Custname, Customer.Custnum, Purchnum
   FROM   Customer, Purchase
  WHERE   Customer.Custnum = Purchase.Custnum;
```

Custname	Customer.Custnum	Purchnum
Armstrong, Inc.	4	1237
Bobby Bon Bons	37	1238
Columberg Sweets	42	1240
Montag, Susie	41	1236
Pickled Pickles	13	1241
Swedish Burgers	12	1242
The Candy Kid	22	1234
Waterman, Al	24	1235
Waterman, Al	24	1239

Figure 7-1 The *Join* Operation

Noga wanted to test her understanding of the *join* operation with a straightforward application. The query in Figure 7-1 links data in the Customer and the Purchase tables. The next step is to *join* the Product table with another table. But which one? The Product table key is the "Prodnum" column. This column occurs in the Purchase table but not in the Customer table. (Customers are linked to products via purchases.) So Noga wrote the query shown in Figure 7-2 to extract information on items to be delivered. Note that the output appears in product-number order, because the "Prodnum" column links the two tables.

```
SELECT   Purchnum, Purchase.Prodnum, Custnum, Pickdel, Unitprice
   FROM   Purchase, Product
  WHERE   Purchase.Prodnum = Product.Prodnum
    AND   Pickdel = 'D';
```

Purchnum	Purchase.Prodnum	Custnum	Pickdel	Unitprice
1234	1	22	D	10.00
1238	1	37	D	10.00
1238	2	37	D	9.00
1240	2	42	D	9.00
1238	3	37	D	10.50
1240	5	42	D	9.50
1241	5	13	D	9.50

Figure 7-2 *Join*ing the Purchase Table and the Product Table

A major reason to introduce the Product table was improved cost control. Noga wanted to determine the gross profit for each complete purchase, identified by a single purchase number. For this she required aggregate functions, presented in Chapter 4. She coded the query shown in Figure 7-3.

```
SELECT   Purchnum, SUM(Kilos), SUM(Kilos*Unitprice),
             SUM(Kilos*Unitcost), SUM(Kilos*(Unitprice-Unitcost))
   FROM   Purchase, Product
  WHERE   Purchase.Prodnum = Product.Prodnum
  GROUP   BY Purchnum;
```

Purchnum	SUM(Kilos)	SUM(Kilos*Unitprice)	SUM(Kilos*Unitcost)	SUM(Kilos*(Unitprice − Unitcost))
1234	3.5	35.00	26.075	8.925
1235	15.0	135.00	86.250	48.750
1236	5.7	58.85	43.575	15.275
1237	3.7	38.85	28.675	10.175
1238	9.3	94.00	68.565	25.435
1239	3.0	27.00	17.250	9.750
1240	18.8	171.60	110.500	61.100
1241	8.6	82.20	54.950	27.250
1242	3.5	33.25	21.875	11.375

Figure 7-3 A *Join* with Aggregate Functions. (For clarity, we present long column headers on two lines. Your SQL implementation may require special "tricks" to generate complete output. For instance, you might have to code a number representing the width of the truncated column, such as SELECT Purchnum=4, *etc.*)

After examining this query, Noga sensed that something was missing: the customer name. But the customer name is in a third table, the Customer table. Fortunately, SQL allows one to *join* three tables. In fact, SQL has no practical limit on how many tables can be *join*ed by a SELECT statement. However, few business applications require *join*ing more than three or four tables.

But an important restriction prevents coding a *join* operation to generate the desired information: When a SELECT statement contains one or more aggregate functions, all columns to be output must appear either in an aggregate function or in the GROUP BY clause. (Chapter 8 furnishes us with the tools necessary to circumvent this restriction.) The query shown in Figure 7-4 processes individual candy orders separately. Note, we restricted the purchase number to a maximum value of 1237, thereby making it easier to verify the output by hand. As you can see, a three-table *join* operation is quite similar to a two-table *join*; it simply includes more tables.

```
SELECT   Purchnum, Customer.Custname, Kilos, Kilos*Unitprice,
             Kilos*Unitcost, Kilos*(Unitprice-Unitcost)
```

```
FROM   Purchase, Product, Customer
WHERE  Purchase.Prodnum = Product.Prodnum
  AND  Purchase.Custnum = Customer.Custnum
  AND  Purchnum <= 1237
ORDER  BY Purchnum;
```

Purchnum	Custname	Kilos	Kilos* Unitprice	Kilos* Unitcost	Kilos*(Unitprice − Unitcost)
1234	The Candy Kid	3.5	35.00	26.075	8.925
1235	Waterman, Al	15.0	135.00	86.250	48.750
1236	Montag, Susie	2.0	20.00	14.900	5.100
1236	Montag, Susie	3.7	38.85	28.675	10.175
1237	Armstrong, Inc.	3.7	38.85	28.675	10.175

Figure 7-4 Processing Individual Candy Orders with a Three-Table *Join*

E X E R C I S E S

1. Write an SQL query generating the purchase number, the product number, the customer number, the description, the unit price, and the unit cost for all purchases. Show the output.

2. Write an SQL query generating the purchase number, the product number, the customer name, the description, and the unit price for all purchases. Show the output.

Self-*Join*s

Noga's new delivery operation was running smoothly. She thought seriously about expanding deliveries. A list of customers paired by zip code could help her decide. Only the Customer table contains zip code information. But processing the Customer table a single time would not generate the needed information. To find out how to obtain this information by computer, we first see how she could get it by hand. She must process this table twice.

She starts with the first customer—Jones, Joe—and checks his zip code against all others in the table. Then she checks the zip code for Armstrong, Inc. against all others in the table. She repeats this process until she is finally checking Columberg Sweets' zip code against all others in the table. In essence she has joined the table to itself—hence, the name **self-*join*.**

Before examining the appropriate SELECT statement, we return to an SQL concept introduced in Chapter 5, the *alias.* Recall that an alias is a temporary table name that obeys the table-naming conventions. Using an alias to abbreviate a table name is optional. In the query shown in Figure 7-5a, X and Y are aliases required to distinguish between different occurrences of a table name.

a

```
SELECT  X.Custname, Y.Custname, Zipcode
  FROM  Customer X, Customer Y
 WHERE  X.Zipcode = Y.Zipcode;
```

X.Custname	Y.Custname	Zipcode
Jones, Joe	Jones, Joe	91212
Jones, Joe	Armstrong, Inc.	91212
Jones, Joe	The Candy Kid	91212
Jones, Joe	Bobby Bon Bons	91212
Armstrong, Inc.	Jones, Joe	91212
Armstrong, Inc.	Armstrong, Inc.	91212

(Remaining output has been suppressed.)

b

```
SELECT  X.Custname, Y.Custname, Zipcode
  FROM  Customer X, Customer Y
 WHERE  X.Zipcode = Y.Zipcode
   AND  X.Custname < Y.Custname;
```

X.Custname	Y.Custname	Zipcode
Jones, Joe	The Candy Kid	91212
Armstrong, Inc.	Jones, Joe	91212
Armstrong, Inc.	The Candy Kid	91212
Armstrong, Inc.	Bobby Bon Bons	91212
Bobby Bon Bons	Jones, Joe	91212
Bobby Bon Bons	The Candy Kid	91212
Susie Montag	Swedish Burgers	91213

Figure 7-5 Two Self-*Join*s. **a,** Original, and **b,** revised to eliminate extraneous rows.

We discuss this query line by line.

Line 1.

```
SELECT  X.Custname, Y.Custname, Zipcode
```

This line lists the three output columns:

1. "X.Custname," the customer name from the table known as X
2. "Y.Custname," the customer name from the table known as Y
3. "Zipcode"

Table names X and Y are aliases; they are defined in line 2.

Line 2.

```
FROM   Customer X, Customer Y
```

This line associates the two aliases, X and Y, with the Customer table. The computer now "knows" that the first output column is the customer name in the first table *join*ed, the Customer table, also called table X. The computer also "knows" that the second output column is the customer name in the second table *join*ed, the Customer table, also called table Y.

Line 3.

```
WHERE   X.Zipcode = Y.Zipcode;
```

This line restricts output to a combination of rows in the first Customer table and the second Customer table whose zip codes are equal.

Let's see how the computer executes a self-*join*. The initial row in the first Customer table (table X) has a customer name Jones, Joe, with a zip code of 91212. Four customers on the second Customer table (table Y) have a zip code of 91212: Jones, Joe; Armstrong, Inc.; The Candy Kid; and Bobby Bon Bons. The computer outputs four rows from the *join*ed tables. It then examines the second row of the first Customer table, whose customer name is Armstrong, Inc., and whose zip code is 91212. The computer examines all rows in the second Customer table, looking for a zip code of 91212. Once again it finds four matches, and so generates four more rows in the combined table. This process repeats until all rows on the first Customer table are compared with all rows on the second Customer table.

A careful examination of the output uncovers two problems. First, the computer pairs Jones, Joe, in table X with Jones, Joe, in table Y. These output rows provide no useful information and should be eliminated. Second, customers Jones, Joe, and Armstrong, Inc., have been paired twice. The first time, Jones, Joe (Customer table X), appears to the left of Armstrong, Inc. The second time, Jones, Joe (Customer table Y), appears to the right of Armstrong, Inc. Duplicate rows occur for all pairs. We must modify the query so that each pair occurs only once rather than twice. (If you had trouble understanding this query, perform the next query by hand.)

Noga reformulated this three-line query by using a second condition to eliminate extraneous rows. Now output is generated only when the customer name on the first table is less (appears earlier in the alphabet) than the customer name on the second table. The revised query is shown in Figure 7-5b.

The self-*join* operation is summarized in Box 7-1.

BOX 7-1

The Self-*Join* Summarized

As the name indicates, a self-*join* joins a table to itself. This operation is useful if we wish to compare different rows within a given table. A self-*join* is coded like a *join,* except that aliases are required to distinguish between different occurrences of table names. A compound WHERE clause is usually coded to eliminate meaningless and redundant output, for example, *join*ing each row to itself and the duplicate output obtained by first *join*ing row A to row B and then *join*ing row B to row A.

TRY IT YOURSELF

1. The exact alias used does not matter, provided it is not a reserved word. Redo the query in Figure 7-5b with different aliases. Show the output.

2. Aliases are not limited to self-*join*s. Rewrite the query in Figure 7-1 by using aliases. Show the output, if any, and compare the output to that of the original query.

E X E R C I S E S

3. Code a query using a self-*join* to generate a list of *triplets,* that is, groups of three customers who share the same zip code. Show the output. Can you think of any application for such a query?

4. Code a query using a self-*join* to pair purchases with the same ready date and the same "Pickdel" status, that is, either both are for pickup or both are for delivery. Show the output.

Review of Nested Queries

Before trying to code any new nested queries, Noga reviewed the nested query in Figure 5-6, which is repeated in Figure 7-6. First the computer analyzes the query inside the parentheses (the inner query). Given the customer name, it finds the customer number (24). Then it automatically supplies the customer number to the query outside the parentheses (the outer query). A nested query enabled Noga to obtain information from the tables even when she forgot such details as Al Waterman's customer number.

```
SELECT   *
  FROM   Purchase
 WHERE   Custnum =
 (SELECT   Custnum
    FROM   Customer
   WHERE   Custname = 'Waterman, Al');
```

Purchnum	Prodnum	Custnum	Purchdat	Readydat	Kilos
1235	2	24	10/28/1992	10/30/1992	15.0
1239	2	24	10/29/1992	10/30/1992	3.0

Figure 7-6 A Nested Query

Noga wanted information on cashew candy sales, but couldn't remember either the product number or the exact product name. No problem. The nested query eliminates the need to know the product number, and the LIKE operator eliminates the need to know the exact product name. This query is shown in Figure 7-7.

```
SELECT   *
  FROM   Purchase
 WHERE   Prodnum =
 (SELECT   Prodnum
    FROM   Product
   WHERE   Description LIKE '%Cashew%');
```

Purchnum	Prodnum	Custnum	Purchdat	Readydat	Kilos	Pickdel
1234	1	22	10/28/1992	10/28/1992	3.5	D
1236	1	41	10/28/1992	10/28/1992	2.0	P
1238	1	37	10/29/1992	10/29/1992	3.7	D
1241	1	13	10/29/1992	10/29/1992	1.0	P

Figure 7-7 A Nested Query Applying the LIKE Operator

She was fairly pleased with the output, but a problem remained. She still didn't know the name of product number 1. To find it she coded a single SELECT statement containing both a nested query and a *join* operation, as shown in Figure 7-8. Most SQL implementations require qualifying data names as in this figure. Note, this query is invalid if the inner query generates more than one value.

Noga suddenly realized she needed the customer name as well. Fortunately, it is also possible to combine a nested query with two *joins*, as shown by the solution to Exercise 5.

```
SELECT   Purchnum, Product.Prodnum, Description, Kilos
  FROM   Purchase, Product
 WHERE   Product.Prodnum =
   (SELECT   Prodnum
      FROM   Product
     WHERE   Description LIKE '%Cashew%')
       AND   Purchase.Prodnum = Product.Prodnum;
```

```
Purchnum     Product.Prodnum     Description                  Kilos
    1234                   1     Celestial Cashew Crunch        3.5
    1236                   1     Celestial Cashew Crunch        2.0
    1238                   1     Celestial Cashew Crunch        3.7
    1241                   1     Celestial Cashew Crunch        1.0
```

Figure 7-8 Combining a Nested Query and a *Join*

TRY IT YOURSELF

3. Repeat the query shown in Figure 7-8, but replace the line

```
WHERE   Description LIKE '%Cashew%'
```

with the line

```
WHERE   Unitprice > 10.00
```

What happens on your SQL implementation?

E X E R C I S E S

5. Write an SQL nested query with two *join*s that modifies the query shown in Figure 7-8 so as to add the customer name. Show the output.

6. Write an SQL nested query that generates all purchases by customers whose name includes a reference to *candy:* Candy, Bon Bons, or Sweets. Include the description and the number of kilos purchased. Show the output.

The EXISTS Operator

Noga wanted a list of active customers, that is, those who make candy purchases. She coded a query using the **EXISTS** operator. The EXISTS operator is a Boolean operator; that is, it has a True or a False value. The EXISTS operator has the value True when at least one row in its associated inner query would be generated. It has the value False when no row in its associated inner query would be generated. It may be used with other Boolean operators: AND, OR, and NOT.

Noga applied the EXISTS operator in the query shown in Figure 7-9. Customer number 4 appears in this query's output because the customer number is 4 for at least one row in the Purchase table. On the other hand, customer number 1 does not appear in the output because the Purchase table contains no rows whose customer number is 1.

```
SELECT   Customer.Custnum, Custname
  FROM   Customer
 WHERE   EXISTS
   (SELECT   *
      FROM   Purchase
     WHERE   Customer.Custnum = Purchase.Custnum);
```

```
Customer.Custnum        Custname
               4        Armstrong, Inc.
              12        Swedish Burgers
              13        Pickled Pickles
              22        The Candy Kid
              24        Waterman, Al
              37        Bobby Bon Bons
              41        Montag, Susie
              42        Columberg Sweets
```

Figure 7-9 The EXISTS Operator

Noga then applied the EXISTS operator to determine which customers ordered more than 10 kilos of a given type of candy. She coded the query shown in Figure 7-10. The upcoming "Common Errors" section shows what can go wrong when coding this query.

```
SELECT   *
  FROM   Customer
 WHERE   EXISTS
   (SELECT   *
      FROM   Purchase
     WHERE   Kilos > 10
       AND   Customer.Custnum = Purchase.Custnum);
```

Custnum	Custname	Custtype	Custaddr	Zipcode	Phone
24	Waterman, Al	P	23 Yankee Blvd.	91234	-0-
42	Columberg Sweets	W	239 East Falls	91209	874-9092

Figure 7-10 The EXISTS Operator Revisited

Box 7-2 summarizes the EXISTS operator.

B O X   7 - 2

The EXISTS Operator Summarized

The EXISTS operator is used with nested queries to determine whether the inner query generates at least one row. Because we are not interested in the inner query's individual columns but simply in whether or not it generates at least one row, the * is used in the inner SELECT statement. The EXISTS operator evaluates as True or False (Boolean operator), and may be combined with the AND, OR, and NOT operators presented in Chapter 3.

Using a Lookup Table

A **lookup table** is a special type of table. It contains values that help to classify values in another table. One common lookup table contains income tax deductions based on salary. A payroll office clerk might consult such a lookup table to determine each employee's deduction. As we will see shortly, an SQL query can accomplish the same kind of task.

To review the Discount table, Noga coded the following query:

```
SELECT  *
  FROM  Discount;
```

which generates the following output:

Reduction	Lowerlim	Upperlim
.02	0	4.99
.05	5	14.99
.10	15	99.99

Let's see what this table means. "Reduction" indicates the fractional discount for a single candy order, depending on the kilos ordered. For instance, a customer who purchases 6.2 kilos of a given type of candy would obtain a .05 (5%) reduction on that candy purchase, because 6.2 is between 5 (Lowerlim) and 14.99 (Upperlim).

Noga wrote the query in Figure 7-11 to determine the final selling price for each individual candy purchase. Note, we restricted the purchase number to a maximum value of 1237, making it easier to verify the output by hand. Let's check one value: Purchase number 1236 includes an order for 2 kilos of product number 1. According to the Discount table, this entitles the customer to a discount (reduction) of .02, or 2% (2 kilos is between 0 and 4.99). Because Reduction = .02, 1 − Reduction = .98. The customer pays 98% of the regular price (Kilos * Unitprice). The regular price of 2 kilos of candy number 1 at $10.00 per kilo is $20.00. The discounted price is 98% of the regular price, or $19.60. (If you are unsure of exactly how to perform this calculation, do several more by hand.) Noga's SQL implementation does not round the results. Does yours?

```
SELECT   Y.Purchnum, Y.Prodnum, Kilos * Unitprice,
         (1-Reduction) * Kilos * Unitprice

  FROM   Purchase Y, Discount, Product

 WHERE   Kilos BETWEEN Lowerlim AND Upperlim

   AND   Y.Prodnum = Product.Prodnum

   AND   Purchnum <= 1237;
```

Y.Purchnum	Y.Prodnum	Kilos * Unitprice	(1-Reduction) * Kilos * Unitprice
1234	1	35.000	34.3
1235	2	135.000	121.5
1236	1	20.000	19.6
1236	3	38.850	38.1
1237	3	38.850	38.1

Figure 7-11 Applying a Lookup Table. (For simplicity, the last column header is presented on two lines.)

EXERCISES

7. Write an SQL query using the EXISTS operator to generate a list of inactive customers. Use aliases. Show the output.

8. Modify the query in Figure 7-11 to generate output in product-number order. Display the discount amount, the discounted price, and the customer name. Show the output.

Correlated Subquery

The delivery issue was still on Noga's mind. She wanted to know which customers made purchases to be delivered. The "Pickdel" column indicates whether individual candy purchases are for pick up (Pickdel = 'P') or for delivery (Pickdel = 'D'). Although she could use a *join* operation to obtain this information, she decided instead to use a **correlated subquery,** that is, a nested query whose inner query processes information generated by the outer query. Correlated subqueries are summarized in Box 7-3.

Figure 7-12 illustrates a correlated subquery. Notice the similarity between the correlated subquery and a *join* operation. In this correlated subquery, the computer fixes a single row in the Customer table and then goes through the Purchase table, row by row, looking for a match. The Purchase table contains information about several purchases to be delivered, for example, purchase number 1241 (for customer number 13).

```
SELECT   Custname, Customer.Custnum, Custaddr, Zipcode, Phone
   FROM   Customer
  WHERE   'D' IN
      (SELECT   Pickdel
         FROM   Purchase
        WHERE   Customer.Custnum = Purchase.Custnum);
```

Custname	Custnum	Custaddr	Zipcode	Phone
Pickled Pickles	13	194 CityView	91289	324-8909
The Candy Kid	22	2121 Main St.	91212	563-4545
Bobby Bon Bons	37	12 Nichi Cres.	91212	434-9045
Columberg Sweets	42	239 East Falls	91209	874-9092

Figure 7-12 A Correlated Subquery for Deliveries. (Custnum column header has been abbreviated.)

Noga coded a similar correlated subquery to generate information on customers who pick up their orders. See Figure 7-13. At first Noga was upset when she reviewed the output of the last two queries, for Pickled Pickles was on both lists. Then she realized the results were correct: Pickled Pickles takes delivery of one candy purchase and picks up another.

```
SELECT   Custname, Customer.Custnum, Custaddr, Zipcode, Phone
   FROM   Customer
  WHERE   'P' IN
      (SELECT   Pickdel
         FROM   Purchase
        WHERE   Customer.Custnum = Purchase.Custnum);
```

Custname	Custnum	Custaddr	Zipcode	Phone
Armstrong, Inc.	4	231 Globe Blvd.	91212	434-7664
Swedish Burgers	12	1889 20th N.E.	91213	434-9090
Pickled Pickles	13	194 CityView	91289	324-8909

Waterman, AL	24	23 Yankee Blvd.	91234	-0-
Montag, Susie	41	981 Montview	91213	456-2091

Figure 7-13 A Correlated Subquery for Pickups

She modified the last query to obtain the purchase number from the Purchase table. This new query is somewhat complicated. The clause

```
Customer.Custnum = Purchase.Custnum
```

in the next-to-last line restricts rows output by the *join* operation. The line

```
AND Pickdel = 'P'
```

selects only pickups for customers, such as Pickled Pickles, who have both pickups and deliveries. The results of eliminating these two lines are discussed in the upcoming "Common Errors" section. The query is shown in Figure 7-14.

This correlated subquery could be replaced by a *join* operation, as shown in Figure 7-15. This query is simpler to code than the one in Figure 7-14. It also runs on the computer more quickly. Why would anybody want to write a complicated query when a simple one is possible? The more powerful correlated subquery might generate information that is otherwise unavailable. For example, Noga coded the query shown in Figure 7-16 for information about deliveries to customers picking up other purchases. Purchase number 1241 is the only delivery going to a customer who picks up at least one purchase.

```
SELECT   Custname, Customer.Custnum, Custaddr, Phone,
         Purchnum, Prodnum
  FROM   Customer, Purchase
 WHERE   'P' IN
   (SELECT   Pickdel
      FROM   Purchase
     WHERE   Customer.Custnum = Purchase.Custnum)
       AND   Customer.Custnum = Purchase.Custnum
       AND   Pickdel = 'P';
```

Custname	Custnum	Custaddr	Phone	Purchnum	Prodnum
Waterman, Al	24	23 Yankee Blvd.	-0-	1235	2
Montag, Susie	41	981 Montview	456-2091	1236	1
Montag, Susie	41	981 Montview	456-2091	1236	3
Armstrong, Inc.	4	231 Globe Blvd.	434-7664	1237	3
Waterman, Al	24	23 Yankee Blvd.	-0-	1239	2
Pickled Pickles	13	194 CityView	324-8909	1241	1
Swedish Burgers	12	1889 20th N.E.	434-9090	1242	5

Figure 7-14 Combining a Correlated Subquery and a *Join*. (Custnum column header has been abbreviated.)

```
SELECT   Custname, Customer.Custnum, Custaddr, Phone,
         Purchnum, Prodnum
  FROM   Customer, Purchase
 WHERE   Customer.Custnum = Purchase.Custnum
   AND   Pickdel = 'P';
```

Figure 7-15 Replacing a Correlated Subquery by a *Join*. The output is the same as in Figure 7-14.

```
SELECT   Custname, Customer.Custnum, Custaddr, Phone,
         Purchnum, Prodnum
  FROM   Customer, Purchase
 WHERE   'P' IN
    (SELECT   Pickdel
       FROM   Purchase
      WHERE   Customer.Custnum = Purchase.Custnum)
   AND   Customer.Custnum = Purchase.Custnum
   AND   Pickdel <> 'P';
```

Custname	Custnum	Custaddr	Phone	Purchnum	Prodnum
Pickled Pickles	13	194 CityView	324-8909	1241	5

Figure 7-16 Obtaining Sophisticated Information with a Sophisticated Query. (Custnum column header has been abbreviated.)

BOX 7-3

The Correlated Subquery Summarized

A correlated subquery is a nested query whose inner query requires information generated by the outer query. Regular (uncorrelated) nested queries execute the inner query only once. In contrast, correlated subqueries execute the inner query once for each row in the outer query. The inner query and the outer query are not independent; they are correlated. The queries in Figures 7-9 and 7-10 applying the EXISTS operator are actually correlated subqueries.

EXERCISES

9. Write an SQL query using a correlated subquery to obtain information about purchases by wholesale customers. Show the output.

10. Modify the query in Exercise 9 to add unit-price information, via a *join* operation. Show the output.

Common Errors

The more complicated the statement, the easier it is to make errors. The material in this chapter is relatively complicated, so we will discuss several common errors. Other errors are possible, of course.

Misuse of Aliases. The alias is an SQL feature that can cause problems. For example, forgetting the aliases after the two Customer tables as in the following query,

```
SELECT  X.Custname, Y.Custname, Zipcode
  FROM  Customer, Customer
 WHERE  X.Zipcode = Y.Zipcode
   AND  X.Custname < Y.Custname;
```

leads to an error message such as the following:

```
-ERROR-  Correlation X not found
```

The computer has not found table X.

If we completely eliminate any reference to aliases X and Y as in the following query,

```
SELECT  Custname, Custname, Zipcode
  FROM  Customer, Customer
 WHERE  Zipcode = Zipcode
   AND  Custname < Custname;
```

then the system generates a message such as the following:

```
-WARNING-  No rows exist or satisfy the specified clause.
```

This should not surprise us, for the computer cannot find a single row whose customer name is less than its customer name.

Misuse of the EXISTS Operator. The EXISTS operator may generate more output than desired. For example, if we recode the query in Figure 7-10 by omitting the last line

```
AND  Customer.Custnum = Purchase.Custnum;
```

then we obtain the query

```
SELECT   *
  FROM   Customer
 WHERE   EXISTS
    (SELECT   *
       FROM   Purchase
      WHERE   Kilos > 10);
```

which generates the entire Customer table. The AND clause in Figure 7-10 is required to select generated output.

Incorrectly Coded Correlated Subqueries. When we presented the sophisticated correlated subquery in Figure 7-16, we stated that the last two lines were necessary. Let's see what happens if these lines are eliminated: If we eliminate only the last line,

```
AND   Pickdel <> 'P'
```

we obtain the query

```
SELECT   Custname, Customer.Custnum, Custaddr, Phone,
         Purchnum, Prodnum
  FROM   Customer, Purchase
 WHERE   'P' IN
    (SELECT   Pickdel
       FROM   Purchase
      WHERE   Customer.Custnum = Purchase.Custnum)
   AND   Customer.Custnum = Purchase.Custnum;
```

which generates the following output:

Custname	Customer.Custnum	Custaddr	Phone	Purchnum	Prodnum
Armstrong, Inc.	4	231 Globe Blvd.	434-7664	1237	3
Swedish Burgers	12	1889 20th N.E.	434-9090	1242	5
Pickled Pickles	13	194 CityView	324-8909	1241	1
Pickled Pickles	13	194 CityView	324-8909	1241	5
Waterman, Al	24	23 Yankee Blvd.	-0-	1235	2
Waterman, Al	24	23 Yankee Blvd.	-0-	1239	2
Montag, Susie	41	981 Montview	456-2091	1236	1
Montag, Susie	41	981 Montview	456-2091	1236	3

The output is now in customer-number order instead of purchase-number order. More important, the output now contains two rows for Pickled Pickles.

The second of these rows corresponds to a purchase to be delivered. This query generates all purchases for any customer who picks up at least one purchase.

If we also eliminate the next-to-last line in Figure 7-16,

```
AND  Customer.Custnum = Purchase.Custnum
```

then we obtain the query

```
SELECT  Custname, Customer.Custnum, Custaddr, Phone,
        Purchnum, Prodnum
  FROM  Customer, Purchase
 WHERE  'P' IN
   (SELECT  Pickdel
      FROM  Purchase
     WHERE  Customer.Custnum = Purchase.Custnum);
```

which generates voluminous output. We present only a few rows:

Custname	Customer.Custnum	Custaddr	Phone	Purchnum	Prodnum
Armstrong, Inc.	4	231 Globe Blvd.	434-7664	1234	1
Armstrong, Inc.	4	231 Globe Blvd.	434-7664	1235	2
Armstrong, Inc.	4	231 Globe Blvd.	434-7664	1236	1
Armstrong, Inc.	4	231 Globe Blvd.	434-7664	1236	3

(Remaining output suppressed.)

The line

```
WHERE  Customer.Custnum = Purchase.Custnum
```

does not choose rows for the *join* operation. It chooses rows for the statement

```
SELECT  Pickdel
```

The one line does *not* do double duty.

Syntax and Applications Summary

A self-*join joins* a table to itself. This operation is useful for comparing different rows within a given table. The first line is

```
SELECT  alias1.column-name1, alias2.column-name2, etc.
```

The second line, the FROM clause, uses an alias to distinguish between dif-

---

TRY IT YOURSELF

4. What happens to the first error message given in the "Common Errors" section if we replace the "less than" symbol in the last line of the associated query with an "equals" sign?

5. What happens to the correlated subquery in the final example of the "Common Errors" section if we reintroduce the clause

```
AND Pickdel = 'P'
```

Explain the contents and the order of any output.

---

ferent occurrences of table names:

```
FROM   table-name alias1, table-name alias2
```

A compound WHERE clause, the succeeding lines, is usually coded to eliminate useless and redundant information:

```
WHERE   alias1.column-name1 = alias2.column-name1
  AND   alias1.column-name2 < alias2.column-name2
```

The EXISTS operator is used with nested queries to determine whether the inner query generates at least one row. The inner SELECT statement uses the * instead of a column name. Whenever the EXISTS operator evaluates as True, the outer query generates a row. The EXISTS operator may be combined with the AND, OR, and NOT operators presented in Chapter 3.

```
SELECT   output-column-name1, output-column-name2, etc.
  FROM   table-name1
 WHERE   EXISTS
    (SELECT   *
       FROM   table-name2
      WHERE   expression);
```

A correlated subquery is a nested query whose inner query requires information generated by the outer query. Correlated subqueries execute the inner query once for each row in the outer query. The inner query and outer query are not independent; they are correlated.

―――――――――――

Productivity Tip:
TEST BY HAND.

―――――――――――

Experienced programmers know that nothing is more time-consuming than trying to correct an error via the method of "I'm not sure what is happening, so I'll just run it by the computer." Mindless testing not only takes a long time, it is also very tiring. Don't rely on chance to solve your problems. It won't.

Playing computer, as we did when introducing the *join* operation, saves time in the long run. When testing nested queries other than correlated subqueries, first execute the inner query. If necessary, run the inner query on the computer. When you know what data the outer query is processing, half the battle is over. And remember Chapter 5's Productivity Tip: Write down your results. Why struggle today with a problem you solved two weeks ago?

Chapter Summary

This chapter continued our examination of the *join* operation and nested queries. We applied the *join* operation to three tables, and combined *joins* and nested queries. We extended the *join* operation to the related self-*join*. We introduced the EXISTS operator and lookup tables. We concluded the chapter by examining correlated subqueries in some detail. But in spite of our sophisticated processing, we still face severe output restrictions when applying aggregate functions. Very basic purchase information remains unavailable.

The next chapter examines *views*. This powerful SQL feature can increase a database's security, simplicity, flexibility, and integrity, advantages that come at a cost, also discussed. It also has an overview of indexes, a tool for increasing a computer's processing speed.

Review Questions

1. Define in your own words the following SQL terms, and describe their use:
   a. self-*join*
   b. EXISTS operator
   c. correlated subquery
   d. lookup table

2. Describe in detail the processing of the following self-*join*:

```
SELECT   First.Purchnum, Second.Purchnum, First.Prodnum,
         Second.Prodnum, First.Readydat
```

```
   FROM   Purchase First, Purchase Second
  WHERE   First.Readydat = Second.Readydat
    AND   First.Purchnum < Second.Purchnum
    AND   First.Prodnum < Second.Prodnum;
```

3. Describe in detail the processing of the following correlated subquery:

```
SELECT   Custname, Customer.Custnum, Custaddr, Zipcode, Phone
  FROM   Customer
 WHERE   '11/02/1992' IN
   (SELECT   Readydat
      FROM   Purchase
     WHERE   Customer.Custnum = Purchase.Custnum);
```

Case Study Exercises

Recall that unstarred questions may be answered using either the full database (tables Cds, Manufs, and Works) or the smaller database (tables Smlcds, Manufs, and Smlworks.) Starred questions require the full database, consisting of tables Cds, Manufs, and Works. Because of the large number of columns in the tables, output only essential columns.

1. Write an SQL query to select the Cdid and title of all CDs with at least one work by Mozart. Show the output.

2. Write an SQL query to select CDs with at least one vocal work. Include the price of the CD. Show the output.

3. Write an SQL query to select single CDs (not part of a box) with at least one vocal work. Include the price of the CD. Show the output.

4. Write an SQL query to select CDs manufactured in Cleveland that include works by Bach. Show the output.

5. Write an SQL query that lists works on CDs with the word *Concert* in the title or the series. Show the output.

6. Repeat the query for Case Study Exercise 5, but include the price of each CD and the discounted price. Show the output.

7. Write an SQL query using the EXISTS operator to select CDs manufactured in Europe (Rome or Paris). Show the output.

8. Repeat the query for Case Study Exercise 7, but include the Wkidcode and the Wkid as well as the price. Show the output.

* **9.** Write an SQL query to show the discount and quality rating of CDs recorded by a chamber orchestra. Show the output.

*10. Repeat the query for Case Study Exercise 9, but include the performing artist and the title of each work. Show the output.

*11. Write an SQL query to select the Cdid and title of all CDs with at least one cello work by Bach. Show the output.

*12. Write an SQL query to select CDs with at least one vocal or violin work. Include the price of the CD, the name of the performing artist, and the name of the orchestra. Show the output.

CHAPTER EIGHT

Views and Indexes

Chapter 7 queried multiple tables by applying some of SQL's sophisticated features, including self-joins and correlated subqueries. We found that we were still unable to process some important, fairly simple queries. This chapter examines views, *a powerful tool for increasing a database's security, simplicity, flexibility, and integrity. These advantages come at a cost, which we also discuss. The chapter concludes with an overview of* indexes, *an SQL feature that increases the computer's speed in processing applications.*

OBJECTIVES

You have met this chapter's objectives when you can:

- Create and update views.
- Discuss the advantages and disadvantages of views.
- Create indexes.
- Discuss the advantages and disadvantages of indexes.
- Apply views to meet business and other information-processing needs.

Introduction

Noga was taking stock, not of the candy but of her experiences in extracting information from the database via SQL. She concluded that her system needed improvements in four areas: data security, simplicity, flexibility, and data integrity.

Data Security. Noga was very busy handling raw materials, making and packaging the candy, and promoting and selling it. And although she wanted to involve her assistant in the computer work, she didn't want him to have access to all of the firm's data.

Simplicity. It was wasteful for Noga to type complicated queries time and time again. And unless she could simplify these queries, her assistant wouldn't be able to help her with the computer work.

Flexibility. Noga had invested countless hours learning multitable *join*s, nested queries, self-*join*s, correlated subqueries, and other SQL features. Yet she still was highly restricted in combining data for the different candies that make up a given purchase order. Aggregate functions limited her queries severely.

Data Integrity. Noga was afraid that sooner or later incorrect data would be stored in the tables, resulting in lost candy, lost orders, and eventually lost customers. SQL should help ensure the validity of data in the tables.

Then Noga found out about views. We will follow her as she applies this important feature that extends SQL tables to meet the four needs just listed.

Views and Their Advantages

A **base table** is a table defined with the CREATE TABLE command. Although we have not used this term previously, all our tables have actually been base tables. SQL allows us to process base tables to create new tables called **views.** Unlike base tables, however, views do not exist physically. They contain no actual data. A view represents people's *perception* of base tables, whether singly or in combination. A single base table may be the foundation of several views. Several tables may be combined to form one view. The relationship among users, views, and base tables is shown in Figure 8-1.

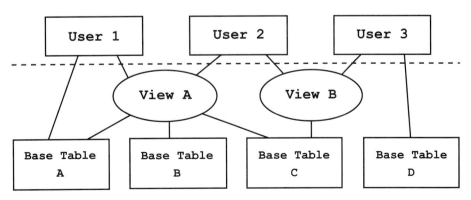

Figure 8-1 Relationship Among Users, Views, and Base Tables

Data Security

Views are defined with the CREATE VIEW statement. Views apply the same naming conventions as do tables. We often terminate a view name with the characters *view* or simply *v,* although this practice is optional.

To increase her database's security, Noga coded the simple view shown in Figure 8-2. If we compare this with the Product table in Figure 8-3, we see that the Prodnum view is identical to the Product table, with a single exception: The view does not contain the "Unitcost" column. No matter how many times Noga's assistant queries the Prodview view, he still won't have any idea of the candies' unit cost. The query

```
SELECT   Prodnum, Unitcost
  FROM   Prodview;
```

generates an error message such as the following:

```
-ERROR- Column Unitcost not found
```

All other data in the original Product table is available.

```
CREATE   VIEW Prodview
    AS   SELECT Prodnum, Description, Unitprice
  FROM   Product;
```

Display the view's contents with the following SELECT statement:

```
SELECT   *
  FROM   Prodview;
```

Prodnum	Description	Unitprice
1	Celestial Cashew Crunch	10.00
2	Unbrittle Peanut Paradise	9.00
3	Mystery Melange	10.50
4	Millionaire's Macadamia Mix	16.00
5	Nuts Not Nachos	9.50

Figure 8-2 A View that Increases Database Security

Prodnum	Description	Unitcost	Unitprice
1	Celestial Cashew Crunch	7.45	10.00
2	Unbrittle Peanut Paradise	5.75	9.00
3	Mystery Melange	7.75	10.50

```
       4    Millionaire's Macadamia Mix          12.50          16.00
       5    Nuts Not Nachos                       6.25           9.50
```

Figure 8-3 Original Product Table

A view need not use the same column names as its associated base table or tables. For example, we could create a view with the command shown in Figure 8-4. The view's column names appear in parentheses and must obey SQL naming conventions. The number of columns listed in parentheses must equal the number of columns in the associated table. In this example, some view column names differ from column names of the associated table. People querying the Pdview view use the names in parentheses. They need not know the column names "Prodnum" and "Description" associated with the base table Product.

```
CREATE    VIEW Pdview (Product, Prodname, Unitprice)
     AS   SELECT   Prodnum, Description, Unitprice
          FROM    Product;
```

Figure 8-4 Explicitly Naming Fields in a View. This view is equivalent to the Prodview view shown in Figure 8-2.

Query Simplicity

Noga had a potential problem with the Cashew supplier and might need to contact all purchasers of Cashew candy. To obtain required information, she coded the query shown in Figure 8-5.

```
                                          ↗CUSTOMER●
SELECT   Purchnum, Purchase.Prodnum, ⌐Custnum, Custname,
         Purchdat, Readydat, Kilos, Pickdel, Phone
   FROM   Purchase, Customer
  WHERE   Purchase.Prodnum =
     (SELECT   Prodnum
        FROM   Product
       WHERE   Description LIKE '%Cashew%')
   AND   Purchase.Custnum = Customer.Custnum;
```

Prch	Pn	Cn	Custname	Purchdat	Readydat	Kilos	Pd	Phone
1234	1	22	The Candy Kid	10/28/1992	10/28/1992	3.5	D	563-4545
1236	1	41	Montag, Susie	10/28/1992	10/28/1992	2.0	P	456-2091
1238	1	37	Bobby Bon Bons	10/29/1992	10/29/1992	3.7	D	434-9045
1241	1	13	Pickled Pickles	10/29/1992	10/29/1992	1.0	P	324-8909

Figure 8-5 A Complex Query. (Column headings have been abbreviated.)

Noga could not reasonably expect her young helper to write such a query. She didn't care to code such a query herself, and she especially didn't like recoding it whenever she required information about Cashew candy purchases and customers. She needed a Cashew candy view. She could query this view herself or even have her assistant code simple queries. She created the view with the command shown in Figure 8-6. The output is the same as that generated by the query in Figure 8-5. But now, the data appears in an easily queried view.

```
CREATE   VIEW Cashewv
    AS   SELECT Purchnum, Purchase.Prodnum, Custnum, Custname,
         Purchdat, Readydat, Kilos, Pickdel, Phone
  FROM   Purchase, Customer
 WHERE   Purchase.Prodnum =
    (SELECT   Prodnum
       FROM   Product
      WHERE   Description LIKE '%Cashew%')
  AND   Purchase.Custnum = Customer.Custnum;
```

Figure 8-6 Replacing a Complex Query with a View

To obtain the Cashew candy data, one need only write the query shown in Figure 8-7. If we can spell the view name, the Cashew candy information is at our fingertips. If necessary, Noga can create the view with a simpler name.

```
SELECT   *
  FROM   Cashewv;
```

Figure 8-7 Querying the Cashewv View. The output would be the same as in Figure 8-5.

Creating the view is slightly more difficult than creating the original query. Creating the Cashewv view requires knowledge about views, the LIKE operator, correlated subqueries, and the *join* operation. But using this view requires only elementary SQL knowledge.

In many firms a single individual creates views for several people. When Noga's Crispy Crunch expands, it could hire a computer specialist whose duties include creating views for nontechnical users.

E X E R C I S E S

1. Use the Purchase table to create a view containing the columns "Purchnum," "Prodnum," "Custnum," "Kilos," and "Pickdel." Write an SQL query to output the contents of this view. Show the output.

2. Use any base tables necessary to create a view containing the columns "Purchnum," "Prodnum," "Custnum," "Custname," "Kilos," and "Unitprice." Write an SQL query to output the contents of this view. Show the output.

3. Use any base tables necessary and a correlated subquery to create a Peanutv view similar to the Cashewv view. Remember that *Nuts Not Nachos* also includes peanuts. Write an SQL query to output the contents of this view. Show the output.

Flexibility

Noga was fed up. She had spent a lot of time learning SQL, including views, and still she couldn't extract desired information from the Purchase table. The limitations imposed by the use of aggregate functions made it difficult to obtain consolidated information about a single purchase. The correct application of views enables users of most SQL implementations to bypass these limitations.

First Noga applied aggregate functions to create a view combining all individual candy orders sharing the same purchase number, as shown in Figure 8-8. Some information has been consolidated per purchase. However, other purchase information, such as the customer number and customer name, is absent. These two columns may not appear in the Tempview view because it was created using aggregate functions.

```
CREATE   VIEW Tempview (Purchnum, Totkilos, Ncandies)
    AS   SELECT   Purchnum, SUM(Kilos), COUNT(Kilos)
         FROM   Purchase
         GROUP  BY Purchnum;
```

Display the view's contents with the following SELECT statement:

```
SELECT   *
   FROM   Tempview;
```

Purchnum	Totkilos	Ncandies
1234	3.5	1
1235	15.0	1
1236	5.7	2
1237	3.7	1
1238	9.3	3
1239	3.0	1
1240	18.8	2
1241	8.6	2
1242	3.5	1

Figure 8-8 A View Using Aggregate Functions

Tempview itself contains output generated by processing aggregate functions, but not aggregate functions themselves. So in most SQL implementations a *join* operation may combine Tempview with columns in other tables, as shown in Figure 8-9.

```
CREATE   VIEW Purchview
     AS   SELECT DISTINCT Tempview.Purchnum,
          Purchase.Custnum, Custname, Totkilos, Ncandies
            FROM   Tempview, Purchase, Customer
          WHERE   Tempview.Purchnum = Purchase.Purchnum
            AND   Purchase.Custnum = Customer.Custnum;
```

Display the view's contents with the following SELECT statement:

```
SELECT   *
    FROM   Purchview;
```

Purchnum	Custnum	Custname	Totkilos	Ncandies
1234	22	The Candy Kid	3.5	1
1235	24	Waterman, Al	15.0	1
1236	41	Montag, Susie	5.7	2
1237	4	Armstrong, Inc.	3.7	1
1238	37	Bobby Bon Bons	9.3	3
1239	24	Waterman, Al	3.0	1
1240	42	Columberg Sweets	18.8	2
1241	13	Pickled Pickles	8.6	2
1242	12	Swedish Burgers	3.5	1

Figure 8-9 A View of a View. (Some column headers have been abbreviated.)

Noga finally had the information she wanted. She could display this information in any desired order, she could process it with aggregate functions such as SUM and AVG, or she could join this view with other tables. She could do whatever she wanted with this information—or could she? What if she wanted to price the orders? Putting a price tag on purchase number 1234 or 1235 is no problem. (She need only *join* the Purchview view with the Purchase and Product tables.) She could not use Purchview to assign a price to purchase number 1236 because this order includes two candies with a different unit price. When base table information was consolidated in the Purchview view, some information was lost. This view contains no information relative to individual candy purchases; it contains only summary information for complete purchases.

Noga returned to the base tables to retrieve information relative to individual candy purchases. First she created a temporary view with aggregate information. She couldn't call it Tempview, because a Tempview view already exists. The view is shown in Figure 8-10.

```
CREATE   VIEW Tempvw2 (Purchnum, Totkilos, Totcost, Totprice)
    AS   SELECT Purchnum, SUM(Kilos), SUM(Unitcost*Kilos),
         SUM(Unitprice*Kilos)
             FROM   Purchase, Product
             WHERE  Purchase.Prodnum = Product.Prodnum
             GROUP  BY Purchnum;
```

Display the view's contents with the following SELECT statement:

```
SELECT   *
    FROM Tempvw2;
```

Purchnum	Totkilos	Totcost	Totprice
1234	3.5	26.075	35.000
1235	15.0	86.250	135.000
1236	5.7	43.575	58.850
1237	3.7	28.675	38.850
1238	9.3	68.565	94.000
1239	3.0	17.250	27.000
1240	18.8	110.500	171.600
1241	8.6	54.950	82.200
1242	3.5	21.875	33.250

Figure 8-10 A View Summarizing Candy Purchases

E X E R C I S E S

4. Create a view using the Tempvw2 view that includes the customer number and customer name. Write an SQL query to output the contents of this view. Show the output.

5. Create a view showing the discounted price as well as the information requested in Exercise 4. Is it possible to use the Tempvw2 view in creating this view? Write an SQL query to output the contents of this view. Show the output.

Data Integrity

We next examine with Noga the fourth aspect of views, data integrity. Before we do so, you should make backups of all existing base tables. Then you can test our examples and attempt the exercises without jeopardizing your original base tables. Use the following table names for the copies: Custcopy, Purchcopy, Prodcopy, and Disccopy. **Important:** Do not try the examples or the exercises on the original base tables; try them only on the copies.

Noga thought about launching a new product, with the following data: product number 6; description Addictive Almond Angels; unit cost 8.50; unit price 12.50. She could add the product directly to the Prodcopy table with the following command:

```
INSERT  INTO Prodcopy
     VALUES  (6, 'Addictive Almond Angels', 8.50, 12.50);
```

But what would happen if she entered the data incorrectly? She might make a mistake and not realize it until much later.

A special feature of views (available on some SQL implementations) called the WITH CHECK OPTION can help validate data inserted into a given base table. Noga does not believe in *loss leaders,* that is, products sold at less than cost price to attract customers. She applied the WITH CHECK OPTION to enforce her policy. She first created a view called Productv, as shown in Figure 8-11.

```
CREATE  VIEW Productv
    AS   SELECT   *
            FROM   Prodcopy
           WHERE   Unitprice > Unitcost
   WITH   CHECK OPTION;
```

Display the view's contents with the following SELECT statement:

```
SELECT   *
   FROM   Productv;
```

Prodnum	Description	Unitcost	Unitprice
1	Celestial Cashew Crunch	7.45	10.00
2	Unbrittle Peanut Paradise	5.75	9.00
3	Mystery Melange	7.75	10.50
4	Millionaire's Macadamia Mix	12.50	16.00
5	Nuts Not Nachos	6.25	9.50

Figure 8-11 A View Enforcing Company Pricing Policy

If she enters the data, via the view, with the following SQL command:

```
INSERT  INTO Productv
     VALUES  (6, 'Addictive Almond Angels', 8.50, 12.50);
```

then the new candy appears on both the Prodcopy base table and the Productv view. But what if she tries to enter a product whose unit price is less than its unit cost? An attempt to enter the following data:

Product Number	Description	Unit Cost	Unit Price
7	Lousy Loss Leader	7.00	6.50

via the view, with the SQL command

```
INSERT   INTO Productv
    VALUES   (7, 'Lousy Loss Leader', 7.00, 6.50);
```

leads to an error message such as

```
    The row violates the WHERE clause
```

No data is entered into either the Productv view or the Prodcopy base table.

TRY IT YOURSELF

1. What happens if you try to insert into the Productv view the following data? product number 8; description Boring Break-Even; unit cost 8.25; unit price 8.25

2. What happens if you try to insert into the Prodcopy table the following data? product number 8; description Boring Break-Even; unit cost 8.25; unit price 8.25

E X E R C I S E S

6. Use the Custcopy table to create a view verifying that the customer type column is 'P', 'R', or 'W'. Test this view using both valid and invalid data. Write SQL queries to output the contents of this view and the associated base table. Show the output.

7. Use the Purchcopy table to create a view verifying that the ready date column is not prior to the purchase date column. Also verify that the number of kilos ordered is not negative. Test this view using both valid and invalid data. Write SQL queries to output the contents of this view and the associated base table. Show the output.

Read-Only Views

We have already seen how to update views. But not all views can be updated. Some views, called **read-only views,** do not allow UPDATE, DELETE, or INSERT commands. For example, in the Tempview view in Figure 8-8 the last row contains the following data: purchase number = 1242, total kilos = 3.5, and number of candies = 1. Suppose we coded the following illegal update query:

```
UPDATE   Tempview
   SET   Ncandies = 5
 WHERE   Purchnum = 1242;
```

If successful, this update would destroy the relationship between the Tempview view and its underlying Purchase base table.That is, for purchase number 1242, Tempview would no longer accurately reflect the Purchase table. Therefore, the system itself rejects this UPDATE query.

In many cases the validity of an UPDATE, DELETE, or INSERT command is not so clear-cut. As we have so often seen, different SQL implementations apply different rules. Box 8-1 presents typical read-only views. As this chapter's Productivity Tip indicates, if you are unsure about whether a given view may be updated, try updating it.

BOX 8-1

Typical Read-Only Views

While the exact restrictions on updating views depend on the specific SQL implementation, the following views commonly are read-only (and therefore are not subject to UPDATE, INSERT, or DELETE commands):

Views defined by SELECT statements containing an ORDER BY clause

Views defined by SELECT statements including a nested query

Views defined by SELECT statements including a *join* operation

Views defined by SELECT statements including a column derived from an expression, such as Kilos/2.2

Views defined by SELECT statements including an aggregate function

Views defined by SELECT statements including the DISTINCT qualifier

Views defined by SELECT statements including the GROUP BY or HAVING clause

Views defined by SELECT statements combined by the UNION operator

Note, on occasion some columns in a view may be updated whereas others may not.

Deleting a View

Deleting a view is quite simple. For instance, the command for deleting the Prodview view is:

```
DROP   VIEW Prodview;
```

Some SQL implementations request you to confirm view deletion. Do *not* automatically confirm: If you haven't been careful with your view names, you may find yourself deleting the wrong view. Once you delete a given view, you may render other views inaccessible. For example, if you deleted the Tempview view, information appearing on the Purchview view would no longer be accessible.

Modifying a View

Although SQL provides no direct means of modifying an existing view, you can still do so as follows: Carefully note down all desired changes, such as revised column names and new selection criteria. Then delete the current view, and create the modified view.

Common Errors

Views reduce but do not eliminate user errors. Some other errors can occur during view creation. Among the most common errors are the following.

Creating a View with a Duplicate Name. If after creating a Prodview view we attempt to create another Prodview view (whether or not the contents are the same), the system responds with an error message such as the following:

```
-ERROR-  New table is a duplicate.
```

and the second Prodview table is not created.

Forgetting Parentheses in the List of Column Names. This error occurs in the following command:

```
CREATE   VIEW Pdview2 Product, Prodname, Unitprice
     AS SELECT  Prodnum, Description, Unitprice
         FROM  Product;
```

which generates an error message such as the following:

```
-ERROR- Syntax is incorrect for the command.
```

Discrepancy in the Number of Columns. A similar but more sophisticated error occurs when the number of columns within parentheses differs from the number of columns in the associated SELECT clause. Perhaps the view coder thought it unnecessary to place the "Unitprice" column within parentheses because it appears within the SELECT clause. This reasoning is incorrect. For instance, the query

```
CREATE   VIEW Pdview3 (Product, Prodname)
     AS SELECT   Prodnum, Description, Unitprice
          FROM   Product;
```

generates an error message such as the following:

```
-ERROR- Syntax is incorrect for the command.
```

Trying to Update a Read-Only View. The Tempview view applies aggregate functions. It may not be updated. The statement

```
INSERT INTO   Tempview
      VALUES   (1243, 5.0, 62.50, 80.00);
```

generates a message such as the following:

```
-WARNING- Unauthorized access to the table
```

The data is not added to the view or to the associated base table.

Disadvantages of Views

While views may be highly advantageous, they have several potential disadvantages, including longer processing time, extra computer memory, and additional administrative complexity.

The computer does not process views directly but must translate queries or updates on views into equivalent queries or updates on the base tables. This additional processing requires extra time. Then the computer must store the view definitions, which takes extra computer memory, a precious commodity in many computer systems. Finally, the more views available, the greater the administrative control required to keep the database running smoothly. (Database administration is the subject of the next chapter.)

The time saved by applying simple views instead of complicated queries often more than balances the extra computer processing time needed.

However, views should not be regarded as a panacea. They must be created and modified to meet a firm's specific information needs.

Indexes

Noga felt she had a good picture of SQL views and their applications, given her present database of only two days' data. But she wondered about the impact on the base tables and the associated views when the data began to multiply. What would happen to system efficiency when the tables and views contained two weeks' or six months' data? For the moment, a newer, faster computer was out of the question. Just as SQL provides the views technique, to make the system more user-friendly, she hoped it could provide a technique to make the system more efficient. It does: indexes.

An **index** acts as a pointer to the location of each row in a table or view. An SQL index resembles a book index; both allow the user to find requested information more rapidly. The computer usually finds selected rows faster by searching the index than by searching the rows themselves, because the index entries, unlike the data rows, are in a predetermined order. However, in contrast to a book index, an SQL index is invisible to users querying a table. SQL systems contain a special section that determines which (if any) indexes to use for maximum efficiency when executing a given query.

Index use does not automatically lead to significant speed improvements. Processing small tables or views containing about a dozen rows may be so rapid that indexation has no appreciable effect. Processing tables or views containing hundreds of rows can take at least several minutes, in which case even a moderate per-row increase may be cumulatively noticeable. Furthermore, the larger the table or view, the greater the percentage of time usually saved by judicious index creation. Box 8-2 presents rules of thumb for efficient index use.

Creating Indexes

To create an index, use the CREATE INDEX command, as shown in Figure 8-12, which presents a schematic image of the index as stored in the database. The computer uses this index to increase processing speed for Customer table queries such as the following:

```
SELECT   *
  FROM   Customer
 WHERE   Custname = 'Bobby Bon Bons';
```

Figure 8-13 illustrates how to create an index in descending order. Note the use of the term *DESC* to put the index in descending order.

BOX 8 - 2

How to Make Efficient Use of Indexes

Indexes are most efficient when the *indexed column* obeys at least one of the following conditions:

a. It is a key column, identifying a row uniquely.

b. It links two or more tables used in a *join* operation.

c. It is referred to frequently in WHERE or ORDER BY clauses.

d. It is a CHAR column whose first four characters are unique.

Because indexes occupy computer memory, they should be created only if truly useful. Unnecessary indexes may actually degrade system performance. For example, indexes tend to slow down INSERT and UPDATE operations, because they require the system to process additional information.

```
CREATE   INDEX Cnameidx
    ON   Customer(Custname);
```

Index Value	Customer Name
1	Armstrong, Inc.
2	Bobby Bon Bons
3	Columberg Sweets
4	Crowsh, Elias
5	Jones, Joe
6	Montag, Susie
7	Pickled Pickles
8	Swedish Burgers
9	The Candy Kid
10	Waterman, Al

Figure 8-12 Creating an Index. The command is shown on the left; a simplified image of the index as stored in the database is shown on the right.

```
CREATE   INDEX Cnameidd
    ON   Customer(Custname DESC);
```

Index Value	Customer Name
1	Waterman, Al
2	The Candy Kid
3	Swedish Burgers
4	Pickled Pickles
5	Montag, Susie
6	Jones, Joe
7	Crowsh, Elias
8	Columberg Sweets
9	Bobby Bon Bons
10	Armstrong, Inc.

Figure 8-13 Creating a Descending-Order Index. The command is shown on the left; a simplified image of the index as stored in the database is shown on the right.

Some implementations accept the UNIQUE INDEX OPTION, as in the following command:

```
CREATE    UNIQUE INDEX Cnameudx
    ON    Customer(Custname);
```

A *unique index* prohibits the adding of a record with a duplicate indexed column or columns. The statement

```
INSERT    INTO Customer
    VALUES    (55, 'Montag, Susie', 'W', '111 NorthSide',
                '91213', '456-0908');
```

generates a message such as the following:

```
-ERROR- Data is not unique
```

and the new record is not added.

Noga thought of indexing the Purchase table. Which column should she index? By the guidelines in Box 8-2, we see that indexing the "Pickdel" column would be a waste of time and computer memory, for its value is far from unique. Similarly, she should not index the "Purchdat" or the "Readydat" column. The "Kilos" column is almost unique, but she should not index it because she so infrequently codes Purchase table queries that reference this column. (The query

```
SELECT    *
    FROM    Purchase
    WHERE    Kilos > 4.8;
```

is an example.) Should Noga ever code many such queries, she could then index the "Kilos" column. However, she often codes Purchase table queries that reference the "Custname" column, so she should index this column, with a statement such as

```
CREATE    INDEX Cnameix2
    ON    Purchase(Custname);
```

Note, this index is different from the index used on the Customer table, even though the two indexed columns have the same name. The name *Cnameidx* is illegal here because it is already in use (see Figure 8-12).

Neither the "Purchnum" column nor the "Prodnum" column is unique, and neither should be indexed separately. However, the following command indexes the combined columns, which *are* unique:

```
CREATE   INDEX Purprdix
    ON   Purchase(Purchnum, Prodnum);
```

Note, when we created the Purchase table (see Chapter 6), we included the line

```
UNIQUE(Purchnum, Prodnum)
```

Deleting an Index

Deleting an index is quite simple. The command used to delete the Purprdix index is:

```
DROP   INDEX Purprdix;
```

Some SQL implementations request that you confirm index deletion. Do *not* automatically confirm. If you haven't been careful with your index names, you may find yourself deleting the wrong index. Deleting an index does not change the data on the associated table or view. Data is still accessible but is no longer indexed. When a table is deleted, all associated index names are automatically deleted.

E X E R C I S E S

8. Code an SQL statement to index the Product table on an appropriate column.

9. Code an SQL statement to delete the index you created in Exercise 8.

TRY IT YOURSELF

3. Note the time it takes to run the query that selects customer Bobby Bon Bons from the Customer table. Delete the Cnameidx index, and note the time it takes to rerun the query. Is the difference appreciable?

4. Note the time it takes to run the query

```
SELECT   * FROM Purchase WHERE Kilos > 4.8;
```

Index the "Kilos" column, and note the time it takes to rerun the query. Is the difference appreciable? Delete the index of the "Kilos" column.

Syntax and Applications Summary

Views. The CREATE TABLE command (see Chapters 1 and 6) creates base tables, which store actual data. Views are created from base tables with the CREATE VIEW statement:

```
CREATE   VIEW viewname (view-column-name1, etc.)
    AS   SELECT
  WITH   CHECK OPTION;
```

The view-column-names are optional, but if used their number must be equal to the number of columns within the SELECT statement. The usual SELECT statement options are available. The WITH CHECK OPTION statement acts to validate data, thereby preventing data that does not meet the constraints of the WHERE clause from being loaded into the view or the underlying base table. It is not available with all SQL implementations. Some views are read-only; they may not be updated (UPDATE, DELETE, or INSERT commands are not allowed). Box 8-1 presents common rules for determining whether a view is read-only. Remember, views do not actually contain stored data; they represent the user's image of the data.

Indexes. SQL employs indexes to process a database more rapidly. Indexes are created with the command

```
CREATE   UNIQUE INDEX index-name
    ON   table-name or view-name (column-name1 DESC, etc.)
```

The UNIQUE clause, which is optional, prevents rows with a duplicate indexed column (or columns) from being entered into the database. The DESC indicates that the index on the given column is in descending order. Box 8-2 discusses how to make efficient use of indexes.

Productivity Tip:
TRY IT OUT.

As we have seen so frequently, specific SQL implementations may obey slightly different rules. For example, the rules for updating views are not always the same: One implementation may allow updating some columns in a given view, while another may forbid updating any columns in the same view. Given a firm's specific needs, slightly different rules may have a vastly different impact. Although it is important to examine the documentation for your SQL version, another excellent way to determine what your system will do is by trying it out yourself. If you need help, document the tests you have run, before approaching an expert. This will save time for all involved.

Chapter Summary

In this chapter we explored two very different SQL techniques for increasing productivity. Views tend to increase a database's security, simplicity, flexibility, and integrity, and may improve the productivity of system users. Indexes may increase the computer's effective processing speed. The next chapter discusses another way of improving productivity, system administration. Subjects covered include data security and integrity, serving multiple users, applying new SQL statements, and organizational suggestions, all important considerations when building a well-running system based on SQL.

Review Questions

1. Define in your own words the following SQL terms, and describe their use:
   a. base table
   b. view
   c. read-only view
   d. index

2. Describe in your own words how views can increase a database's security, simplicity, flexibility, and integrity.

3. Describe in detail how views can overcome the restrictions on columns output when aggregate functions are used.

4. Discuss the disadvantages of views. How can a firm decide whether the advantages outweigh the disadvantages?

5. When should indexes be used? How can you determine which columns to index?

Case Study Exercises

Recall that unstarred questions may be answered using either the full database (tables Cds, Manufs, and Works) or the smaller database (tables Smlcds, Manufs, and Smlworks). Starred questions require the full database, consisting of tables Cds, Manufs, and Works. Because of the number of columns in the tables, present only essential columns in the output.

   1. Create a view of the Cds or Smlcds base table that does not include the "Price" column or the "Number of Copies" column. Write an SQL query to output this view's contents. Show the output.

2. Create a view of the Cds or Smlcds base table that does not include the "Price" column or the "Number of Copies" column. Include only individual CDs and not boxes. Write an SQL query to output this view's contents. Show the output.

3. Create a view of the Cds or Smlcds base table that includes only 'DDD' CDs. Write an SQL query to output this view's contents. Show the output.

4. Create a view of the Cds or Smlcds base table that includes only 'DDD' CDs produced by manufacturers whose quality rating for that series is at least 7. Write an SQL query to output this view's contents. Show the output.

5. Create a view of the Cds or Smlcds base table that includes only CDs with *Mozart* in the title. Write an SQL query to output this view's contents. Show the output.

6. Select all works from the appropriate table for all CDs in the view created in Case Study Exercise 5. Show the output.

7. Create a view of the Works or Smlworks base table that includes only works with *Mozart* in the title. Write an SQL query to output this view's contents. Show the output. Compare this output to that generated in Case Study Exercise 6. Explain the differences, if any.

8. Create a view of the necessary base tables that includes the price, the number of copies, the total price, and the discounted price for all CDs. Write an SQL query to output this view's contents. Show the output.

9. Copy one of the base tables. Create a view of the chosen table that includes the WITH CHECK OPTION for a single column. Test this view using both valid and invalid data for that column. Write SQL queries to output this view's contents and the associated base table. Show the output.

10. Copy the same base table as in Case Study Exercise 9 or another base table. Create a view of the chosen table that includes the WITH CHECK OPTION for two columns. Test this view using both valid and invalid data for the two columns. Write SQL queries to output this view's contents and the associated base table. Show the output.

11. For a table of your choice, note the time it takes to run a query involving a given column. Index the column, and note the time it takes to rerun the query. Is the difference appreciable?

12. Repeat Case Study Exercise 11 for a *join* operation. First note the time it takes to run the query without indexes. Then index the column or columns used to *join* the two base tables, and note the time it takes to rerun the query. Is the difference appreciable?

*13. Create a view of compact disks recorded by a chamber orchestra that does not include the "Price" column or the "Number of Copies" column. Write an SQL query to output this view's contents. Show the output.

* 14. Create a view of violin works that includes the recording orchestra. Write an SQL query to output this view's contents. Show the output.

Administering the System

The previous chapter illustrated how views may provide an excellent method of increasing data security. SQL's GRANT statement extends security provisions by permitting potential users different degrees of access to database tables. The larger the database, the greater the likelihood of system failure. We will discuss specific measures available in many SQL systems to reduce the impact of system failure. This chapter presents other SQL features that (a) reduce interference among users, (b) increase the probability that data is correct and consistent, and (c) provide authorized parties with precise information on the database contents. Along the way we introduce a formal description of SQL syntax.

OBJECTIVES

You have met this chapter's objectives when you can:

- Code SQL statements to GRANT and REVOKE access to tables in the database.
- Understand a formal description of SQL statements.
- Code SQL statements to COMMIT and ROLLBACK transactions.
- Code SQL statements to LOCK tables.
- Describe, in detail, primary key integrity and referential integrity.
- Describe the contents of your system catalog, if accessible.
- Apply these SQL statements and concepts to meet business and other information-processing needs.

Administering Multiuser Databases

We are now peering several years into the future. Noga's candy has become a bestseller. The firm has incorporated under the name *Noga's Crispy Crunch,*

Inc., also known by its initials, *NCCI*. NCCI's product line has expanded from five to over two dozen candies. It now has 17 full-time employees and several part-timers for the holiday rush season. Noga ships candy across the country and to selected locations in Canada. Next week she will meet with three European distributors, at their request.

All these business changes have caused changes in the company's computer system. After years of faithful service, Uncle Mike's gift computer now graces her den, though not retired, but linked to NCCI's computer network. For two years the business has relied on a network encompassing a dozen microcomputers and three printers, including a high-speed laser printer. Both the business and its supporting computer system are on the verge of major expansion.

Business pressures prevent Noga from spending much time at the computer. While she still runs occasional queries, she rarely updates any tables. She chairs the firm's Computer Policy Committee and retains ultimate control over the database. She recently assigned day-to-day control of the computer system to the Computer Systems Officer, her first employee.

Life has changed for the former delivery boy. He is now completing a degree in Microcomputer Systems at the local college. Next semester he plans to teach SQL at night. In line with the firm's expansion, he and Noga have had to address five interrelated issues associated with administering multiuser databases:

Controlling Access. Database access must be strictly controlled. Authorized users must have relatively easy access to required data. On the other hand, users must be denied access to data not authorized to them. SQL's GRANT statement provides users with such access. The REVOKE statement removes it.

Protecting the Database Against System Failure. The likelihood of system failure increases with the increasing size and complexity of a computer system. This potential damage cannot be eliminated but must be limited. SQL's transaction processing mode and the appropriate use of COMMIT and ROLLBACK statements reduce the impact of system failure.

Interuser Interference. A database is continuously being accessed by many users, who must be protected from one another. For example, two users may not update the same data simultaneously. The LOCK TABLE statement or its equivalent, found in many versions of SQL, reduces the probability of user interference.

Ensuring Only Correct and Consistent Data. Without such data integrity, the database's value is sharply reduced. Some SQL implementations provide facilities that tend to increase data integrity. More will in the future.

Professional Management. The database should not be managed on an amateur, ad hoc basis. An individual must be assigned active responsibility for the computer system. Like all other managers, this person requires up-to-date information on which to base decisions. SQL's system catalog supplies such information.

Before examining each of these points in greater detail, we introduce a feature familiar to many of you, *passwords.*

Controlling Access

Like most stand-alone microcomputers, Uncle Mike's computer made no provision for passwords. Users accessed the system by simply turning on the computer. NCCI's network works differently. All users must enter an individual password before being allowed access to the system. The Computer Policy Committee soon realized the network security system was insufficient. The committee felt that individuals should be granted access to specific tables rather than to the entire computer system. For example, kitchen employees should be denied access to payroll tables, but have access to the recipes table. Counter employees should be given limited access to tables containing customer and purchase information. SQL's GRANT and REVOKE statements accord and remove such table access.

The GRANT Statement

The GRANT statement provides (or grants) one or more individuals with various rights (or privileges) affecting one or more tables. It is defined as follows:

```
GRANT   {ALL | ALL PRIVILEGES | {ALTER | DELETE | INDEX |
    INSERT  | SELECT | UPDATE[({column-name},...)]},...}
   ON  {table-name},...
   TO  {user-id | PUBLIC},...
[WITH GRANT OPTION]
```

The GRANT statement provides our first example of the widely used **formal SQL syntax,** also employed in describing elements of many other programming languages. See Box 9-1 for details on formal SQL syntax.

Most versions of SQL restrict system access to approved users who can produce on demand a correct **authorization identification,** which may be considered a user-id. In addition, most multiuser computer systems require users to furnish a password before logging onto the system. Check your system manuals to determine how your specific SQL implementation handles authorization identifications and passwords. We simplify the following discussion by employing short, easy-to-remember authorization identifications such as *Joe* and *Mary.* In real-life situations, you should use hard-to-remember and hard-to-guess authorization identifications and passwords, to improve system security, as discussed in this chapter's Productivity Tip.

The GRANT statement is our first Data Control Language statement. It does not change data in the database, but specifies database access. The complete GRANT statement, presented in Box 9-1, controls table access in the following ways:

a. It accords access privileges varying from read-only (SELECT) to all privileges (ALTER, DELETE, INDEX, INSERT, SELECT, and UPDATE on one or several columns).

b. It names the tables or views to which access is granted.

c. It indicates to whom access is granted, including PUBLIC access, that is, access to all who log on the computer system.

d. It may allow users receiving access to pass on this permission to others.

As with many other SQL statements, the exact syntax of the GRANT statement may vary from implementation to implementation.

In spite of her busy schedule, Noga decided to retain ultimate control of the database. She is the Database Administrator (DBA), whose system privileges are discussed in Box 9-2 on page 161. Perhaps when the Computer Systems Officer has proven himself in his new capacity, Noga will assign him ultimate control of the database. But on a day-to-day basis, he is responsible for the database. Therefore Noga accorded him (password *THEKID*) full access privileges to the Customer, Purchase, and Discount tables. She accomplished this with the SQL command shown in Figure 9-1a. There was too little time for Noga to control all business operations. She decided to share the load with her excellent team. Noga considered two different table access policies and their ensuing SQL commands: She assigned her Computer Systems Officer the right to grant access privileges to the Customer and Purchase tables. She implemented this policy with the command shown in Figure 9-1b. In a sense, these two tables have become his; he can GRANT or REVOKE (take away) access privileges as he sees fit. Notice that while he has full access to the Discount table, he may *not* GRANT others access to this table.

```
a                                           b
GRANT   ALL                                 GRANT   ALL
    ON  Customer, Purchase, Discount            ON  Customer, Purchase
    TO  THEKID;                                 TO  THEKID
                                               WITH GRANT OPTION;
```

Figure 9-1 Two Ways of Granting Access Privileges. Only the privileges granted in query **b** may be passed on to others.

BOX 9-1

Formal SQL Syntax

Symbols used in Formal SQL Syntax.

Spelling/Punctuation	*Example*	*Meaning*
All uppercase letters	GRANT	Reserved word, must be spelled correctly.
All lowercase letters	column-name	User supplied, spelled according to SQL naming conventions.
Unpunctuated word	ON	Mandatory.
{ | }	{user-id | PUBLIC}	Object is chosen from within the braces separated by a vertical mark.
,...	ON {table-name},...	Object may be repeated.
[ ]	[WITH GRANT OPTION]	Object is optional.

Formal SQL Syntax for the GRANT Statement. Here we dissect the GRANT statement, line by line. Because the first line is relatively complex, we shall leave it for last.

Line 2.

```
ON {table-name},...
```

The GRANT statement affects one or more tables. The GRANT statement also operates on views, subject to implementation-dependent restrictions.

Line 3.

```
TO {user-id | PUBLIC},...
```

The GRANT statement may affect one or more user-ids or it may be PUBLIC, in other words, accorded to all users.

Line 4.

```
[WITH GRANT OPTION]
```

The GRANT statement may include the term WITH GRANT OPTION, that is, the ability to pass on the GRANT to other users. We discuss this option in greater detail later.

Continued on next page.

Formal SQL Syntax (continued)

Line 1.

```
GRANT {ALL | ALL PRIVILEGES | {ALTER | DELETE | INDEX |
    INSERT | SELECT | UPDATE[({column-name},...)]},...}
```

The GRANT statement starts with the mandatory reserved word GRANT (this should be no surprise). The final punctuation,

```
...}
```

allows listed privileges to be repeated as often as desired. What are these privileges? The first two options, ALL and, equivalently, ALL PRIVILEGES, designate all six listed privileges, namely, ALTER, DELETE, INDEX, INSERT, SELECT, and UPDATE. The braces surrounding the ALTER and the statement

```
UPDATE[({column-name},...]
```

permit selection of one or more listed privileges. The UPDATE option requires further explanation: The portion

```
[({column-name},...)]
```

immediately following the term UPDATE means that UPDATE may appear alone or may be followed by one or more column names. The GRANT statement may accord the privilege to UPDATE all columns or only listed columns.

You now should be able to analyze any formal SQL syntax specifications appearing in your system manuals. Many SQL statements are simpler than the GRANT statement. However, the all-important SELECT statement is even more complicated.

Noga rejected another table access option. She could have allowed full access to all employees via the following SQL query:

```
GRANT   ALL
    ON  Customer, Purchase
    TO  PUBLIC;
```

She chose not to because she felt it went too far: It would allow anyone logging on the computer network to make any changes whatsoever to these two key tables. Clearly, such a command could lead to trouble.

E X E R C I S E S

1. Code an SQL statement that allows the Computer Systems Officer full access to the Product table.
2. Code an SQL statement that allows the Computer Systems Officer read-only (SELECT) access to the Discount table.
3. Code an SQL statement that allows a user whose password is *MaryJo* read-only (SELECT) access to the Customer, Purchase, and Product tables. She may pass these privileges on to other users.

In many SQL implementations, users other than the owner must refer to a table, supplying the owner's identification as a prefix. For example, with many SQL implementations, while Noga could code the following query:

```
SELECT   *
    FROM   Customer;
```

other users would have to code the following:

```
SELECT   *
    FROM   Noga.Customer;
```

Such systems often permit users to code synonyms such as the following:

```
CREATE   SYNONYM Customer
    FOR   Noga.Customer;
```

Some implementations provide PUBLIC synonyms, that is, synonyms available to all authorized users.

TRY IT YOURSELF

1. Repeat Exercise 1 to see whether your SQL implementation requires users other than the owner to designate the Product table with the owner's name.

2. If the answer to the preceding question is yes, determine whether your SQL implementation allows synonyms.

Albert Newbridge (password *Albert*) was the head of NCCI's order desk. He required almost complete access to the Purchase table. He was not allowed to DELETE this table. Noga accorded him such access with the SQL command shown in Figure 9-2a. Because Albert was a junior manager, he did not receive full discretionary power to grant privileges to others. But the Computer Systems Officer coded the command shown in Figure 9-2b to empower Albert to grant others read-only access to the Purchase table.

a

```
GRANT   ALTER, INDEX, INSERT, SELECT, UPDATE
    ON  Purchase
    TO  Albert;
```

b

```
GRANT   SELECT
    ON  Purchase
    TO  Albert
  WITH  GRANT OPTION;
```

Figure 9-2 Two Ways of Granting Partial Access Privileges. Only the privileges granted in query **b** may be passed on to others.

Eva Whittaker (password *Eva*) was the head of Customer Relations. She was the second employee hired and knew the business like the back of her hand. She received full access to the Customer table, except for DELETE. The SQL statement giving her these privileges is shown in Figure 9-3a. Her assistant, Joe Leahy (password *Joe*), had the same access, but with two exceptions: Joe was not allowed to pass access privileges on to other employees, and he did not have the right to update the "Custtype" column. These privileges are expressed in the SQL statement in Figure 9-3b.

a

```
GRANT   ALTER, INDEX, INSERT, SELECT, UPDATE
    ON  Customer
    TO  Eva
  WITH  GRANT OPTION;
```

b

```
GRANT   ALTER, INDEX, INSERT, SELECT,
        UPDATE(Custnum, Custname, Custaddr, Zipcode, Phone)
    ON  Customer
    TO  Joe;
```

Figure 9-3 Two Ways of Granting UPDATE Privileges. **a,** Full privileges; **b,** partial privileges.

EXERCISES

4. Code an SQL statement that allows a user whose password is *Ralph* read-only (SELECT) and UPDATE privileges on the Customer table. Limit UPDATE access to the "Custaddr," "Zipcode," and "Phone" columns.

Although a single GRANT statement may not directly affect more than one table, we can circumvent this restriction via the use of views. Eva required access to both customer and purchase information. This access could not be granted directly. To meet these needs, the Computer Systems Officer first created a view by *join*ing these two tables with the command shown in Figure 9-4.

Creating the view:

```
CREATE   VIEW Purchcus
    AS   SELECT  Custname, Customer.Custnum, Purchnum
         FROM   Purchase, Customer
         WHERE  Customer.Custnum = Purchase.Custnum;
```

Granting access to the view:

```
GRANT   ALL
    ON   Purchcus
    TO   Eva;
```

Figure 9-4 Creating and Granting Access to a View

E X E R C I S E S

5. Grant MaryJo read-only access to a view that includes the purchase number, sum of kilos, sum of kilos times the unit price, sum of kilos times the unit cost, and sum of the kilos times the unit price minus the unit cost (as presented in Figure 7-3). Do not allow her to grant others access to this view.

6. Grant MaryJo read-only access to a view that includes the purchase number, sum of kilos, and sum of kilos times the unit price. Allow her to grant others access to this view.

The REVOKE Statement

The REVOKE statement removes access privileges. It is not part of the ANSI standard. However, virtually all SQL implementations include some form of the REVOKE statement. Its syntax resembles the syntax of the GRANT statement, except that no clause corresponds to the WITH GRANT OPTION.

When Albert resigned from NCCI, his database privileges were removed with the simple statement shown in Figure 9-5. Depending on the specific SQL implementation, this command may also remove all privileges Albert granted others.

```
REVOKE   ALL
    ON   Purchase
  FROM   Albert;
```

Figure 9-5 Revoking Access

E X E R C I S E S

7. Revoke all privileges assigned to MaryJo.

Recall from Figure 9-3a that Eva Whittaker has full access privileges to the Customer table, except for the DELETE option. This access was accorded by a single GRANT statement stating the five explicit privileges. This access could also have been achieved by according ALL six privileges and then removing the DELETE privilege. These two SQL queries are shown in Figure 9-6. In this case, two short SQL queries replace one longer SQL query. There is a danger in using the two SQL queries: If the computer system fails after executing the GRANT statement but before executing the REVOKE statement, Eva Whittaker will have been accorded an extra privilege, which is against company policy. These two SQL queries should be handled as a unit, or **transaction,** and be accepted or rejected together.

```
GRANT   ALL
    ON   Customer
    TO   Eva
  WITH   GRANT OPTION;

REVOKE   DELETE
    ON   Customer
  FROM   Eva;
```

Figure 9-6 Granting Partial Access Privileges

Transaction Processing

Until now we have considered SQL commands separately, except for the rarely used UNION statement. Often, however, several SQL statements are intimately related and should be processed together. From the user's viewpoint, a transaction is a useful unit of work, independent of how many SQL statements are required. For example, the pair of GRANT and REVOKE statements discussed earlier form one transaction. NCCI's new computerized billing system provides another example. When an order is processed, the fol-

---

BOX 9-2

The Database Administrator (DBA) and System Privileges

We have assumed that any authorized user may create his or her own tables and GRANT privileges on these tables to any other authorized users. This policy of decentralization often leads to inefficiency and duplication, especially in systems with many users. An alternate approach is to centralize database control in one individual, often called the *database administrator,* or *DBA.* The GRANT statement in some SQL implementations provides additional privileges, including CONNECT, RESOURCE, and DBA. The CONNECT privilege allows users to log on the system, access base tables, and perhaps create their own views. The RESOURCE privilege allows users to create base tables. The DBA privilege allows total database manipulation, including the ability to access and modify the system catalog (discussed elsewhere in the chapter).

---

lowing tables are affected: Purchase table—a new row is created; Billing table—the customer's amount due is modified.

The SQL statements affecting the Purchase table and the Billing table form a transaction. In case of system malfunction, they all should be rejected. For example, recording a purchase without updating the Billing table is a serious error. Charging the wrong customer for a purchase is equally serious.

Until now we have assumed that all SQL statements modifying the database, such as INSERT, UPDATE, and DELETE, take effect immediately. This is not necessarily true. After the user selects transaction processing (the exact command varies among SQL implementations), the database is processed with the COMMIT and the ROLLBACK statements.

The COMMIT Statement and the ROLLBACK Statement

SQL statements do not cause permanent changes to the database unless "frozen" by the COMMIT statement. Until the user issues a COMMIT statement, the changes may be undone with a ROLLBACK statement. A short example of transaction processing shows how these statements operate.

Statement	*Effect*
BEGIN TRANSACTION	Initiates SQL transaction processing.
INSERT INTO Purchase VALUES(. . .);	Creates first new Purchase table row.
UPDATE Billing SET . . . WHERE . . .;	Processes first Billing table row

At this point, the user visually inspects these last two statements to make sure they are correct before proceeding to COMMIT.

COMMIT	Updates the database so it reflects the day's first purchase.

Continued on next page.

```
INSERT INTO Purchase VALUES(1555, 5, 26, . . .);
```
Creates second new Purchase table row.
```
UPDATE Billing SET . . . WHERE . . . Custnum = 25;
```
Processes second new Billing table row.

Again the user visually inspects the last two statements to make sure they are correct before proceeding to COMMIT. In this case the user notices a discrepancy between the customer number in the INSERT statement (26) and the customer number in the UPDATE statement (25). To undo the two discrepant statements, the user enters a ROLLBACK command:

```
ROLLBACK
```
Deletes the preceding INSERT and UPDATE statements so the database still reflects the day's first purchase.

The user then enters the corrected statements:

```
INSERT INTO Purchase VALUES(1555, 5, 25, . . .);
```
Creates second new Purchase table row.
```
UPDATE Billing SET . . . WHERE . . . Custnum = 25;
```
Processes second new Billing table row.

The user visually inspects the corrected transaction to make sure it is correct before issuing the COMMIT statement.

```
COMMIT
```
Updates the database so it reflects the day's second purchase.
```
INSERT INTO Purchase VALUES(. . .);
```
Creates third new Purchase table row.

At this point a power outage occurs. This event automatically triggers a ROLLBACK, and the database still reflects the day's second purchase. Data for the third purchase has been lost. When power is restored, the user must reenter the INSERT command for the third purchase, followed by the associated UPDATE command.

When the system is in transaction-processing mode, it is strongly recommended that you regularly issue COMMIT statements to reduce the number of statements lost should a power outage occur. As advised in Chapter 1, perform regularly scheduled backups to reduce the impact of inevitable system malfunctions, which may cause data loss even when COMMIT statements are issued frequently.

E X E R C I S E S

8. Code and then erase a transaction, including two UPDATE statements, that modifies the Custcopy table. Use the COMMIT and ROLLBACK statements.

Locking Tables

In contrast, the computer network enabled many people to use the system simultaneously, although at a price: user interference. No problem occurred if Eva accessed the Customer table while Albert or Eloise (his replacement) was accessing the Purchase table. But simultaneous access to a given table, say the Product table, could cause problems. (The Product table has been modified to include the quantity of product in stock.) For example, let's suppose that with only three kilos of Macadamia nuts left in stock, MaryJo entered a purchase requiring two kilos while at the same time Ralph entered an UPDATE statement reflecting the arrival of five kilos from the supplier. Here is a possible error scenario:

1. MaryJo's transaction reads the "Quantity" column for the Macadamia nuts row and finds three kilos.

2. Ralph's transaction reads the "Quantity" column for the Macadamia nuts row and finds three kilos.

3. MaryJo's transaction subtracts the quantity of Macadamia nuts ordered, two kilos, from the present value of three kilos, generating a new quantity of one kilo. It writes this value in the Product table.

4. Ralph's transaction adds the quantity of Macadamia nuts received, five kilos, to the presumed value of three kilos, generating a new quantity of eight kilos. It writes this value in the Product table. Because Ralph's transaction didn't wait for MaryJo's transaction to finish, part of her transaction is lost. The system now shows eight kilos of Macadamia nuts, whereas it should show six kilos.

A similar problem could occur when Ralph queries the database via the SELECT statement to generate statistics from the Product table: If his first few queries are entered before MaryJo's transaction, they would show inventory of three kilos of Macadamia nuts. If his final queries occurred *after* MaryJo's transaction, they would show inventory of one kilo of Macadamia nuts, clearly a contradiction.

The system must prevent other users from accessing the table while a transaction modifying the database is in process, a transaction which might include several SQL statements.

Statements for Locking Tables

Different SQL implementations handle the simultaneous-update problem differently. Many SQL implementations include a LOCK TABLE command that allows a given user exclusive access to one or more tables for a limited time. Here is a representative syntax:

```
LOCK TABLE {table-name | view-name} IN {SHARE | EXCLUSIVE} MODE
```

The SHARE MODE allows other users read-only (SELECT) access to the table or view. Several users may place a SHARE lock on a given table or view simultaneously. The EXCLUSIVE MODE denies other users the right to modify a table or view, or to place any lock on it. Either version of this command restricts table access until the user issues either a COMMIT or a ROLLBACK command. Before the system LOCKs the table, it must check to see that no other user has already placed an exclusive LOCK on the table.

The LOCK TABLE command involves a few potential problems: A negligent user might effectively monopolize access to one or more tables for a long time. The system should look for such problems and take any necessary action to enable all authorized users access within a reasonable time period.

A more dangerous problem is *deadlock*. This occurs when user A has an exclusive LOCK on table X and is waiting for access to table Y and simultaneously user B has an exclusive LOCK on table Y and is waiting for access to table X. If left to their own devices, the two users would wait forever. The system can break the deadlock by sacrificing one of the two users.

Some SQL implementations provide a sophisticated table-LOCKing command, allowing a user to LOCK only required rows rather than LOCKing the entire table. This may be done with the following syntax:

```
SELECT   {column-name},...
  FROM   {table-name}...
 WHERE   search-condition
   FOR   UPDATE OF {column-name},...
```

which allows other users full access to all rows except those selected by the WHERE clause. If you are entering data for customers whose zip code is

```
    IN  (91212, 91213, 91214)
```

you should use that syntax to reduce the waiting time on the Customer table for users accessing customers with other zip codes.

Note, the SELECT...FOR UPDATE OF statement does not UPDATE the table; it merely SELECTs rows to be updated, reserving access to those rows. The ensuing UPDATE statement actually modifies the data within the table, after LOCKing the entire table's contents. Once the UPDATE statement is COMMITted (or ROLLed BACK) the entire table is unLOCKed and may be accessed by any authorized user.

The exact nature of LOCKs available depends on the specific SQL implementation. The database administrator should have complete information on the LOCKs in force on the database at any given time. Such information is usually unavailable to users.

EXERCISES

9. Start transaction processing. Code a LOCK transaction for each of the tables in the database. Code a ROLLBACK statement.

10. Redo Exercise 9, but LOCKing the Customer table by using the SELECT...FOR UPDATE OF statement.

Data Integrity

Noga's business conducts operations and makes decisions based on data within the database. Incorrect data leads to erroneous operations, such as underbilling or overbilling customers, and consequently financial and customer relations problems. Incorrect data also leads to poor decisions, further endangering the company. Ensuring data integrity, the accuracy and consistency of data, is a major concern. Data integrity depends on both users and the computer system.

Users have a major role in ensuring data integrity. They must pay careful attention when entering data. As the well-known saying goes, "Garbage in, garbage out." Data entry errors tend to decline when users themselves are responsible. But even the most careful user will make errors entering data. The computer system should help detect input errors and notify users of these errors before any damage occurs.

SQL itself may also help ensure data integrity. Chapter 8 described the WITH CHECK OPTION used with views. This SQL feature reduces data entry errors, for example, rejecting a value outside predefined limits. Data entry errors may be further reduced by validating entries against lookup tables, such as described in Chapter 7. With such a system, phone numbers and zip codes could be validated against each other. (NCCI's Computer Systems Officer is presently engaged in analyzing which additional lookup tables to create, and the additional processing time and resources that such tables will entail.)

Primary key integrity means that primary keys must be unique and not null. While ANSI SQL does not include primary key integrity, many versions of SQL do. The CREATE TABLE commands in Chapter 1 illustrate the UNIQUE and NOT NULL clause for primary keys. Chapter 8 presented the CREATE UNIQUE INDEX statement, which has a similar effect. Unfortunately, not all versions of SQL enforce primary key integrity. In its absence, users adding data to a table must ensure that no rows with duplicate primary keys exist. The concept of *referential integrity* is often associated with primary key integrity.

Referential Integrity

Starting in Chapter 5 we applied the *join* operation to link two or more tables. For example, we consolidated data from the Customer and Purchase tables with the following query:

```
SELECT  Custname, Customer.Custnum, Purchnum
  FROM  Customer, Purchase
 WHERE  Customer.Custnum = Purchase.Custnum;
```

In this query the "Customer.Custnum" column is the primary key of the Customer table. It is matched to a *foreign key,* the "Custnum" column of the Purchase table. A **foreign key** is a column in one table whose values match those of a primary key in another table. A foreign key is usually not the primary key of its own table. **Referential integrity** means that each foreign key takes on either NULL values or values equal to its associated primary key. Consider the following Purchase table and Customer table:

Purchnum	Prodnum	Custnum	Purchdat	Readydat	Kilos
1234	1	22	10/28/1992	10/28/1992	3.5
1235	2	24	10/28/1992	10/30/1992	15.0
1236	1	41	10/28/1992	10/28/1992	2.0
1236	3	41	10/28/1992	10/28/1992	3.7
1237	3	4	10/28/1992	11/02/1992	3.7
1238	1	37	10/29/1992	10/29/1992	3.7
1238	2	37	10/29/1992	10/29/1992	1.2
1238	3	37	10/29/1992	10/29/1992	4.4
1239	2	24	10/29/1992	10/30/1992	3.0
1240	2	42	10/29/1992	10/31/1992	14.0
1240	5	42	10/29/1992	11/02/1992	4.8
1241	1	13	10/29/1992	10/29/1992	1.0
1241	5	13	10/29/1992	10/30/1992	7.6
1242	5	12	10/29/1992	10/29/1992	3.5

Custnum	Custname	Custtype	Custaddr	Zipcode	Phone
1	Jones, Joe	P	1234 Main St.	91212	434-1231
4	Armstrong, Inc.	R	231 Globe Blvd.	91212	434-7664
12	Swedish Burgers	R	1889 20th N.E.	91213	434-9090
13	Pickled Pickles	R	194 CityView	91289	324-8909
22	The Candy Kid	W	2121 Main St.	91212	563-4545
24	Waterman, Al	P	23 Yankee Blvd.	91234	-0-
37	Bobby Bon Bons	R	12 Nichi Cres.	91212	434-9045
39	Crowsh, Elias	P	7 77th Ave.	91211	434-0007
41	Montag, Susie	P	981 Montview	91213	456-2091
42	Columberg Sweets	W	239 East Falls	91209	874-9092

We check for referential integrity by examining the values of the foreign key "Custnum" in the Purchase table. This foreign key's first value is 22. The

Customer table has a primary key with this value (The Candy Kid). The second value of the foreign key is 24; this value is also found in the Customer table (Waterman, Al). We can see that each value of the foreign key in the Purchase table is equal to a value of the primary key in the Customer table. Thus, referential integrity is maintained with respect to the customer-number column.

Consider the consequences if referential integrity is not maintained. If the Purchase table contained the row

Purchnum	Prodnum	Custnum	Purchdat	Readydat	Kilos
1243	5	7	10/29/1992	10/29/1992	3.5

then referential integrity would not be maintained, because there is no customer number 7 in the Customer table. In this case, order 1243 could not be picked up, delivered, or paid for. Perhaps the customer number was incorrectly entered as 7 instead of 4. Or perhaps customer number 7 has ceased doing business with NCCI, and its purchases have not been completely dealt with.

Most SQL versions do not automatically verify referential integrity; but leave this task to those responsible for the database. Many installations write custom programs to help ensure referential integrity, for example, deleting all rows for customer number 7 from the other tables before removing the row for customer number 7 from the Customer table.

E X E R C I S E S

11. Describe referential integrity as it applies to the candy database. Be precise; discuss specific columns.

System Catalog

The collection of system tables is known as the **system catalog.** As may be expected, the exact nature of the system tables varies from one SQL implementation to another. In many cases, full access to system tables is restricted to the database administrator and perhaps a few associates. At NCCI, only Noga has unrestricted access to the central system catalog. The Computer Systems Officer has access to most catalog information. Other users do not have access to the central system catalog. System security is best maintained when system catalog access is available on a need-to-know basis.

The contents of system tables vary from one SQL implementation to another. Box 9-3 describes system tables for dBASE IV SQL.

E X E R C I S E S

12. Display the system catalog for your database if available. Note any "authorizations table" changes when you issue GRANT and REVOKE statements.

BOX 9-3

dBASE IV SQL System Tables

SQL as implemented on the popular microcomputer database management program dBASE IV includes ten system tables:

SYSTABLS "System tables" contains ten fields, including table name, table creator, column count, date created, and date updated.

SYSCOLS "System columns" contains 12 fields, including column name, table name, table creator, and column type.

SYSIDXS "System indexes" contains 12 fields, including index name, index creator, table name, and table creator.

SYSKEYS "System keys" contains six fields, including index name, index creator, and column name.

SYSVIEWS "System views" contains seven fields, including view name, view creator, and the view creation command.

SYSVDEPS "Additional system view information" contains four fields: view name, table number, table name, and creator.

SYSSYNS "System synonyms" contains four fields: synonym name, table number, table name, and table creator.

SYSAUTH "System authorization" contains 11 fields, including grantor, table name, user-id, and grant option (Y or N).

SYSCOLAU "System column authorization" contains six fields, including grantor, table name, grantee, column name, and grant option (Y or N).

SYSTIMES "System update information" contains three fields: name, update date, and update time.

All of these tables are read-only, and are available to users who have created their own database, not necessarily to other users.

Syntax and Applications Summary

The GRANT statement controls access to the database by providing more individuals with table or view privileges. It is defined as follows:

```
GRANT  {ALL | ALL PRIVILEGES | {ALTER | DELETE | INDEX |
   INSERT  | SELECT | UPDATE[({column-name},...)]},...}
  ON {table-name},...
  TO {user-id | PUBLIC},...
[WITH GRANT OPTION]
```

Users may have to reference the table with a prefix indicating the table owner's name. Some versions of the GRANT statement allow the database administrator to accord users the privilege to create tables, effectively centralizing control. The REVOKE statement removes privileges.

A transaction is a useful unit of work, independent of how many SQL statements are required. Until the user issues a COMMIT statement, the statements composing a transaction may be undone with a ROLLBACK statement.

When several users simultaneously access a given table, problems often arise. The command

```
LOCK   TABLE {table-name | view-name} IN {SHARE | EXCLUSIVE} MODE
```

allows users to have shared read-only or exclusive access to a given table or view. Advanced versions of this command LOCK only affected rows rather than the entire table.

Versions of SQL provide several features that increase database integrity, the likelihood that the data is free from error. The UNIQUE NOT NULL command and the CREATE UNIQUE INDEX command offer primary key integrity, enforcing the uniqueness of primary keys. A foreign key is a column in one table whose values match those of a primary key in another table. Referential integrity means that each foreign key takes on either NULL values or values equal to its associated primary key.

The collection of system tables, the system catalog, can serve as a source of information about the database to help the database administrator administer the database.

Productivity Tip:

MAKE USERS IDENTIFY THEMSELVES.

This tip may appear contradictory at first glance. When you are anxious to get on the computer system, pausing to enter a password seems counterproductive. And yet the proper use of passwords and authorization identifications increases productivity. A computer system that does not require passwords is similar to a bank with open safe deposit boxes: The valuables are there for the taking. If all employees have open access to all files and tables, it is hard to have confidence in the data.

Password selection is important. A password is worthwhile only if it remains secret. Passwords should be hard to guess and should be changed often. For instance, *Joseph Smolic* should not use passwords such as *Joseph, Joe, Hpesoj,* or *Ciloms.* Other risky passwords include the names of his wife, children, or pets, and his street address. And, of course, a password scribbled on the memo pad next to the keyboard is useless.

We have seen in this chapter that the notion of password is extended by SQL's GRANT and REVOKE statements. Their use increases system productivity by restricting resources to those who need to know. When passwords and the GRANT and REVOKE statements are properly applied, little time is wasted cleaning up the damage caused by unauthorized users.

Chapter Summary

This chapter examined administering multiuser databases. We addressed issues of database access, protecting the database against system failure, interuser interference, ensuring only correct and consistent data, and professional management. We presented the SQL syntax related to the above issues.

We know from previous chapters that SQL often lacks power and flexibility when handling either input or output. Chapter 10 will examine how to combine SQL with either of two widely used microcomputer database software packages, dBASE IV and R:BASE, to take advantage of the best that each component has to offer. It will also include an introduction to embedded SQL, that is, SQL within another programming language, an alternative way to deal with SQL's shortcomings.

Review Questions

1. Define in your own words the following SQL reserved words, and describe their use:
   a. GRANT
   b. PUBLIC
   c. WITH GRANT OPTION
   d. REVOKE
   e. COMMIT
   f. ROLLBACK
   g. LOCK TABLE
   h. SHARE MODE
   i. EXCLUSIVE MODE

2. Define in your own words the following terms associated with SQL, and describe their use:
   a. formal SQL syntax
   b. authorization identifier
   c. transaction
   d. transaction processing
   e. deadlock
   f. data integrity
   g. primary key integrity

   h. foreign key
   i. referential integrity
   j. system catalog

3. Describe five issues that must be addressed when administering multiuser SQL databases.

4. What are the advantages of the formal SQL syntax? List any disadvantages you can think of.

Case Study Exercises

These questions may be answered using either the full database (tables Cds, Manufs, and Works) or the smaller database (tables Smlcds, Manufs, and Smlworks).

 1. Code an SQL statement or statements allowing a user with the password *Rufus* read-only access to all tables for your compact disk database. *Rufus* may accord this access to others.

 2. Code an SQL statement or statements allowing a user with the password *Edna* complete read-only access and UPDATE access to all nonfinancial columns in all tables for your compact disk database.

 3. Code an SQL statement or statements allowing a user with the password *SuperUser* complete access to your entire compact disk database. *SuperUser* may accord read-only access to anyone else, at her discretion.

 4. Code an SQL statement or statements removing UPDATE privileges from *Edna*, except for the Manufs table.

 5. Code two UPDATE transactions for the Manufs table. Use the COMMIT and ROLLBACK statements.

 6. Redo Case Study Exercise 5, but LOCKing the Manufs table.

 7. Code an INSERT transaction for each table in your compact disk database. Use the COMMIT and ROLLBACK statements.

 8. Redo Case Study Exercise 7, but LOCKing all tables.

 9. Describe referential integrity as it applies to your compact disk database. Be precise; discuss specific columns.

10. Display your compact disk database's system catalog if available. Note changes in the "authorizations table" when you issue GRANT and REVOKE statements.

Interfacing SQL with Other Systems

This final chapter examines how to tie together SQL with three other systems. First we link SQL with dBASE IV, the widely used microcomputer database software package. We see how SQL and dBASE IV combined are more powerful and easier to use than SQL alone. Then we repeat the analysis using R:BASE, another popular microcomputer database software package. Again, SQL and R:BASE combined are more powerful and easier to use than SQL alone. We conclude the chapter with another method of improving SQL's power and flexibility: embedding it in a programming language such as COBOL, C, FORTRAN, or Pascal. Because COBOL is widely used for commercial and administrative applications, we chose it as the vehicle for embedded SQL. However, this discussion requires no previous COBOL knowledge; the principles illustrated apply to embedding SQL in other common programming languages.

OBJECTIVES

You have met this chapter's objectives when you can:

- Discuss the need for interfacing SQL with other software packages and programming languages.
- Interface SQL with dBASE IV (suggested for those with access to dBASE IV).
- Interface SQL with R:BASE (suggested for those with access to R:BASE).
- Write SQL code embedded in elementary COBOL programs (suggested for those with any computer programming experience).

Introduction

NCCI's Computer Policy Committee was facing a difficult decision. Both experienced and inexperienced users continually complained about SQL's drawbacks. Nobody liked its totally nonvisual data-entry facilities. Although the Computer Systems Officer spent countless hours coding views applying the WITH CHECK OPTION, the error rate remained high.

SQL reports were as unpopular as its data-entry facilities. The generated output was unattractive and inflexible. Many seemingly straightforward information requests were cumbersome or even impossible to fulfill. As discussed in Chapter 8, determining the total amount of candy ordered in a given purchase number is a multistep process involving several views, beyond the capacity of most NCCI employees.

After conducting a preliminary inquiry, the committee assigned newly hired Leona Miller, a recent Management Information Systems graduate, to analyze the problem and recommend improvements. The committee's guideline was clear: Don't abandon SQL; do whatever you must to make it work better. Miller examined NCCI's internal forms and reports, interviewed selected personnel at all levels, and submitted a report outlining the firm's requirements. She then screened available software packages and programming languages to determine their SQL interface capabilities, narrowing the list down to three contenders: dBASE IV, R:BASE, and COBOL. (The first two, dBASE IV and R:BASE are popular microcomputer database management software packages. COBOL, a widely used computer programming language, is available for computers of all sizes.) Portions of her report on the three SQL interfaces follow. *Note:* Each of the following three sections, dBASE IV, R:BASE, and COBOL, is independent; you may read any or all sections.

SQL–dBASE IV Interface

The most popular database management program for microcomputers, dBASE, first incorporated SQL commands and features with the release of dBASE IV, so SQL is unavailable on previous versions. The following material is not intended to teach dBASE. Rather, it simply shows you how to interface dBASE with SQL, to take advantage of both products.

Unlike previous dBASE versions, dBASE IV runs in two modes: SQL mode and non-SQL mode. If you are unsure which mode is active, look closely at your screen: The letters *SQL* to the left of the (.) indicate SQL mode. To change modes, enter either of the following commands from dBASE's famous dot prompt:

```
SET SQL ON
```

or

```
SET SQL OFF
```

Use SQL mode to run SQL examples and exercises.

Appendix C presents some of the quirks of the dBASE IV version of SQL.

The remainder of this section applies the non-SQL mode. Unless otherwise noted, commands in this section are valid for all versions of dBASE.

SQL and dBASE employ different terminology:

dBASE Term	SQL Term
File	Table
Field	Column
Record	Row

Many people use a subdirectory or a diskette for each dBASE database. In dBASE, SQL and non-SQL tables (files) have a different internal format, which is transparent to users.

Ms. Miller started dBASE, and proceeded to the dot prompt. (The exact start-up procedure may differ from one installation to another.) She opened the database called *Candy,* and entered the following command to select the Purchase table:

```
USE PURCHASE
```

She then displayed the entire contents of this table with the command

```
LIST
```

She obtained various purchase lists by entering commands such as the following:

```
LIST ALL FOR Purchnum > 1238
```

Note: The FOR clause belongs to the dBASE language. It does *not* have the exact same syntax as the familiar SQL WHERE clause. See Box 10-1 for a discussion of data-entry problems with SQL.

BOX 10-1

SQL Data-Entry Problems

While data entry is never very easy or pleasant, it is particularly difficult and time-consuming in SQL. Because SQL provides no help in the data-entry process, users who enter data directly into SQL must know the language. By choice, our tables contain few rows and few columns, to save time and effort. Most installations apply other software to augment SQL's data-entry capabilities.

All dBASE versions are considerably more visual than SQL. Consequently, they result in less tiring data entry, with fewer errors. As with previous versions, dBASE IV provides its well-known data-entry box.

For example, we might try to add a row to the Purchase table with the APPEND command. The dBASE APPEND command is similar to the SQL INSERT INTO VALUES command, but with an important difference: The APPEND command displays a characteristic data-entry box, as shown in Figure 10-1a. The line at the top of the screen is a menu of options, such as *Go To* to access a particular record. The line at the bottom of the screen indicates which record in which file is ready for processing. The data-entry box in the middle of the screen contains one row for each field in the record. The field name, in capital letters, appears at the left. The highlighted area is available for data entry. Position the cursor using the arrow keys, and then enter the data. The width of the highlighted area corresponds to the field size, and indicates the zone in which data entry is permitted. It is impossible to enter data outside highlighted areas. For example, the system rejects any purchase number greater than four digits. The system also rejects invalid dates and letters in numeric fields such as *Kilos*.

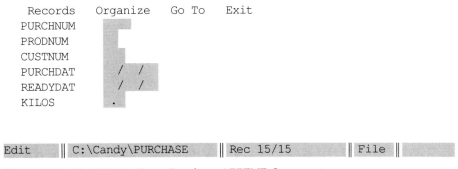

Figure 10-1 dBASE Data-Entry Box from APPEND Statement

Because errors are rejected on the spot, they can be corrected immediately. This is important, because the sooner a user realizes a data-entry error, the more easily the error can be corrected.

The dBASE EDIT command is similar to SQL's UPDATE command, but with an important difference: The dBASE EDIT command processes a single row that must be specified, perhaps by row number, whereas the SQL UPDATE command processes one or more rows, which may be specified by the familiar WHERE clause. For many applications the SQL method is preferable, because it enables users to specify what they want rather than making them count records. Furthermore, a single SQL UPDATE command may affect several related records, such as all wholesale customers. On the other hand, the dBASE EDIT may be preferable because it displays the data-entry box, reducing the pain and errors associated with data entry. Figure 10-2 presents such a data-entry box.

```
   Records    Organize    Go To    Exit
 PURCHNUM     1242
 PRODNUM      5
 CUSTNUM      12
 PURCHDAT     10/29/92
 READYDAT     10/29/92
 KILOS        3.5
```

```
Edit    ‖ C:\Candy\PURCHASE    ‖ Rec 14/14    ‖ File ‖
```

Figure 10-2 dBASE Data-Entry Box from EDIT Statement

Changing the data structure is a lot easier with dBASE than with SQL. Recall from Chapter 6 that copying an SQL table requires several steps: You first CREATE the new table structure (as done in Chapters 1 and 6) and then INSERT the old table data INTO the new table. Contrast this process with the dBASE COPY FILE command. Miller copied the Purchase table to a table called *Newpurch* with the following commands:

```
USE Purchase

COPY TO Newpurch
```

Those familiar with dBASE should note that the MODIFY STRUCTURE command may not be used directly with tables created in SQL.

Both SQL and dBASE make it very easy to delete a table. In SQL, you simply enter

```
DROP tablename
```

In dBASE, you simply enter

```
ERASE filename.DBF
```

and then

```
USE
```

to close the file.

E X E R C I S E S

D1. Use dBASE to copy the Customer file to a file called *Custcopd*. Use SQL to copy the Customer table to a table called *Custcops*. Compare these two processes. Use Custcopd and Custcops in the following exercises.

BOX 10-2

Formatting Reports

The output generated by standard SQL is rudimentary and inflexible. On occasion we were forced to modify actual query results to show legible output. Many SQL implementations provide additional output capabilities known as *report formatting*.

Among the available report-formatting facilities are:

Titles and subtitles

Page and report footers

Modified column headers

Dollar signs (or other currency indicators) and commas in numbers

Rounding numbers to any desired degree of accuracy

Control breaks (for example, skipping lines or to a new page for every new purchase number)

Totals and subtotals

D2. Compare output for the Custcopd file using the dBASE LIST command with that for the Custcops table generated by the SQL SELECT command.

D3. Compare adding two records to the Custcopd file using the dBASE APPEND command to using the SQL INSERT command with the Custcops table. Which is easier? Would your answer be the same if you were to add 20 records?

D4. Compare deleting two records from the Custcopd file using the appropriate dBASE commands to using the appropriate SQL commands with the Custcops table. Which is easier? Would your answer be the same if you were to delete 20 records? Would your answer be the same if you were to delete the entire file or table?

We are familiar with SQL's shortcomings in generating output. Some SQL implementations provide a special FORMAT command for output, discussed in Box 10-2. A special dBASE IV report module allows a nontechnical user to create a report based on one or more SQL tables. Report generation, though fairly straightforward, is too lengthy to be shown here.

Of course, Miller must carry out many additional tests before drawing conclusions about the suitability of the SQL–dBASE IV interface for NCCI's needs. Space limitations force us to conclude this part of Miller's findings.

SQL–R:BASE Interface

R:BASE, a popular database management program for microcomputers, first incorporated SQL commands and features with the release of version 3.0. SQL is unavailable on previous versions. Many non-SQL commands and features found in earlier versions have been carried forward to R:BASE 3.0 and later versions with little or no change. The rest of this section assumes version 3.0 or later. The following material is not intended to teach R:BASE. Rather, it simply shows you how to interface R:BASE with SQL, to take advantage of both products.

Unlike dBASE IV, which can run in two modes—the SQL mode and the non-SQL mode—R:BASE employs a single mode that includes both SQL and non-SQL commands. SQL and R:BASE both use the same terminology for tables, columns, and rows. When processing reports, R:BASE often uses the term *field* instead of *column*. Unlike dBASE, R:BASE does not store tables individually.

Miller enters the following command to open a database called *Candy:*

```
CONNECT CANDY
```

She then displays the entire contents of the Purchase table with the command

```
BROWSE    *
   FROM   Purchase
```

or the SQL equivalent

```
SELECT    *
   FROM   Purchase;
```

She obtains various purchase lists with commands such as the following:

```
BROWSE    *
   FROM   Purchase
  WHERE   Purchnum > 1238
```

Note, the WHERE clause in this display follows SQL syntax rules. R:BASE uses a somewhat more restricted WHERE clause when processing forms, reports, and labels; these objects are not part of SQL. See Box 10-1 for a discussion of data-entry problems with SQL. All R:BASE versions are somewhat more visual than SQL. Consequently, they result in less tiring data entry, with fewer errors. For example, to add one or more rows to the Purchase table, enter the following R:BASE command:

```
LOAD PURCHASE WITH PROMPTS
```

The R:BASE LOAD WITH PROMPTS command is similar to the SQL INSERT INTO VALUES command, but with two important differences: The LOAD WITH PROMPTS command displays each column name with its data type, and prompts data entry for the column. For example, a customer-name column defined as

```
Custname CHAR(18)
```

displays

```
Custname (TEXT)
```

on the screen. The system limits customers names to 18 characters, rejecting all additional characters for this field. The LOAD WITH PROMPTS command also rejects illegal values for numeric or date data types.

Because errors are rejected on the spot, they can be corrected immediately. This is important, because the sooner a user realizes such data-entry errors are made, the more easily they can be corrected.

The R:BASE EDIT command (the SQL WHERE clause is optional) is similar to SQL's UPDATE command, but with an important difference: The R:BASE EDIT command displays all candidate rows on the screen, and each change is made individually. A single SQL UPDATE command may affect several related records, such as all wholesale customers. On the other hand, the R:BASE EDIT may be preferable, because it provides limited error checking, reducing the pain and errors associated with data entry.

Changing the data structure is a lot easier with R:BASE than with SQL. Recall from Chapter 6 that copying an SQL table requires several steps. You first CREATE the new table structure (as done in Chapters 1 and 6) and then INSERT the old table data INTO the new table. Contrast this with the R:BASE PROJECT command. Miller copied the Purchase table to a table called Newpurch with the following command:

```
PROJECT  Newpurch FROM Purchase USING *
```

Both SQL and R:BASE make it very easy to delete a table. In SQL, you simply enter

```
DROP  tablename
```

In R:BASE, you simply enter

```
DROP  tablename
```

or

```
REMOVE   tablename
```

E X E R C I S E S

R1. Use R:BASE to copy the Customer table to a table called *Custcopr.* Use SQL to copy the Customer table to a table called *Custcops.* Compare these two processes. Use Custcopr and Custcops in the following exercises.

R2. Compare adding two records to the Custcopr table using the R:BASE LOAD WITH PROMPTS command to using the SQL INSERT command with the Custcops table. Which is easier? Would your answer be the same if you were to add 20 records?

R3. Compare deleting two records from the Custcopr table using the appropriate R:BASE commands to using the appropriate SQL commands with the Custcops table. Which is easier? Would your answer be the same if you were to delete 20 records? Would your answer be the same if you were to delete the entire table?

What about output? We are familiar with SQL's shortcomings in generating output, sometimes met by report-formatting commands, discussed in Box 10-2. A special R:BASE report module allows a nontechnical user to create a report based on one or more SQL tables. Report generation, though fairly straightforward, is too lengthy to be shown here. Of course, Miller must carry out many additional tests before drawing conclusions about the suitability of the SQL–R:BASE interface for NCCI's needs. Space limitations force us to conclude this part of Miller's findings.

Embedded SQL

SQL may be applied in two modes, interactive SQL and embedded SQL. *Interactive SQL* accesses a database directly, generating output destined for people rather than computer files. Until now we have used only interactive SQL. **Embedded SQL** is SQL within a programming language called a *host language.* The American National Standards Institute document ANSI X3.168–1989 defines embedded SQL for six host languages; Ada, C, COBOL, FORTRAN, Pascal, and PL/1. While the general principles governing embedded SQL are the same for all host languages, specific details may vary from one host language to another. No matter which host language is used, embedded SQL offers advantages in three important areas: data entry, processing, and output. We examine each of these in turn.

Data Entry

See Box 10-1 for a discussion of data-entry problems with interactive SQL. Data entry via embedded SQL requires no familiarity with SQL or with the host language. Programs written to facilitate data entry generate screens that tell users what to do, offering additional help on demand. They may include data-validation routines to detect errors as they occur, enabling users to correct the data on the spot. As with dBASE or R:BASE, they verify a given entry's length, and reject letters entered into numeric columns. They may invoke lookup tables (see Chapter 7), applying rules such as limiting private customers to $500 credit. In summary, embedding SQL in a host language smooths the data-entry process.

Processing

Interactive SQL executes commands one at a time, and has no facilities for repeating commands. An employee using interactive SQL must enter dozens of INSERT commands to modify the database to account for the day's candy orders. All host languages include structures that direct programs to repeat statements as required. For example, if inflation forced Noga to increase her selling prices, the exact amount might differ from product to product and might not be expressible with a simple formula. Interactive SQL would require one UPDATE statement per product. An embedded SQL program could repeatedly read rows in the price-change table and apply the changes automatically, stopping at the end of the table. This is simpler and less error-prone than entering dozens of statements, one by one, to update the price table. Interactive SQL processing is particularly cumbersome for transactions involving several tables. Noga didn't computerize her operations so that her employees would process the tables in a semimanual fashion.

Another useful programming structure missing from interactive SQL is the IF...THEN...ELSE. This structure commands the program to carry out different activities to meet different situations. We know that some candy orders are picked up and others are delivered. With interactive SQL, an individual entering a candy order must decide whether or not to access the Delivery table. With embedded SQL, the program itself makes the decision.

As any programming student knows, it is not always easy to find and correct a program's errors. Leona Miller is a competent computer programmer. It won't take her very long to write a program that makes fewer errors than an equally competent counterperson with a heavy workload.

The Computer Systems Officer must analyze programming projects to see whether they are cost-effective. Some such projects are worth doing; others are not. But embedded SQL makes them possible. Miller's next assignment was developing a program to calculate the profit on each candy purchase. The additional information generated might pay for purchasing the host language and the cost of program development. Such calculations were totally unfeasible with interactive SQL.

Output

Neither Miller nor the Computer Policy Committee believe in generating fancy output without a reason. NCCI's management style is hands-on. NCCI executives are not impressed by resumes with fancy designs or by internal memos using six different typefaces. They all agree that unadorned SQL output is fine for many internal purposes, as long as it is legible. But the output situation had to change.

Interactive SQL's basic output facilities are extremely rudimentary. Its reports are unattractive. In many cases, column headers are so wide they render the output difficult to read. In the age of desktop publishing and high-resolution computer graphics, such output could no longer be tolerated for management reports, even if it was acceptable for many working documents.

Host languages provide the necessary support to generate more attractive reports. Their output formats are virtually unlimited. They go beyond the SQL report-formatting facilities discussed in Box 10-2. Some offer report-writer modules, similar to the dBASE IV and R:BASE report facilities. Miller has the COBOL experience needed to create such reports.

Embedding SQL in COBOL

In this section we examine two short COBOL programs that employ embedded SQL. We introduce the syntax of embedded SQL as required. The first program generates output coming from a single row in the Purchase table. The second program generates output from all rows in the Purchase table. No prior COBOL knowledge is required to follow this discussion.

COBOL programs consist of four divisions:

IDENTIFICATION DIVISION, which identifies the program.

ENVIRONMENT DIVISION, which describes the computer hardware and software used.

DATA DIVISION, which describes data used by the program.

PROCEDURE DIVISION, which describes computer processing.

Embedded SQL statements appear only in the DATA DIVISION and in the PROCEDURE DIVISION.

The DATA DIVISION itself is composed of two sections:

FILE SECTION, which describes the files processed by the program.

WORKING-STORAGE SECTION, which describes variables used by the program.

Within the DATA DIVISION, embedded SQL statements appear only in the WORKING-STORAGE SECTION.

The first COBOL program outputs a single row from the Purchase table, the row whose purchase number is 1237. In addition to the regular COBOL entries, the first program's WORKING-STORAGE SECTION includes three additional types of information, namely, the host variables associated with SQL columns, the SQL table declaration, and the SQL communications area.

Declaring the Host Variables. Both interactive and embedded SQL use column names such as "Purchnum" to identify the "containers" for the data that it processes. Host languages may process SQL data only after it is transferred to host variables. The four SQL columns to be output are "Purchnum," "Prodnum," "Custnum," and "Kilos." For ease in identification, the four corresponding host variables are named "HPurch," "HProd," "HCust," and "HKilos." These variables are defined in the WORKING-STORAGE SECTION, as shown in Figure 10-3. The two EXEC statements mark the beginning and the end of host variable definitions. The four other statements are standard COBOL statements that define the four host variables, and indicate their sizes and interrelationships.

```
EXEC SQL BEGIN DECLARE SECTION END-EXEC.
01   HPURCH   PIC  S9999 COMP.
01   HPROD    PIC  S9 COMP.
01   HCUST    PIC  S99 COMP.
01   HKILOS   PIC  S999V9 PACKED-DECIMAL.
     EXEC SQL END DECLARE SECTION END-EXEC.
```

Figure 10-3 Declaring the Host Variables in COBOL

Declaring the SQL Table. The Purchase table was created with an interactive SQL command such as shown in Figure 10-4a. (Not all versions of interactive SQL provide the INTEGER, NOT NULL, and UNIQUE clauses.) This table is declared in some versions of COBOL with the statement shown in Figure 10-4b. This declaration is not required in the programs shown in Figures 10-6 and 10-11.

Establishing the SQL Communications Area. The WORKING-STORAGE SECTION also contains the following statement:

```
EXEC SQL INCLUDE SQLCA END-EXEC.
```

```
                                    b

a                                   EXEC SQL

CREATE TABLE Purchase               DECLARE TABLE Purchase

   (Purchnum  INTEGER,                 (Purchnum  INTEGER,

    Prodnum   INTEGER,                  Prodnum    INTEGER,

    Custnum   INTEGER,                  Custnum    INTEGER,

    Purchdat  DATE,                     Purchdat   DATE,

    Readydat  DATE,                     Readydat   DATE,

    Kilos     DECIMAL(3,1) );           Kilos      DECIMAL(3,1) )

                                    END-EXEC.
```

Figure 10-4 An SQL Table as Coded in COBOL: **a**, interactive SQL; **b**, COBOL.

Before the program is executed, the system replaces this statement with several others, one of which defines the SQLCODE variable in the program. The SQLCODE variable indicates whether an error occurred during processing. If no error occurred, its value is 0. The SQLCODE variable is tested in the PROCEDURE DIVISION.

The PROCEDURE DIVISION describes the actions taken by a program. It contains the SELECT...INTO statement that transfers data from the SQL table into the host variables. The following discussion assumes that only a single row of data is processed. The next program presents the changes required to process more than one row of data.

The interactive SQL statement shown in Figure 10-5a generates a single row of output from the present Purchase table. The equivalent embedded SQL statement appearing in COBOL's PROCEDURE DIVISION is shown in Figure 10-5b.

```
a                               b
SELECT   Purchnum, Prodnum      EXEC SQL
         Custnum, Kilos            SELECT   PURCHNUM, PRODNUM,
   FROM  Purchase                           CUSTNUM, KILOS
  WHERE  Purchnum = 1237;          INTO   :HPURCH,  :HPROD,
                                          :HCUST,  :HKILOS
                                   FROM   PURCHASE
                                  WHERE   PURCHNUM = 1237
                                END-EXEC.
```

Figure 10-5 The SELECT Statement as Coded in COBOL: **a**, interactive SQL; **b**, COBOL.

As previously, the EXEC SQL clause tells the system to expect embedded SQL. The END-EXEC. clause indicates the end of the embedded SQL statement. The SELECT INTO statement SELECTs chosen SQL variables and then assigns them to host language variables. After this statement is executed, host variables such as HPurch are available to the COBOL program for further processing as described shortly.

The PROCEDURE DIVISION includes a test of the SQLCODE variable to determine whether processing occurred without error. The program code is shown in Figure 10-6.

```
IDENTIFICATION DIVISION.
PROGRAM-ID. EMBDSQL1.
AUTHOR. LEVI REISS.
ENVIRONMENT DIVISION.
CONFIGURATION SECTION.
SOURCE-COMPUTER. IBM.
OBJECT-COMPUTER. IBM.
DATA DIVISION.
WORKING-STORAGE SECTION.
01   K-O     PIC   999.9.
         EXEC SQL BEGIN DECLARE SECTION END-EXEC.
01   HPURCH  PIC   S9999 COMP.
01   HPROD   PIC   S9 COMP.
01   HCUST   PIC   S99 COMP.
01   HKILOS  PIC   S999V9 PACKED-DECIMAL.
         EXEC SQL END DECLARE SECTION END-EXEC.
         EXEC SQL INCLUDE SQLCA END-EXEC.


PROCEDURE DIVISION.
         EXEC SQL WHENEVER SQLWARNING CONTINUE END-EXEC.
         PERFORM A100-INITIALIZE.
         PERFORM A200-PROCESS-AND-OUTPUT.
         PERFORM A300-TERMINATE.
         STOP RUN.
A100-INITIALIZE.
         EXEC SQL SELECT  PURCHNUM, PRODNUM, CUSTNUM, KILOS
                   FROM  PURCHASE END-EXEC.
         DISPLAY "                  PURCHASE REPORT".
         DISPLAY "PURCH #  PROD #   CUST # KILOS".
```

```
A200-PROCESS-AND-OUTPUT.
    EXEC SQL SELECT PURCHNUM, PRODNUM, CUSTNUM, KILOS
               INTO :HPURCH, :HPROD, :HCUST, :HKILOS
               FROM PURCHASE WHERE PURCHNUM = 1237
    END-EXEC.
    IF SQLCODE = 0
        MOVE HKILOS TO K-O
        DISPLAY HPURCH," ", HPROD, " ", HCUST, " ", K-O
    ELSE
        DISPLAY "THE ERROR CODE IS", SQLCODE.
```

Figure 10-6 First COBOL Program. This program runs on an IBM9370 using SQL/DS. For simplicity, all cursor-related instructions (see Figures 10-7 to 10-10) required for this SQL implementation have been removed.

The first COBOL example applies the SELECT INTO statement, which processes only a single row from an SQL table. Single-row processing may involve a relatively simple SQL–COBOL interface, because COBOL itself processes only one record at a time. On the other hand, SQL queries generate a group or set of rows. When the set includes more than one row, the SQL–COBOL interface becomes more complicated. The interface is handled by a cursor structure, which for COBOL requires additional DATA DIVISION statements and the PROCEDURE DIVISION statements.

The second COBOL example applies the cursor structure to generate a purchase report, including the sum of the kilos sold. More sophisticated reports are left as exercises for students with programming experience.

The Cursor Structure

The cursor structure bridges the gap between SQL, which generates several rows at once, and programming languages such as COBOL, which process a single record at a time. Many people feel that the word *cursor* is a misnomer in this context, for there is no direct connection between SQL's cursor and a cursor blinking on the screen. The SQL cursor points to one row in the set of rows generated by the query. This pointed row becomes available to the COBOL program for processing. A repetitive control structure steps the cursor through the set of rows, enabling COBOL to process them, one at a time.

Applying the cursor structure to a COBOL program requires four steps:

1. *Declaring (defining) the cursor.* This is done in the DATA DIVISION.
2. *Opening the cursor.* This step and the remaining steps are done in the PROCEDURE DIVISION.

3. *Retrieving the records* one at a time with the aid of the cursor. This step requires a repetitive control structure, as discussed previously.

4. *Closing the cursor.*

We examine these steps one by one.

Declaring the Cursor. The statement shown in Figure 10-7 declares the cursor used with the Purchase table. The cursor name *PURCHCUR* indicates its use. Cursor names obey SQL naming conventions. The DECLARE CURSOR statement defines the cursor; it does not transfer any rows. Note, the SELECT INTO clause is not used with the cursor structure. An optional WHERE clause chooses the rows, as in interactive SQL.

```
EXEC SQL
DECLARE PURCHCUR CURSOR FOR
    SELECT PURCHNUM, PRODNUM, CUSTNUM, KILOS
    FROM PURCHASE
END-EXEC.
```

Figure 10-7 Declaring the Cursor

Opening the Cursor. Opening the cursor executes the SELECT clause defined in the associated DECLARE CURSOR statement. Rows selected are available for processing by the host program language. The OPEN statement only makes rows available for processing; it does not actually process them. The OPEN statement is shown in Figure 10-8.

```
EXEC SQL OPEN PURCHCUR END-EXEC.
```

Figure 10-8 Opening the Cursor

Fetching the Records. After the OPEN statement has executed, the available rows may be processed using the FETCH INTO statement shown in Figure 10-9. The FETCH INTO statement moves the cursor before transferring a row of SQL data into a COBOL record containing the host variables. Each time the FETCH INTO statement is executed, the next SQL row is processed. When all rows have been processed, the system sets the SQLCODE variable to 100. (Recall that the SQLCODE variable is generated by the DATA DIVISION statement INCLUDE SQLCA.) It is the programmer's responsibility to test this variable and to take appropriate action when its value equals 100.

```
EXEC SQL FETCH PURCHCUR
    INTO :HPURCH, :HPROD, :HCUST, :HKILOS END-EXEC.
```

Figure 10-9 Fetching the Records

```
EXEC SQL

     CLOSE PURCHCUR

END-EXEC.
```

Figure 10-10 Closing the Cursor

Closing the Cursor. Closing the cursor deletes the pointer to the set of rows. These rows may no longer be accessed until another OPEN statement is executed. The CLOSE statement is shown in Figure 10-10.

The program code is shown in Figure 10-11.

```
IDENTIFICATION DIVISION.

PROGRAM-ID. EMBDSQL2.

AUTHOR. LEVI REISS.

ENVIRONMENT DIVISION.

CONFIGURATION SECTION.

SOURCE-COMPUTER. IBM.

OBJECT-COMPUTER. IBM.

DATA DIVISION.

WORKING-STORAGE SECTION.

01   K-O            PIC 999.9.

01   T-K            PIC 999V9.

01   T-K-O          PIC 999.9.

     EXEC SQL BEGIN DECLARE SECTION END-EXEC.

01   HPURCH         PIC S9999 COMP.

01   HPROD          PIC S9 COMP.

01   HCUST          PIC S99 COMP.

01   HKILOS         PIC S999V9 PACKED-DECIMAL.

     EXEC SQL END DECLARE SECTION END-EXEC.

     EXEC SQL INCLUDE SQLCA END-EXEC.


PROCEDURE DIVISION.

     EXEC SQL WHENEVER SQLWARNING CONTINUE END-EXEC.

     PERFORM A100-INITIALIZE.

     PERFORM A200-PROCESS-AND-OUTPUT

        UNTIL SQLCODE = NOT = 0.

     PERFORM A300-TERMINATE.

     STOP RUN.
```

```
A100-INITIALIZE.
    EXEC SQL DECLARE PURCHCUR CURSOR FOR
        SELECT PURCHNUM, PRODNUM, CUSTNUM, KILOS
            FROM PURCHASE END-EXEC.
    DISPLAY "                        PURCHASE REPORT".
    DISPLAY "PURCH # PROD # CUST # KILOS".
    MOVE 0.0 TO T-K.
    PERFORM B100-OPEN-CURSOR.
A200-PROCESS-AND-OUTPUT.
    EXEC SQL FETCH PURCHCUR
    INTO :HPURCH, :HPROD, :HCUST, :HKILOS END-EXEC.
    IF SQLCODE = 0 THEN
        MOVE HKILOS TO K-O
        DISPLAY HPURCH, "  ", HPROD, "  ", HCUST, "  ", K-O
        ADD HKILOS TO T-K.
A300-TERMINATE.
    IF SQLCODE = 100
        MOVE T-K TO T-K-O
        DISPLAY " TOTAL NUMBER OF KILOS = " T-K-O
    ELSE
        DISPLAY "THE ERROR CODE IS ", SQLCODE.
    PERFORM B300-CLOSE-CURSOR.
B100-OPEN-CURSOR.
    EXEC SQL OPEN PURCHCUR END-EXEC.
B300-CLOSE-CURSOR.
    EXEC SQL CLOSE PURCHCUR END-EXEC.
```

Figure 10-11 Second COBOL Program. This program runs on an IBM9370 using SQL/DS.

EXERCISES

P1. If you have programming experience in a host language other than COBOL, rewrite the first program in that language.

P2. If you have programming experience in a host language other than COBOL, rewrite the second program in that language.

P3. If you have sufficient programming experience in any host language, write a program creating a purchase report, printing two blank lines before each new purchase number (control break). Include the total number of kilos purchased for each purchase number and the grand total.

P4. *(For skilled programmers only)* Extend the program written in Exercise P3, but pricing the orders with the aid of other tables in the database. Present appropriate sums.

Syntax and Applications Summary

Users of dBASE can manipulate SQL tables (which dBASE calls files) using certain commands, including USE, LIST, APPEND, EDIT, COPY, and DELETE. However, some traditional dBASE commands, such as MODIFY STRUCTURE, do not work on SQL tables.

Users of R:BASE (version 3.0 or later) can manipulate SQL tables using the commands CONNECT, BROWSE, LOAD, EDIT, PROJECT, and DROP or REMOVE.

Host languages such as COBOL serve as a vehicle for embedded SQL, bringing the power and flexibility of programming languages to SQL. SQL statements known to generate a single row of output may be easily embedded in host languages. SQL statements that may generate more than one row of output are embedded in host languages with the aid of a special structure known as a cursor.

Productivity Tip:

DON'T REINVENT THE WHEEL.

In the classroom environment, programs are written to meet specific teaching goals. Very often a program receives a grade and is then thrown away, perhaps after the final exam. The business environment is quite different. Businesses cannot afford to start each project from scratch. Before starting to write a program, the employee should determine the availability of existing, potentially useful programs or program segments. Programming code is often modified to meet project needs. Computer programming courses and textbooks discuss specific techniques that render program segments more flexible. Some programming languages are known for their ability to create reusable programs.

The recycling principle is not restricted to computer programming. The Cashewv view example in Figures 8-6 and 8-7 showed how views can be designed to isolate a query's complexity, enabling virtually untrained users to obtain information painlessly. An installation may find it worthwhile to keep statistics on issued queries, in particular those with a high error rate. This information may be applied to create appropriate views, reducing user stress and improving their productivity.

Chapter Summary

This chapter examined the shortcomings of interactive SQL and how to overcome them by linking SQL to three other systems. We examined combining SQL with two popular microcomputer database software packages, dBASE IV and R:BASE. Then we discussed embedded SQL, placing SQL commands in a host language. Our examples used COBOL but several other programming languages could have been used.

This is the last chapter. But in a real sense this is the beginning. You can now apply SQL to meet business and other information needs. Keep this book. SQL's increasing popularity on computer systems of all sizes makes it likely that, sooner or later, you will be asked to generate SQL queries. And remember, if you can't, someone else can.

Review Questions

1. What are the disadvantages of interactive SQL?

2. How can the microcomputer database software package dBASE IV remedy the disadvantages of interactive SQL? How can previous versions of the microcomputer database software package dBASE remedy these disadvantages?

3. How can the microcomputer database software package R:BASE remedy the disadvantages of interactive SQL?

4. What is embedded SQL? How can embedded SQL remedy the disadvantages of interactive SQL?

5. Describe the changes necessary to embed SQL in a host program processing a single record.

6. Describe the changes necessary to embed SQL in a host program processing several records.

Case Study Exercises

These exercises may be performed using either the full database (tables Cds, Manufs, and Works) or the smaller database (tables Smlcds, Manufs, and Smlworks).

1. Use COBOL or another host language to create a report listing the compact disks in alphabetical order. *Hint:* Sort the compact disk file or table before creating the report.

2. Use COBOL or another host language to create a report listing the manufacturers in alphabetical order. *Hint:* Sort the manufacturers' file or table before creating the report.

3. Use COBOL or another host language to create a report listing the compact disks in alphabetical order for each manufacturer. Include the count of compact disks for each manufacturer, the control break identifier. *Hint:* Sort the compact disk file or table before creating the report.

Case Study Database

Introduction

The case study applies SQL in processing a classical music compact disk database. Because different classes have widely varying needs, this case study comes in two versions, the full version and the smaller version. The smaller version is similar to the full version, but processes tables containing fewer columns. Corresponding tables include the same number of rows. End-of-chapter exercises are given for both the full version and the smaller version.

One table describes individual classical compact disks, usually abbreviated *CDs*, to meet the information needs of a vendor. The full version of the database includes a Cds table. The smaller version of the database includes a Smlcds table. (Most of the data appearing in these tables was found on CDs in the writer's own collection.)

The Manufs table describes CD manufacturers. For simplicity, the Manufs table is the same in both versions and does not change during the life of the case study.

Full Version of the Database—First Cut

The initial database is composed of two tables, Cds and Manufs. The Cds table contains an entry for each compact disk. The Manufs table contains an entry for each manufacturer's series of compact disks. The two tables are interrelated; with the aid of SQL facilities such as the *join* operation, it is possible to link data on the two tables.

After reading about the Cds table, enter the CREATE statement shown in Figure A-1. (Table creation is discussed in Chapter 6. Note that with many computer systems it is possible to create the tables with a product other than SQL and then process these tables via SQL commands.) A single row in the Cds table contains 11 columns, with a maximum of approximately 120 characters. Compare this to the Smlcds table, with 8 columns and a maximum of approximately 90 characters. A brief description of the columns and their interrelationships follows.

```
CREATE TABLE Cds
   (Cdid       CHAR(15) UNIQUE NOT NULL,
    Manucode   CHAR(2),
    Series     CHAR(20),
    Cdcode     CHAR(3),
    Title      CHAR(40),
    Price      DECIMAL(4,2),
    Numwks     SMALLINT,
    Fstrec     SMALLINT,
    Orch       CHAR(24),
    Durmin     SMALLINT,
    Copies     SMALLINT );
```

Figure A-1 Creating the Cds Table

Column Descriptions for the Cds Table and the Smlcds Table

1. *Cdid*. This column is the product number appearing on the CD package. Because there is presently no fully accepted industry standard for product numbers, this column alone may be insufficient to identify the CD. However, in our present system the Cdid column is the key and identifies the CD. Examples of the Cdid are: *CDZ 7 62508 2*, and *SCD 6008*.

2. *Manucode*. This column identifies the CD manufacturer. Examples are *31* and *MM*. We choose to use a code instead of the complete manufacturer name to reduce both the size of the database and the amount of data entry required. This code is vendor assigned. Note, this column is also found on the Manufs table.

3. *Series*. This column contains the manufacturer's series name, used to identify a group of CDs; for example, *Baroque Series*. Note, this column is also found on the Manufs table.

4. *Cdcode*. This column contains a standard industry code describing the recording process. The values are as follows:

DDD—Digital tape recorder used during session recording, mixing and/or editing, and mastering (transcription).

ADD—Analog tape recorder used during session recording; digital tape recorder used during subsequent mixing and/or editing; digital tape recorder used during mastering (transcription).

AAD—Analog tape recorder used during session recording and subsequent mixing and/or editing; digital tape recorder used during mastering (transcription).

It is probably fair to say that all other factors being equal, the top quality is DDD, and the second quality is ADD. However, all other factors are not necessarily equal. Furthermore, even though a standard industry code describing the recording process exists, it does not appear on every compact disk.

5. *Title*. This column shows the CD title, wherever possible as it appears on the edge of the CD pack or on the box; for example, *Vivaldi The Four Seasons* etc.

6. *Price*. This column lists the selling price of the CD.

7. *Numwks*. This column contains the number of works or separate entries on the CD. A symphonic movement is not considered a work and is not separately identified in this table. This column is *not* included in the Smlcds table.

8. *(Column 7 in the Smlcds table) Fstrec*. This column shows the year in which the music was first recorded. In the case of ADD and AAD compact disks, the original performance may have been recorded during the 1960s or before. (We are assuming that all works on a given CD are recorded in the same year.)

9. *Orch*. This column indicates the orchestra performing the CD. (We are assuming that all works on a given CD are performed by the same orchestra.) This column is *not* included in the Smlcds table.

10. *Durmin*. This column lists the duration of the CD, in minutes. This value may be greater than 60, and is rounded according to the number of seconds. If no recording time is given for the CD but recording times are given for the individual works, this time must be calculated manually. This column is *not* included in the Smlcds table.

11. *(Column 8 on the Smlcds table) Copies*. The number of copies on hand is shown in this column.

The Manufs table contains an entry for each manufacturer's series of compact disks. The primary key to the Manufs table is the combined "Manucode" and "Series" columns. After reading about this table, enter the CREATE statement shown in Figure A-2. A single row in the Manufs table contains six columns and a maximum of approximately 50 characters. A brief description of the columns and their interrelationships follows.

```
CREATE TABLE Manufs
    (Manucode   CHAR(2) NOT NULL,
    Series      CHAR(20) NOT NULL,
    City        CHAR(15),
    Discount    DECIMAL(3,1),
    Deltime     SMALLINT,
    Quality     SMALLINT )
    UNIQUE      (Manucode, Series) );
```

Figure A-2 Creating the Manufs Table. Note, the UNIQUE clause might not be available on your SQL implementation.

Column Descriptions for the Manufs Table

1. *Manucode.* This column identifies the CD manufacturer. Examples are *31* and *MM.* We choose to use a code instead of the complete manufacturer name to reduce both the size of the database and the amount of data entry required. This code is vendor assigned. Note, this column is also found on the Cds table.

2. *Series.* Here is listed the manufacturer's series name, used to identify a group of CDs; for example, *Baroque Series.* Note, this column is also found on the Cds table.

3. *City.* The city from which we order more CDs is given in this column. In real life we would have to include the street address, a telephone number, and probably a contact name. But we are omitting these columns to simplify the database.

4. *Discount.* This column gives the percent discount the vendor offers on CDs of this particular series. Examples are *25.0* and *37.5.* We have simplified the true process of calculating discounts.

5. *Deltime.* This lists the number of days it takes to receive the CDs once the order is placed.

6. *Quality.* This column contains a subjective quality rating of this series of CDs. Values run from 0 ("Don't sell") to 10 ("Highest quality").

Smaller Version of the Database—First Cut

Some groups will find they don't have enough time to complete the case study using the full classical music database. For this reason we have included a smaller version of the database. End-of-chapter exercises are included for both versions of the database. It is important to realize that the smaller version of the database cannot supply as much information as the full version. For example, in the smaller compact disk table (Smlcds) we have included the "Price" column, for obvious reasons, but eliminated the "Orch" column. Thus, if you use the smaller database, you won't be able to list CDs by orchestra. The smaller version of the database provides a reduced benefit at a reduced cost. (A key aspect of any system design is calculating the cost/benefit ratio.)

The initial database is composed of two tables, Smlcds and Manufs. The Smlcds table holds an entry for each compact disk. The Manufs table contains an entry for each manufacturer's series of compact disks. The two tables are interrelated; with the aid of SQL features such as the *join* operation, it is possible to link data on the two tables. After reading about this table enter the CREATE statement shown in Figure A-3. (Table creation is discussed in Chapter 6. Note that with many computer systems it is possible to create the tables with a product other than SQL and then process these tables via SQL commands.)

```
CREATE TABLE Smlcds
    (Cdid       CHAR(15) UNIQUE NOT NULL,
    Manucode    CHAR(2),
    Series      CHAR(20),
    Cdcode      CHAR(3),
    Title       CHAR(40),
    Price       DECIMAL(4,2),
    Fstrec      SMALLINT,
    Copies      SMALLINT );
```

Figure A-3 Creating the Smlcds Table

A single row in the Smlcds table contains 8 columns and a maximum of approximately 90 characters. Compare this to the Cds table, with 11 columns and a maximum of approximately 120 characters. (See "Column Descriptions for the Cds Table and the Smlcds Table" in the "Full Version of the Database—First Cut," earlier, for the relevant column descriptions.)

The Manufs table contains an entry for each manufacturer's series of compact disks. It is exactly the same as that used for the full version of the database, where it is described in detail.

Entering Data into the Tables

Data entry is discussed in Chapter 6. We indicate next the commands necessary to enter data into the tables for either of the two databases. Note that with

Cdid	Manucode	Series	Cdcode	Title	Price	Numwks	Fstrec	Orch	Durmin	Copies
CDZ 7 62508 2	31	DRM	ADD	Vivaldi The Four Seasons etc.	10.95	6	1960	Virtuosi Di Roma	62	3
422 472-2	P9	Classics	ADD	Chopin Piano Concertos Nos 1 & 2	12.50	2	1958	Wiener Symphoniker	72	8
SCD-6036	AZ	Stradivari Classics	DDD	Mozart Piano Concerti K 414 K 488	11.75	2	1984	Israel Chamber	52	2
SCD 6008	AZ	Stradivari Classics	DDD	Tchaikovsky Symphony No 6	11.75	2	1984	Ljubljana Symphony	45	8
CDZ 7 62511 2	31	DRM	ADD	Mozart Symphonies Nos 40 & 41	12.50	2	1968	English Chamber	61	2
422 494-2	P9	Baroque Classics	ADD	Bach Cello Suites 1 4 & 6	13.75	3	1964	-0-	73	9
422 481-2	P9	Concert Classics	ADD	Haydn Boccherini Cello Concertos	13.75	2	1965	London Symphony	46	3

Figure A-4 Table CDs. The first entry in the original full version of the compact disk table can be interpreted as follows: Compact disk ID is CDZ 7 62508 2, Manufacturer code is 31, Series is DRM, Cdcode is ADD, Title is Vivaldi The Four Seasons etc., Price is 10.95, Number of works is 6, Year first recorded is 1960, Orchestra is Virtuosi Di Roma, Duration in minutes is 62, and Number of copies available is 3.

Cdid	Manucode	Series	Cdcode	Title	Price	Fstrec	Copies
CDZ 7 62508 2	31	DRM	ADD	Vivaldi The Four Seasons etc.	10.95	1960	3
422 472-2	P9	Classics	ADD	Chopin Piano Concertos Nos 1 & 2	12.50	1958	8
SCD-6036	AZ	Stradivari Classics	DDD	Mozart Piano Concerti K 414 K 488	11.75	1984	2
SCD 6008	AZ	Stradivari Classics	DDD	Tchaikovsky Symphony No 6	11.75	1984	8
CDZ 7 62511 2	31	DRM	ADD	Mozart Symphonies Nos 40 & 41	12.50	1968	2
422 494-2	P9	Baroque Classics	ADD	Bach Cello Suites 1 4 & 6	13.75	1964	9
422 481-2	P9	Concert Classics	ADD	Haydn Boccherini Cello Concertos	13.75	1965	3

Figure A-5 Table Smlcds. The first entry in the original smaller version of the compact disk table can be interpreted as follows: Compact disk ID is CDZ 7 62508 2, Manufacturer code is 31, Series is DRM, Cdcode is ADD, Title is Vivaldi The Four Seasons etc., Price is 10.95, Year first recorded is 1960, and Number of copies available is 3.

many computer systems it is possible to enter data into the tables with a product other than SQL and then process these tables via SQL commands.

Entering Data into the Cds Table. If you are using the full version of the case study database, enter the appropriate insert commands to produce the Cds table shown in Figure A-4.

Entering Data into the Smlcds Table. If you are using the smaller version of the case study database, enter the appropriate insert commands to produce the Smlcds table shown in Figure A-5.

Entering Data into the Manufs Table. If you are using either version of the case study database, enter the appropriate insert commands to produce the Manufs table shown in Figure A-6.

Chapter 6 discusses updating of the Cds and Smlcds tables and loading data into these tables. The Manufs table is not modified during the case study.

Manucode	Series	City	Discount	Deltime	Quality
31	DRM	Chicago	25.0	3	7
P9	Classics	New York	32.5	4	6
AZ	Stradivari Classics	Rome	28.5	14	7
P9	Baroque Classics	Cleveland	28.5	4	8
ZX	-0-	Newark	40.0	3	7
MM	Virtuoso	New York	35.0	2	7
P9	Concert Classics	Cleveland	25.0	4	8
LM	El Cheapo	Nameless	65.0	70	2
LM	Maestro	Paris	25.0	10	7

Figure A-6 Table Manufs. The first entry in the manufacturers table can be interpreted as follows: Manufacturer code is 31, Series is DRM, City from which CDs delivered is Chicago, Discount is 25.0%, Delivery time is 3 days, and Quality is 7.

Modifying the
Case Study Database

Introduction

This appendix reviews principles and commands presented in Chapter 6. Since this involves modifying and creating tables that are used throughout the rest of this textbook, any error here has repercussions elsewhere.

No matter which version you are using, the process of modifying the database can be divided into four steps. It is imperative that you verify your work at the end of each step before proceeding to the next step.

1. Modify either the Cds or the Smlcds table by adding new columns, which enable the vendor to record data for CD boxes as well as individual CDs. The Cds table is also modified to include a column indicating whether the CD or box contains a descriptive booklet.

2. Load the modified Cds table or the Smlcds table with data for the new columns, and the new rows.

3. Create a new table to record data for individual works in the compact disks. Depending on the database version used, create either the Works table or the Smlworks table.

4. Load the Works table or the Smlworks table with data.

Step I   Modifying the Cds Table or the Smlcds Table

The two tables of the present compact disk database—either Cds and Manufs, or Smlcds and Manufs—describe the vendor's CDs. They do not take into account CD boxes, that is, single packages containing two or more CDs, such as Beethoven's nine symphonies packaged together. A box may contain several CDs, each with the same value in the "Cdid" column. Both the Cds table and the Smlcds table require two new columns: The "Cdseqnum" column indicates the sequence number of the CD, whether in a box or not; the "Numcds" column indicates the number of Cds packaged together. In addition, the Cds table is modified to include a column entitled "Booklet," which indicates whether a descriptive booklet is enclosed. Users of the full version of the database should do Exercise 1A. Users of the small version of the database should do Exercise 1B.

Modifying the Cds Table Structure

Exercise 1A. Enter the commands shown in Figure B-1 to add three columns to the Cds table. The modified Cds table contains 14 columns. A single row now contains a maximum of approximately 140 characters. Compare this to the modified Smlcds table, with 10 columns and a maximum of approximately 100 characters per row. These three new columns are added at the end of the Cds table and are interpreted in the list that follows.

```
ALTER TABLE Cds
     ADD Cdseqnum   SMALLINT UNIQUE NOT NULL;
ALTER TABLE Cds
        ADD Numcds   SMALLINT;
ALTER TABLE Cds
     ADD Booklet    CHAR(1);
```

Figure B-1 Modifying the Cds Table Structure

12. *Cdseqnum.* This column indicates the sequence number of the CD in its box. Individually sold CDs have a Cdseqnum of 1. The Cdseqnum helps indentify CDs in a box uniquely, with the "Cdid" column it forms the primary key.

13. *Numcds.* This column denotes the number of CDs sold together. For an individual package the value is 1; for a box the value is greater than 1.

14. *Booklet.* This column contains a Y or N indicating whether a descriptive booklet is included with the CD or box.

Note, although we have modified the Cds table, we have not added any data. At present the columns "Cdseqnum," "Numcds," and "Booklet" contain NULLs. Proceed to Exercise 2A to load these new columns with data.

Modifying the Smlcds Table Structure

Exercise 1B. Enter the commands shown in Figure B-2 to add two columns to the Smlcds table. The modified Smlcds table contains 10 columns. A single row now contains a maximum of approximately 100 characters. Compare this to the modified Cds table, with 14 columns and a maximum of approximately 140 characters per row. These two new columns are added at the end of the Cds table and are interpreted in the list that follows.

```
ALTER TABLE Smlcds
    ADD Cdseqnum  SMALLINT UNIQUE NOT NULL;
ALTER TABLE Smlcds
    ADD Numcds  SMALLINT
```

Figure B-2 Modifying the Smlcds Table Structure

9. *Cdseqnum.* This column indicates the sequence number of the CD in its box. Individually sold CDs have a Cdseqnum of 1. The Cdseqnum helps indentify CDs in a box uniquely, with the "Cdid" column it forms the primary key.

10. *Numcds.* This column denotes the number of CDs sold together. For an individual package the value is 1; for a box the value is greater than 1.

Note, although we have modified the Smlcds table, we have not added any data. At present the columns "Cdseqnum" and "Numcds" contain NULLs. Proceed to Exercise 2B to load these new columns with data.

Step II   Loading Data into the Cds Table or the Smlcds Table

The Cds and Smlcds tables were modified to process boxes as well as individual compact disks. Loading either of them with data is a two-part operation: First load data into the columns created in Exercise 1A or 1B; then load the tables with new data for a single box containing five CDs. Users of the full version of the database should do Exercise 2A. Users of the smaller version of the database should do Exercise 2B.

Entering Data into the Cds Table

Exercise 2A. First we load data into the three new columns created in Step I. Then we load data for a five-CD box containing Beethoven's nine symphonies. (In this specific case, performing these two operations in reverse order is more complicated.)

Part 1.
Because all seven rows in the present Cds table represent individual compact disks, the values for Cdseqnum and Numcds are always 1. This simplifies data entry for these two columns. Code the following statement:

```
UPDATE   Cds
  SET    Cdseqnum=1, Numcds=1;
```

The "Booklet" column does not contain a single value for all of the seven CDs. No booklet is included for five of them. A booklet is included for compact disks with the following Cdids: '422 494-2' and '422 481-2'. While there are different ways to enter the booklet data, perhaps the simplest is as follows.

First set all Booklet columns to 'N':

```
UPDATE   Cds
  SET    Booklet = 'N';
```

Then set the two appropriate "Booklet" columns to 'Y':

```
UPDATE   Cds
  SET    Booklet = 'Y'
WHERE    Cdid IN ('422 494-2', '422 481-2');
```

Part 2.
We load data for a box containing five compact disks. Of course, this data must also contain values for the "Cdseqnum," "Numcds," and "Booklet" columns. The "Cdseqnum" column ranges from 1 to 5. The "Numcds" column equals 5 for all CDs in this box. The "Booklet" column equals 'Y' for all CDs in this box. Enter the appropriate insert commands to produce the Cds table shown in Figure B-3. These five new rows are appended to the end of the Cds table. Our Cds table is now ready to go. Proceed to Step III to create the Works table.

Entering Data into the Smlcds Table

Exercise 2B. First we load data into the two new columns created in Step I. Then we load data for a five-CD box containing Beethoven's nine symphonies. (In this specific case, performing these two operations in reverse order is more complicated.)

Part 1.
Because all seven rows in the present Smlcds table represent individual compact disks, the values for Cdseqnum and Numcds are always 1. This simplifies data entry for these two columns. Code the following statement:

```
UPDATE   Smlcds
  SET    Cdseqnum=1, Numcds=1;
```

Part 2.
We load data for a box consisting of five compact disks. Of course, this data must also contain values for the "Cdseqnum" and "Numcds" columns. The "Cdseqnum" column ranges from 1 to 5. The "Numcds" column equals 5 for all CDs in this box. Enter the appropriate insert commands to produce the Smlcds table shown in Figure B-4. These five new rows are appended to the end of the Smlcds table. Our Smlcds table is now ready to go. Proceed to Step III to create the Smlworks table.

Step III   Creating the Works Table or the Smlworks Table

None of the existing tables gives information on the individual works comprising a compact disk. One prospective buyer may wish to know if a given compact disk contains a particular work, such as Beethoven's Ninth Symphony. Another prospective buyer may want to know if a given CD contains vocal works. The best way to supply such data is to create a new table with information on a compact disk's individual works. The Works table is added to the full database. A smaller table known as the Smlworks table is added to the smaller database. As did the Cds and Smlcds tables, the Works and Smlworks tables both contain the same number of rows. Users of the full version of the database should do Exercise 3A. Users of the smaller version of the database should do Exercise 3B.

Creating the Works Table

Exercise 3A. After reading about the Works table, enter the CREATE statement shown in Figure B-5. A single row in the Works table contains 15 columns and a maximum of approximately 140 characters. Compare this to the Smlworks table, with 10 columns and a maximum of approximately 90 characters per row.

Before examining the individual columns, we wish to make a few comments about the Works table as a whole: System design is somewhat complicated, because manufacturers may package different composers on a single CD. As with the Cds table, data for the Works table is taken from the compact disk package itself. (Most of the data appearing in the database was found on CDs in the writer's own collection.) A brief description of the columns and their interrelationships follows.

Column Descriptions for the
Works Table and the Smlworks Table

1. *Cdid.* This column is the product number appearing on the CD package. Because presently there is no fully accepted industry standard for product

Cdid	Manucode	Series	Cdcode	Title	Fstrec	Numwks	Price	Orch	Durmin	Copies	Cdseqnum	Numcds	Booklet
CDZ 7 62508 2	31	DRM	ADD	Vivaldi The Four Seasons etc.	1960	6	10.95	Virtuosi Di Roma	62	3	1	1	N
422 472-2	P9	Classics	ADD	Chopin Piano Concertos Nos 1 & 2	1958	2	12.50	Wiener Symphoniker	72	8	1	1	N
SCD-6036	AZ	Stradivari Classics	DDD	Mozart Piano Concerti K 414 K 488	1984	2	11.75	Israel Chamber	52	2	1	1	N
SCD 6008	AZ	Stradivari Classics	DDD	Tchaikovsky Symphony No 6	1984	2	11.75	Ljubljana Symphony	45	8	1	1	N
CDZ 7 62511 2	31	DRM	ADD	Mozart Symphonies Nos 40 & 41	1968	2	12.50	Erglish Chamber	61	2	1	1	N
422 494-2	P9	Baroque Classics	ADD	Bach Cello Suites 1 2 & 6	1964	3	13.75	-0-	73	9	1	1	Y
422 481-2	P9	Concert Classics	ADD	Haydn Boccherini Cello Concertos	1965	2	13.75	London Symphony	46	3	1	1	Y
429036-2	ZX	-0-	ADD	Beethoven Karajan 1	1963	2	33.95	Berliner Philharmoniker	75	12	1	5	Y
429036-2	ZX	-0-	ADD	Beethoven Karajan 1	1963	2	33.95	Berliner Philharmoniker	62	12	2	5	Y
429036-2	ZX	-0-	ADD	Beethoven Karajan 1	1963	2	33.95	Berliner Philharmoniker	67	12	3	5	Y
429036-2	ZX	-0-	ADD	Beethoven Karajan 2	1963	2	33.95	Berliner Philharmoniker	60	12	4	5	Y
429036-2	ZX	-0-	ADD	Beethoven Karajan 2	1963	1	33.95	Berliner Philharmoniker	67	12	5	5	Y

Figure B-3 Table Cds. The first entry in the updated full version of the compact disk table can be interpreted as follows: Compact disk ID is CDZ 7 62508 2, Manufacturer code is 31, Series is DRM, Cdcode is ADD, Title is Vivaldi The Four Seasons etc., Price is 10.95, Number of works is 6, Year first recorded is 1960, Orchestra is Virtuosi Di Roma, Duration in minutes is 62, Number of copies available is 3, CD sequence number is 1, Number of CDs sold together is 1, and no booklet is enclosed.

Cdid	Manucode	Series	Cdcode	Title	Price	Fstrec	Copies	Cdseqnum	Numcds
CDZ 7 62508 2	31	DRM	ADD	Vivaldi The Four Seasons etc.	10.95	1960	3	1	1
422 472-2	P9	Classics	ADD	Chopin Piano Concertos Nos 1 & 2	12.50	1958	8	1	1
SCD-6036	AZ	Stradivari Classics	DDD	Mozart Piano Concerti K 414 K 488	11.75	1984	2	1	1
SCD 6008	AZ	Stradivari Classics	DDD	Tchaikovsky Symphony No 6	11.75	1984	8	1	1
CDZ 7 62511 2	31	DRM	ADD	Mozart Symphonies Nos 40 & 41	12.50	1968	2	1	1
422 494-2	P9	Baroque Classics	ADD	Bach Cello Suites 1 2 & 6	13.75	1964	9	1	1
422 481-2	P9	Concert Classics	ADD	Haydn Boccherini Cello Concertos	13.75	1965	3	1	1
429036-2	ZX	-0-	ADD	Beethoven Karajan 1	33.95	1963	12	1	5
429036-2	ZX	-0-	ADD	Beethoven Karajan 1	33.95	1963	12	2	5
429036-2	ZX	-0-	ADD	Beethoven Karajan 1	33.95	1963	12	3	5
429036-2	ZX	-0-	ADD	Beethoven Karajan 2	33.95	1963	12	4	5
429036-2	ZX	-0-	ADD	Beethoven Karajan 2	33.95	1963	12	5	5

Figure B-4 Table Smlcds. The first entry in the updated smaller version of the compact disk table can be interpreted as follows: Compact disk ID is CDZ 7 62508 2, Manufacturer code is 31, Series is DRM, Cdcode is ADD, Title is Vivaldi The Four Seasons etc., Price is 10.95, Year first recorded is 1960, Number of copies available is 3, CD sequence number is 1, and Number of CDs sold together is 1.

numbers, in reality this column alone may be insufficient to identify the CD or the work. However, in our system the Cdid, the Cdseqnum, and the Wkseqnum form the primary key to the Works or Smlworks table. Examples of the Cdid are *CDZ 7 62508 2*, *429036-2*, and *SCD 6008*.

```
CREATE TABLE Works
    (Cdid       CHAR(15) NOT NULL,
    Manucode    CHAR(2),
    Cdseqnum    SMALLINT NOT NULL,
    Wkseqnum    SMALLINT NOT NULL,
    Numcuts     SMALLINT,
    Worktitl    CHAR(25),
    Worksubt    CHAR(15),
    Wkidcode    CHAR(1),
    Wkid        SMALLINT,
    Thekey      CHAR(1),
    Keydash     CHAR(3),
    Composer    CHAR(20),
    Artist      CHAR(20),
    Instrum     CHAR(20),
    Vocal       CHAR(1),
    UNIQUE   (Cdid, Cdseqnum, Wkseqnum) );
```

Figure B-5 Creating the Works Table

2. *Manucode.* This column identifies the CD manufacturer. Examples are *31* and *MM*. We choose to use a code instead of the complete manufacturer name to reduce both the size of the database and the amount of data entry required. This code is vendor assigned. Note, this column is also found on the other tables in the compact disk database.

3. *Cdseqnum.* This number indicates the sequence number of the CD in its package. Individually sold CDs have a Cdseqnum of 1. The second CD in a box (a group of CDs packed and sold together) has a Cdseqnum value of 2. Because different CDs in a box may have the same Cdid, this column is required as part of the CD identification and the work identification.

4. *Wkseqnum.* This number indicates the sequence number of the work in its CD. In contrast to pop music, a classical music CD usually contains a fairly small number of works, although there are exceptions. We chose not to include

in the database our version of Glenn Gould playing Johann Sebastian Bach's Goldberg Variations, BWV 988. This magnificent CD contains two arias and 30 numbered variations, and would have added 32 rows to the Works table for a single CD. In such a case, an alternate cataloging method would be preferable.

5. *Numcuts.* This column holds the number of cuts for a given work, sometimes indicative of the work's length. The "Numcuts" column is not included in the Smlworks table.

6. *(Column 5 on the Smlworks table).* *Worktitl.* This column lists the title of the work, wherever possible as it appears on the CD package; for example, *The Four Seasons.*

7. *(Column 6 on the Smlworks table) Worksubt.* This column gives the subtitle of the work, wherever possible as it appears on the CD package; for example, *Spring.* Note, this column is often empty.

8. *(Column 7 on the Smlworks table) Wkidcode.* This column lists a code used in conjunction with the following column, Wkid. Many works have a standard identification, often the opus number. Mozart's works are identified with a *K* (Koechel number).

9. *(Column 8 on the Smlworks table) Wkid.* This gives the standard number of the work. For instance, a work identified as *Opus 23* has a Wkidcode of *O* and a Wkid of *23.* Mozart's 40th Symphony is identified as *K 550.* In the case of a well-known work such as Mozart's 40th Symphony, the Koechel identification may be superfluous. However, lesser known works, such as K 414 and K 488, are both identified as *Concerto in A Major,* so the Koechel identification clearly is required.

10. *Thekey.* This column shows the key in which a given work is recorded; for example, *C.* This column, used in conjunction with the next column, is not included in the Smlworks table.

11. *Keydash.* This gives the complement of the key in which a given work is recorded; for example, *Ma* for major, *Mi* for minor, *F* for flat, and *Fma* for flat major. The "Keydash" column is not included in the Smlworks table.

12. *(Column 9 on the Smlworks table) Composer.* This column indicates the composer of the work; for example, *Vivaldi.*

13. *Artist.* The lead artist featured for the work is given in this column. The artist may be the conductor or the lead instrumentalist. The "Artist" column is not included in the Smlworks table.

14. *Instrum.* This column shows the major instrument of the work; for example, *piano.* The "Instrum" column is not included in the Smlworks table.

15. *(Column 10 on the Smlworks table) Vocal.* A single character *Y* or *N* in this column indicates whether or not the work includes singing. (The only vocal work in this database is Beethoven's Ninth Symphony.)

Note, although we have created the Works table, we have not added any data. Proceed to Exercise 4A to load this new table with data.

Creating the Smlworks Table

Exercise 3B. After reading about the Smlworks table, enter the CREATE statement shown in Figure B-6. A single row in the Smlworks table contains 10 columns and a maximum of approximately 90 characters. Compare this to the Works table, with 15 columns and a maximum of approximately 140 characters per row.

```
CREATE TABLE Smlworks
     (Cdid      CHAR(15) NOT NULL,
     Manucode   CHAR(2),
     Cdseqnum   SMALLINT NOT NULL,
     Wkseqnum   SMALLINT NOT NULL,
     Worktitl   CHAR(25),
     Worksubt   CHAR(15),
     Wkidcode   CHAR(1),
     Wkid       SMALLINT,
     Composer   CHAR(20),
     Vocal      CHAR(1),
     UNIQUE     (Cdid, Cdseqnum, Wkseqnum) );
```

Figure B-6 Creating the Smlworks Table

Before examining the individual columns we wish to make a few comments about the Smlworks table as a whole: System design is somewhat complicated, because manufacturers may package different composers on a single CD. As with the Smlcds table, data for the Smlworks table is taken from the compact disk package itself. (Most of the data appearing in the database was found on CDs in the writer's own collection.) See "Column Descriptions for the Cds

Cdid	Manucode	Cdseqnum	Wkseqnum	Numcuts	Worktitl	Worksubt	Wkidcode	Wkid	TheKey	Keydash	Composer	Artist	Instrument	Vocal
CDZ 7 62508 2	31	1	1	3	The Four Seasons	Spring	C	1	E	Ma	Vivaldi	Renato Fasano	Violin	N
CDZ 7 62508 2	31	1	2	3	The Four Seasons	Summer	C	2	G	Mi	Vivaldi	Renato Fasano	Violin	N
CDZ 7 62508 2	31	1	3	3	The Four Seasons	Autumn	C	3	F	Ma	Vivaldi	Renato Fasano	Violin	N
CDZ 7 62508 2	31	1	4	3	The Four Seasons	Winter	C	4	F	Mi	Vivaldi	Renato Fasano	Violin	N
CDZ 7 62508 2	31	1	5	3	La tempesta di mare	-0-	-	-0-	E	Fma	Vivaldi	Renato Fasano	Violin	N
CDZ 7 62508 2	31	1	6	3	Il piacere	-0-	-	-0-	C	Ma	Vivaldi	Renato Fasano	Violin	N
422 472-2	P9	1	1	3	Piano Concerto No 1	-0-	O	11	E	Mi	Chopin	Adam Harasiewicz	Piano	N
422 472-2	P9	1	2	3	Piano Concerto No 2	-0-	O	21	F	Mi	Chopin	Adam Harasiewicz	Piano	N
SCD-6036	AZ	1	1	3	Concerto in A Major	-0-	K	414	A	Ma	Mozart	Arie Vardi	Piano	N
SCD-6036	AZ	1	2	3	Concerto in A Major	-0-	K	488	A	Ma	Mozart	Arie Vardi	Piano	N
SCD 6008	AZ	1	1	4	Symphony No 6	Pathetique	O	74	B	Mi	Tchaikovsky	Marko Munich	-0-	N
CDZ 7 62511 2	31	1	1	4	Symphony No 40	-0-	K	550	G	Mi	Mozart	Daniel Barenboim	-0-	N
CDZ 7 62511 2	31	1	2	4	Symphony No 41	-0-	K	551	C	Ma	Mozart	Daniel Barenboim	-0-	N
422 494-2	P9	1	1	6	Suite No 1	-0-	B	1007	G	-0-	J S Bach	Maurice Gendron	Cello	N
422 494-2	P9	1	2	6	Suite No 4	-0-	B	1010	E	F	J S Bach	Maurice Gendron	Cello	N
422 494-2	P9	1	3	6	Suite No 6	-0-	B	1012	D	-0-	J S Bach	Maurice Gendron	Cello	N
422 481-2	P9	1	1	3	Cello Concerto in C	H.VIIb No 1	-	-0-	C	-0-	Haydn	Maurice Gendron	Cello	N
422 481-2	P9	1	1	3	Cello Concerto in G	-0-	-	-0-	G	-0-	Boccherini	Maurice Gendron	Cello	N
429036-2	ZX	1	1	4	Symphony No 1	-0-	O	21	C	Ma	Beethoven	Herbert von Karajan	-0-	N
429036-2	ZX	1	2	4	Symphony No 3	Eroica	O	55	E	Fma	Beethoven	Herbert von Karajan	-0-	N
429036-2	ZX	2	1	4	Symphony No 2	-0-	O	36	D	Ma	Beethoven	Herbert von Karajan	-0-	N
429036-2	ZX	2	2	4	Symphony No 4	-0-	O	60	B	Fma	Beethoven	Herbert von Karajan	-0-	N
429036-2	ZX	3	1	5	Symphony No 5	-0-	O	67	C	Ma	Beethoven	Herbert von Karajan	-0-	N
429036-2	ZX	3	2	5	Symphony No 6	Pastoral	O	68	F	Ma	Beethoven	Herbert von Karajan	-0-	N
429036-2	ZX	4	1	4	Symphony No 7	-0-	O	92	A	Ma	Beethoven	Herbert von Karajan	-0-	N
429036-2	ZX	4	2	4	Symphony No 8	-0-	O	93	F	Ma	Beethoven	Herbert von Karajan	-0-	N
429036-2	ZX	5	1	5	Symphony No 9	-0-	O	125	D	Mi	Beethoven	Herbert von Karajan	-0-	Y

Figure B-7 Table Works. The first entry in the full version of the works table can be interpreted as follows: Compact disk ID is CDZ 7 62508 2, Manufacturer code is 31, CD sequence number is 1, Work sequence number is 1, Number of cuts is 3, Work title is The Four Seasons, Work subtitle is Spring, Work id code is C (for concerto), Work id is 1, Key is E, Key dash is Ma (for Major), Composer is Vivaldi, Artist is Renato Fasano, Instrument is Violin, and Work is not a vocal.

209

Cdid	Manucode	Cdseqnum	Wkseqnum	Worktitl	Worksubt	Wkidcode	Wkid	Composer	Vocal
CDZ 7 62508 2	31	1	1	The Four Seasons	Spring	C	1	Vivaldi	N
CDZ 7 62508 2	31	1	2	The Four Seasons	Summer	C	2	Vivaldi	N
CDZ 7 62508 2	31	1	3	The Four Seasons	Autumn	C	3	Vivaldi	N
CDZ 7 62508 2	31	1	4	The Four Seasons	Winter	C	4	Vivaldi	N
CDZ 7 62508 2	31	1	5	La tempesta di mare	-0-	-	-0-	Vivaldi	N
CDZ 7 62508 2	31	1	6	Il piacere	-0-	-	-0-	Vivaldi	N
422 472-2	P9	1	1	Piano Concerto No 1	-0-	O	11	Chopin	N
422 472-2	P9	1	2	Piano Concerto No 2	-0-	O	21	Chopin	N
SCD-6036	AZ	1	1	Concerto in A Major	-0-	K	414	Mozart	N
SCD-6036	AZ	1	2	Concerto in A Major	-0-	K	488	Mozart	N
SCD 6008	AZ	1	1	Symphony No 6	Pathetique	O	74	Tchaikovsky	N
CDZ 7 62511 2	31	1	1	Symphony No 40	-0-	K	550	Mozart	N
CDZ 7 62511 2	31	1	2	Symphony No 41	-0-	K	551	Mozart	N
422 494-2	P9	1	1	Suite No 1	-0-	B	1007	J S Bach	N
422 494-2	P9	1	2	Suite No 4	-0-	B	1010	J S Bach	N
422 494-2	P9	1	3	Suite No 6	-0-	B	1012	J S Bach	N
422 481-2	P9	1	1	Cello Concerto in C	H. VIIb No 1	-	-0-	Haydn	N
422 481-2	P9	1	1	Cello Concerto in G	-0-	-	-0-	Boccherini	N
429036-2	ZX	1	1	Symphony No 1	-0-	O	21	Beethoven	N
429036-2	ZX	1	2	Symphony No 3	Eroica	O	55	Beethoven	N
429036-2	ZX	2	1	Symphony No 2	-0-	O	36	Beethoven	N
429036-2	ZX	2	2	Symphony No 4	-0-	O	60	Beethoven	N
429036-2	ZX	3	1	Symphony No 5	-0-	O	67	Beethoven	N
429036-2	ZX	3	2	Symphony No 6	Pastoral	O	68	Beethoven	N
429036-2	ZX	4	1	Symphony No 7	-0-	O	92	Beethoven	N
429036-2	ZX	4	2	Symphony No 8	-0-	O	93	Beethoven	N
429036-2	ZX	5	1	Symphony No 9	-0-	O	125	Beethoven	Y

Figure B-8 Table Smlworks. The first entry in the small version of the works table can be interpreted as follows: Compact disk ID is CDZ 7 62508 2, Manufacturer code is 31, CD sequence number is 1, Work sequence number is 1, Work title is The Four Seasons, Work subtitle is Spring, Work id code is C (for concerto), Work id is 1, Composer is Vivaldi, and Work is not a vocal.

Table and the Smlcds Table" in Exercise 3A, earlier, for the relevant column descriptions.

Note, although we have created the Smlworks table, we have not added any data. Proceed to Exercise 4B to load this new table with data.

Step IV Loading Data into the Works Table or the Smlworks Table

Unlike Step II, in which we loaded data into the tables in two parts, loading data in Step IV is straightforward. Once you have loaded the data, verify it carefully; use the UPDATE. . .SET command to correct data when needed. Users of the full version of the database should do Exercise 4A. Users of the smaller version of the database should do Exercise 4B.

Entering Data into the Works Table

Exercise 4A. Enter the appropriate insert commands to produce the Works table, shown in Figure B-7 on page 209. Be careful in handling NULL values.

Congratulations! Your modified database containing the Cds, Manufs (see Figure B-9), and Works tables is now ready.

Entering Data into the Smlworks Table

Exercise 4B. Enter the appropriate insert commands to produce the Smlworks table, shown in Figure B-8 on page 210. Be careful in handling NULL values.

Congratulations! Your modified database containing the Smlcds, Manufs (see Figure B-9), and Smlworks tables is now ready.

Manucode	Series	City	Discount	Deltime	Quality
31	DRM	Chicago	25.0	3	7
P9	Classics	New York	32.5	4	6
AZ	Stradivari Classics	Rome	28.5	14	7
P9	Baroque Classics	Cleveland	28.5	4	8
ZX	-0-	Newark	40.0	3	7
MM	Virtuoso	New York	35.0	2	7
P9	Concert Classics	Cleveland	25.0	4	8
LM	El Cheapo	Nameless	65.0	70	2
LM	Maestro	Paris	25.0	10	7

Figure B-9 Table Manufs. The first entry in the manufacturers table can be interpreted as follows: Manufacturer code is 31 , Series is DRM, City from which CDs delivered is Chicago, Discount is 25.0%, Delivery time is 3 days, and Quality is 7.

Getting Started with dBASE IV SQL

Introduction

This appendix concretely illustrates compatibility between dBASE IV SQL and the approximately standard SQL applied throughout the text. Using SQL on dBASE IV 1.1 (educational version), the author created and loaded Noga's tables and ran the SQL commands appearing in the figures of Chapters 1 to 8 on an IBM-compatible 386 microcomputer. Version 1.0 is full of bugs, and should not be used. dBASE IV was the first dBASE product to offer SQL. Some of the following results may be related to the specific hardware and software setup the author used. Run all examples yourself, and record your findings.

General Comments

Users of dBASE IV can apply non-SQL commands for activities such as data entry and table manipulation, as discussed in Chapter 10. Note any differences between *your* installation's start-up procedure and the following start-up steps:

1. Start the computer, and enter the appropriate directory. We used directory DBSAMPLE on drive C.
2. Enter DBASE to start the program.
3. In response to dBASE's initial screen, press a *carriage return* to assent to the license agreement.
4. After the system displays the dBASE IV Control Center screen, press the *Esc* key and *Y*(es) to confirm.
5. Enter

   ```
   SET SQL ON
   ```

   In response,

```
SQL.
```

is displayed to the left of the flashing cursor.

6. If you haven't created any tables in the database, enter

```
CREATE DATABASE CANDY;
```

Otherwise, enter

```
START DATABASE CANDY;
```

Note, every SQL command must terminate with a semicolon (;). Erroneous commands generate a window containing the command, an error message such as

```
Incomplete SQL statement
```

and the options Cancel, Edit, and Help. The Edit option allows you to modify the incorrect command and rerun it. The Help option tends to be inconsistent.

Commands are repeated using the up-arrow or the down-arrow. When repeating a command, use the *control* key and the left-arrow key or the right-arrow key to move the cursor from word to word. Use the *Home* key to position the cursor at the beginning of the command. The system is normally in Typeover mode. Press the *Ins* key to access the Insert mode, indicated in the highlighted status line on the screen. Press the *Ins* key again to return to Typeover mode. Press the *Ctrl-Home* keys for full-screen data entry. Press the *Ctrl-End* keys followed by a *carriage return* to execute the command.

Individual Chapters

Chapter 1. The following commands can be used to create the two central tables:

```
CREATE TABLE Customer
    (Custnum    SMALLINT,
    Custname    CHAR(18),
    Custtype    CHAR(1),
    Custaddr    CHAR(15),
    Zipcode     CHAR(5),
    Phone       CHAR(8) );
```

and

```
CREATE TABLE Purchase
    (Purchnum    SMALLINT,
    Prodnum     SMALLINT,
    Custnum     SMALLINT,
    Purchdat    DATE,
    Readydat    DATE,
    Kilos       DECIMAL(3,1) );
```

The NOT NULL and UNIQUE options are not available. Because the zip code field of the Customer table has been defined as a character field, zip codes such as 91212 must be enclosed in single quotes. Note the use of the comma with the DECIMAL data type.

When inserting the date *October 29, 1992,* legal variations include the following:

```
CTOD('10/29/92')  CTOD("10/29/92")  {10/29/92}  {10/29/1992}
```

Chapter 2. The query shown in Figure 2-8 may be expressed as

```
SELECT * FROM Purchase WHERE Readydat = {10/29/1992};
```

or other forms, as shown above. Quotes are necessary when testing for strings such as

```
SELECT * FROM Customer WHERE Zipcode = '91212';
```

Chapter 3. Strings in dBASE IV SQL are case-sensitive (that is, uppercase vs. lowercase); thus, 'R' and 'r' are different. No message appears when a query such as the one shown in Figure 3-8a and b generates no output.

Chapter 4. Column headers involving arithmetic, such as

```
Kilos*2.2
```

appear as EXP1; aggregate functions generate column headers such as SUM1. The clause

```
GROUP BY Purchnum
```

generates a column header G_PURCHNUM. Calculated values include two digits after the decimal point. NULL values appear as blanks; the ORDER BY clause places them at the bottom of the table.

Chapter 5. When tables are joined, the column headers include the table name and the column name for all output columns. Liberal use of aliases makes the output easier to read and may keep a single row from generating two output lines.

The text uses aliases X, Y, and Z, because dBASE IV reserves letters A to J (both uppercase and lowercase) as database aliases. dBASE IV SQL does *not* support the UNION ALL command.

Chapter 6. Because column names are restricted to 10 characters, we changed column name "Description" to "Descript" in the Product table. When loading data into this table, code the description as

```
'Millionaire"s Macadamia Mix'
```

Copying a table with dBASE SQL is fairly easy. For example, to copy the Custtomer table to the Custtest table, code the following:

```
SELECT * FROM Customer SAVE TO TEMP Custtest KEEP;
```

Note, omit the KEEP if you only want a temporary table.

The ALTER TABLE statement is coded as follows:

```
ALTER TABLE Purchase ADD (Pickdel CHAR(1) );
```

When entering the following command shown in Figure 6-5,

```
UPDATE Purchase SET Pickdel = 'P';
```

the system responds with a box containing the message

```
Warning — No WHERE clause specified in UPDATE statement
Cancel Proceed Help
```

If you choose to proceed, the update occurs without any problem.

Chapter 7. Testing these lengthy commands can be quite tedious. Remember to use the *Ctrl-Home* and *Ctrl-End* keys.

Chapter 8. dBASE IV SQL does not allow views defined with a GROUP BY (see Figures 8-8 and 8-9) to be used in a *join*. This serious restriction prevents us from using a series of views to obtain total values per purchase order.

To reject entries with duplicate key values, code a CREATE UNIQUE INDEX for the key in question.

When the WITH CHECK OPTION is coded (see Figure 8-11), the system rejects illegal data, generating the following error message:

```
SQL run-time error
Row violates view definition — INSERT/UPDATE row rejected
```

and displays the offending row.

Getting Started with Oracle SQL

Introduction

This appendix concretely illustrates compatibility between Oracle SQL and the approximately standard SQL applied throughout the text. Using Oracle SQL and UFI (user-friendly interface), the author created and loaded Noga's tables and ran the SQL commands appearing in the figures of Chapters 1 to 8 on an IBM-compatible 386 microcomputer. Some of the following results may be related to the specific hardware and software setup we used. Run all examples yourself, and record your findings.

General Comments

Note any differences between your installation's start-up procedure and the following start-up steps:

1. Start the computer, and enter the appropriate directory. We used

   ```
   C:\ORACLE\DEMO
   ```

2. Start Oracle with the appropriate command. (We entered *IORW*, followed by a carriage return, and then entered *UFI.*)
3. In response to system prompts, enter your preassigned user name and password.

When you have completed this process, the screen displays a prompt such as

```
UFI>
```

Note, every SQL command must terminate with a semicolon (;). In response to a carriage return, the system automatically enters a line number, such as 2, and waits for the command to be continued or to be terminated with a semicolon. Erroneous commands generate an error message such as

```
ERROR at line 1: table or view does not exist
```

The last command line entered may be repeated using the right-arrow to generate the command, character by character.

Individual Chapters

Chapter 1. The following commands can be used to create the two central tables:

```
CREATE TABLE Customer
    (Custnum    SMALLINT,
    Custname    CHAR(18),
    Custtype    CHAR(1),
    Custaddr    CHAR(15),
    Zipcode     CHAR(5),
    Phone       CHAR(8)  );
```

and

```
CREATE TABLE Purchase
    (Purchnum   SMALLINT,
    Prodnum     SMALLINT,
    Custnum     SMALLINT,
    Purchdat    DATE,
    Readydat    DATE,
    Kilos       DECIMAL(3,1)  );
```

The UNIQUE option is not available in some older versions of Oracle. Note the use of the comma with the DECIMAL data type.

When inserting the date *October 29, 1992,* legal variations include the following:

```
'29-Oct-92'    '29/Oct/92'
```

Oct may be expressed as *OCT.*

Chapter 2. On occasion, output is generated in a different order; for example, the following query shown in Figure 2-3b,

```
SELECT DISTINCT Zipcode FROM Customer;
```

generates the following zip codes:

```
91212, 91213, 91289, 91234, 91211, 91209
```

The query shown in Figure 2-8 may be expressed as

```
SELECT * FROM Purchase WHERE Readydat = '29/Oct/92';
```

Other legal date variations such as '29-Oct-92' may be used. The single quote marks are necessary.

Chapter 3. Strings in Oracle SQL are case-sensitive (uppercase vs. lowercase); thus, 'R' and 'r' are different. Older versions of Oracle use

```
! =
```

instead of

```
<>
```

to express "not equals," as in Figure 3-6b.

Chapter 4. Calculated values include two digits after the decimal point, except for whole numbers, which are displayed without a decimal point. NULL values appear as blanks; the ORDER BY clause places them at the beginning of the rows.

Chapter 5. The query illustrated in Figure 5-1 generates output in purchase-number order. To generate output in customer-number order, reverse the order of the tables in the FROM clause.

The UNION and UNION ALL commands (Figures 5-4a, 5-4b, and 5-5) do not work with some older versions of Oracle.

Chapter 6. When loading data into the Product table, code the description as

```
'Millionaire''s Macadamia Mix'
```

The data appears in the table as

```
'Millionaire's Macadamia Mix'
```

The ALTER TABLE statement is coded as follows:

```
ALTER TABLE Purchase ADD (Pickdel CHAR(1) );
```

Chapter 7. The order, and sometimes the number, of rows output may differ from the in-text queries. For example, the Oracle SQL version of the query shown in Figure 7-5b generates output whose order is somewhat different from that in the text.

The EXISTS command (Figures 7-9 and 7-10) does not work with some older versions of Oracle.

Chapter 8. The query shown in Figure 8–9 generates output in customer-number order. To reject entries with duplicate key values, code a CREATE UNIQUE INDEX for the key in question. The WITH CHECK OPTION command (Figure 8-11) does not work with some older versions of Oracle.

Saving Queries

As we will see shortly, it can be very practical to run a given query repeatedly. Oracle enables users to do this with an extension to standard SQL. The SAVE command stores a query for future use. The START command retrieves the query from storage and executes it. For example, run the familiar query

```
SELECT * FROM Purchase;
```

and then enter the SAVE ALLPURCH command. To display the entire Purchase table, simply enter the START ALLPURCH command. We apply this feature in the next section.

Report Formatting

We have already noted standard SQL's inflexible output. Oracle remedies these drawbacks in several ways. Simple commands provide titles, changed column headers, and a dollar sign and commas for numbers, and compute subtotals for groups of rows. We illustrate some of these features with the following query:

```
SELECT   Purchnum, Kilos, Kilos*Unitprice
  FROM   Purchase, Product
 WHERE   Purchase.Prodnum = Product.Prodnum
   AND   Purchnum <= 1236
 ORDER   BY Purchnum;
```

which generates the following results:

PURCHNUM	KILOS	KILOS*UNITPRICE
1234	3.5	35
1235	15	135
1236	2	20
1236	3.7	38.85

To improve the output, first enter the SAVE PURCH command to save the query. Test the effect of the following commands by entering the given command and then the START PURCH command. (Do *not* enter a semicolon (;) after any of these commands.)

Command	*Effect*
COLUMN Kilos*Unitprice HEADING 'Price'	Creates a shorter column header.
COLUMN Kilos*Unitprice FORMAT $999.99	Makes the column more legible, lining up values and adding a $.
COLUMN Kilos FORMAT 99.9	
BREAK ON Purchnum SKIP 1	Separates each group of purchase-number rows.
COMPUTE SUM OF Kilos ON Purchnum	Calculates total kilos for each group of purchase-number rows.
COMPUTE SUM OF Kilos*Unitprice ON Purchnum	

The final output should look something like:

PURCHNUM	KILOS	Price
1234	3.5	$35.00
*********	3.5	$35.00
1235	15.0	$135.00
*********	3.5	$135.00
1236	2.0	$20.00
	3.7	$38.85
*********	5.7	$58.85

Consult your system manuals for further information on improving system output.

Getting Started with SQL/DS

Introduction

This appendix concretely illustrates compatibility between SQL/DS and the approximately standard SQL applied throughout the text. Using an IBM 9370 mainframe computer running VM and SQL/DS Version 2 Release 2, the author created and loaded Noga's tables and ran the SQL commands appearing in the figures of Chapters 1 to 8. We accessed this computer via an IBM-compatible 386 microcomputer. Some of the following results may be related to the specific hardware and software setup we used. Run all examples yourself, and record your findings.

General Comments

Note any differences between your installation's start-up procedure and the following steps:

1. Start the computer. (In response to system prompts, we entered our pre-assigned user name and password.)
2. Start SQL/DS with the appropriate command. (We entered *ISQL* (for interactive SQL) followed by a carriage return.)

When you have completed this process, the screen displays a message such as

```
PLEASE ENTER AN ISQL OR SQL COMMAND
```

Note, SQL/DS commands need not terminate with a semicolon (;). Entering a minus sign (−) at the end of a line continues input onto the next line. Erroneous commands generate several lines, including an error message such as

```
ARI0503E AN SQL ERROR HAS OCCURRED. SQL COMMAND BEGINS PROPERLY
```

```
BUT IS INCOMPLETE
```

followed by technical information.

On our implementation, entered commands may be repeated using the F12 function key. The Insert mode is obtained by pressing the *Ins* key, and is indicated by a boldface ^ on the right-hand side of the screen. It must be activated for each query. Use the *Control* key and the left-arrow key or the right-arrow key on the numeric keypad to move the cursor from word to word.

Individual Chapters

Chapter 1. The following commands can be used to create the two central tables:

```
CREATE TABLE Customer
    (Custnum      SMALLINT,
    Custname      CHAR(18),
    Custtype      CHAR(1),
    Custaddr      CHAR(15),
    Zipcode       CHAR(5),
    Phone         CHAR(8) );
```

and

```
CREATE TABLE Purchase
    (Purchnum     SMALLINT,
    Prodnum       SMALLINT,
    Custnum       SMALLINT,
    Purchdat      DATE,
    Readydat      DATE,
    Kilos         DECIMAL(3,1) );
```

The UNIQUE option is not available. Note the use of the comma with the DECIMAL data type.

The date *October 29, 1992,* is inserted as

```
'10/29/1992'
```

It is displayed as

```
1992-10-29
```

Chapter 2. The query shown in Figure 2-8 is expressed as:

```
SELECT * FROM Purchase WHERE Readydat = '10/29/1992';
```

Chapter 3. Strings in SQL/DS SQL are not case-sensitive (that is, uppercase vs. lowercase); thus 'R' and 'r' are treated exactly the same. In all our examples, SQL/DS displays uppercase characters only.

Chapter 4. The number of digits after the decimal point depends on the specific calculation. One column in the query shown in Figure 4-2 contains data with 12 digits after the decimal point. Unlike many SQL implementations, all data within any given column have the same number of digits after the decimal point in SQL/DS.

NULL values appear as blanks; the ORDER BY clause places them at the beginning of the rows. Column headers are often long. The last header for the query shown in Figure 4-8 is

```
COUNT(EXPRESSION 1)
```

The query in Figure 4-13 is illegal in SQL/DS. It generates an error message that includes the following:

```
"AN ARITHMETIC EXPRESSION WITH A DATE/TIME IS INVALID"
```

Chapter 5. The query illustrated in Figure 5-4b generates customer numbers in the following order: 22, 41, 41, 1, 24, 39, 41. The query in Figure 5-5 generates CUSTNUM CUSTNUM as column headers.

Chapter 6. When loading data into the Product table, code the description as

```
'Millionaire''s Macadamia Mix'
```

The data appears in the table as

```
'Millionaire's Macadamia Mix'
```

The ALTER TABLE statement is coded as follows:

```
ALTER TABLE Purchase ADD (Pickdel CHAR(1) );
```

After this command executes, the "Pickdel" column shows question marks to indicate that values should be entered. As the HELP screen indicates,

```
"The ALTER TABLE is also used to add referential constraints,
```

and to add, drop, activate, or deactivate primary and foreign keys."

Chapter 7. The order, and sometimes the number, of rows output may differ from the in-text queries. For example, the SQL/DS version of the query in Figure 7-5b generates output whose order is somewhat different from that in the text.

The query in Figure 7-11 generates output in different order than that shown within the body of the text. The first expression is displayed with three digits after the decimal point; the second expression is displayed with five digits after the decimal point.

Chapter 8. The query in Figure 8-8 will not run as such.

```
COUNT(Kilos)
```

must be replaced by

```
COUNT(*)
```

or

```
COUNT(DISTINCT Kilos)
```

The query in Figure 8-9 is rejected with an error message indicating

```
"YOU CANNOT PERFORM A JOIN ON A VIEW CONTAINING A GROUP-BY
CLAUSE OR A DISTINCT KEYWORD"
```

The WITH CHECK OPTION shown in Figure 8-11 does not work. To reject entries with duplicate key values, code a CREATE UNIQUE INDEX for the key in question.

Saving Queries

It can be very practical to run a given query repeatedly. SQL/DS enables users to do this with an extension to standard SQL. The STORE command stores a query for future use. The START command retrieves the query from storage and executes it. For example, we run the familiar query

```
SELECT * FROM Purchase;
```

and then enter the STORE ALLPURCH command. To display the entire Purchase table, simply enter the START ALLPURCH command.

Report Formatting

We have already noted standard SQL's inflexible output. SQL/DS remedies these drawbacks in several ways. Simple commands provide titles, changed column headers, and commas for numbers, and compute subtotals for groups of rows. We illustrate some of these features with the following query:

```
SELECT  Purchnum, Kilos, Kilos*Unitprice
  FROM  Purchase, Product
 WHERE  Purchase.Prodnum = Product.Prodnum
   AND  Purchnum <= 1236
 ORDER  BY Purchnum;
```

which generates the following results:

PURCHNUM	KILOS	EXPRESSION 1
1234	3.5	35.000
1235	15.0	135.000
1236	2.0	20.000
1236	3.7	38.850

To improve the output first, enter the STORE PURCH command to save the query. Test the effect of the following commands by entering the given command and then the START PURCH command. (Do *not* enter a semicolon (;) after any of these commands.)

Command	Effect
FORMAT COLUMN 'EXPRESSION 1' NAME 'Price'	Creates a shorter column header.
FORMAT COLUMN 'Price' DPLACES 2	Puts two decimal places in the Price column
FORMAT GROUP (PURCHNUM)	Separates each group of purchase-number rows; the space after the P in GROUP is mandatory.
FORMAT SUBTOTAL (KILOS Price)	Calculates total kilos and price for each group of purchase-number rows; no comma is allowed between these two fields.

The final output should look something like the following:

PURCHNUM	KILOS	Price
1234	3.5	35.00
**********	3.5	35.00
1235	15.0	135.00
**********	3.5	135.00

```
    1236           2.0           20.00
                   3.7           38.85
                   ___           _____
**********         5.7           58.85
```

Consult your system manuals for further information on improving system output.

Glossary

Aggregate function   function that generates elementary statistics, summarizing data for an entire table or for selected rows within a table.

Alias   temporary table name that obeys the SQL table-naming conventions; used with self-*joins* and other operations.

ALL operator   operator found in nested queries that determines whether a condition is satisfied by *all* values generated by the subquery.

ALTER TABLE   command used to modify a table's structure, such as adding a column.

AND operator   operator that combines two conditions, generating a True value if and only if both of the combined conditions are True.

ANY   operator found in nested queries that determines whether a condition is satisfied by *any* values generated by the subquery; equivalent to the SOME operator.

Arithmetic operator   special symbol used in calculations. SQL provides five arithmetic operators: ** or ^ for exponentiation, * for multiplication, / for division, + for addition, and − for subtraction.

Authorization identifier   user-supplied character string that, when validated, allows the user to access SQL.

AVG   aggregate function that calculates the average, or mean, of all selected values for a given column.

Base table   table defined with the CREATE TABLE command.

BETWEEN operator   the part of a SELECT statement that determines whether a column contains values within a given range.

CHARACTER   data type indicating that a column may contain letters, numbers, and special symbols such as (%); often abbreviated as CHAR.

Character string   group of characters, such as a name or an address.

Column   series of similar data items, such as customer numbers.

Command   single SQL instruction; also called *statement*.

COMMIT   statement that renders permanent a transaction's effect.

Compound condition   combination of two or more conditions, using operators such as AND and OR.

Condition   part of the WHERE clause that may be either True or False; for example, Zipcode = '91212'.

Correlated subquery   nested query whose inner query processes information generated by the outer query.

COUNT   aggregate function that counts the number of items in a table. COUNT(column) calculates the number of selected values for a given column. COUNT(*) calculates the total number of rows in a table.

CREATE INDEX   command used to define an index in a table.

CREATE UNIQUE INDEX   command used to define an index in a table; prohibits adding a record with a duplicate key.

CREATE TABLE   command used to define the columns in a table.

Cursor structure   part of an embedded SQL program that enables the host language, such as COBOL, to process a set of rows generated by SQL. Not to be confused with a cursor that points to part of the screen display.

Data   facts and figures that comprise the raw material supplied to a computer for processing.

Data control statements   commands, such as GRANT and REVOKE, that deal with users' right to access and process databases.

Data definition statements   commands, such as CREATE TABLE and ALTER TABLE, that operate on SQL table structures.

Data integrity   accuracy and consistency of data within a database. SQL provides several features that help ensure data integrity.

Data manipulation statements   commands, such as INSERT INTO and UPDATE, that enter, modify, or delete data within the SQL tables.

Data query statements   commands that retrieve data from one or more tables within a database. The key data query statement is the SELECT command, which is the single most widely used SQL command.

Data type   indication of the kind of data allowed in a given column.

Database   organized collection of associated data.

Database management system (DBMS)   collection of computer software that creates, organizes, and manages databases.

DATE   data type indicating that a column may contain legal dates.

DECIMAL   data type indicating that a column may contain numbers with decimal points.

DELETE   command used to erase rows in a table that meet specified conditions.

DISTINCT qualifier   part of a SELECT statement that suppresses rows that are exactly the same, and sorts the output.

DROP INDEX   command used to remove an index in a table.

DROP TABLE   command used to remove a table from a database.

DROP VIEW   command used to delete a view.

Embedded SQL   processing mode in which SQL statements are placed within another programming language.

Equi*join*   *join* operation in which rows are generated whenever the contents of the relevant columns are equal.

EXISTS operator   operator used with nested queries that has the value True when at least one row in the inner query would be generated.

Field   dBASE term corresponding to an SQL column.

File   dBASE term corresponding to an SQL table.

FLOAT   data type indicating that a column may contain numbers with decimal points.

Foreign key   column in one table whose values match those of a primary key in another table.

Formal SQL syntax   way to present SQL statements using special symbols such as '[ ]', which means that the enclosed item is optional.

FROM statement   part of a SELECT statement that indicates which table supplies the data.

GRANT statement   part of a SELECT statement that gives users access privileges to SQL objects such as tables.

GROUP BY clause   part of a SELECT statement that processes rows sharing a common characteristic such as purchase number; used with aggregate functions.

HAVING clause   part of a SELECT statement that applies a condition to a group of rows.

Hierarchy of operations   order in which the computer executes operations; for example, parentheses are executed prior to the AND operator.

Host language   programming language in which SQL statements are embedded.

Host variable   variable within a host programming language that is associated with a given column in an SQL table.

IN operator   part of a SELECT statement that determines whether the contents of a given column is among a list of values.

Index   pointer to the location of each row in a table or view; used to increase system efficiency.

Inner query   in a nested query the query within parentheses; also called *subquery*.

INSERT INTO   command used to fill a table with data.

INTEGER data type indicating that a column may contain whole numbers, that is, those without decimal points.

Interactive SQL processing mode that directly accesses a database, generating output destined for people rather than computer files.

join **operation** one operation that combines data from two or more tables.

Key one or more columns that uniquely identify rows within a table; also called *primary key*.

LIKE operator part of a SELECT statement that determines whether a column contains a character string that is similar to a user-supplied pattern.

Loading data entering data into a table; performed by using the INSERT INTO command.

Locking a table preventing users from accessing a table while another user is processing it. Some systems lock only affected records instead of locking the entire table.

Logic error error in which the query did not correctly express the user's information need but was executed by the computer.

Lookup table table containing values that help to classify values in another table; often used for data validation.

MAX aggregate function that calculates the maximum of all selected values for a given column.

MIN aggregate function that calculates the minimum of all selected values for a given column.

Naming conventions rules for assigning names to objects such as tables and columns.

Nested query query within another query.

NOT operator operator that generates a True value if the original value is False, and generates a False value if the original value is True.

NULL value missing or unknown value. Not the same as a blank value.

NUMERIC data type indicating that a column may contain numbers with decimal points.

OR operator operator that combines two conditions, generating a True value if one or both of the combined conditions is True.

ORDER BY clause part of a SELECT statement that sorts the output rows.

Outer query in a nested query the query outside the parentheses, which processes the value generated by the query within the parentheses.

Primary key one or more columns that uniquely identify rows within a table; also called *key*.

Primary key integrity   restriction that primary keys must be unique and not null.

Query   user-coded request for information from an SQL table.

Read-only view   view that does not allow UPDATE, DELETE, or INSERT commands.

REAL   data type indicating that a column may contain numbers with decimal points.

Record   dBASE term corresponding to an SQL row.

Referential integrity   restriction that each foreign key takes on either NULL values or values equal to that of the associated primary key.

Relational DBMS   database management system processing databases based on a series of tables.

Reserved words   terms that compose SQL's technical vocabulary. Should be used only as SQL intends.

REVOKE statement   statement that removes access privileges.

ROLLBACK   statement that reverses the effect of a transaction.

Row   collection of associated data items; for example, referring to a given customer or a given purchase.

SELECT statement   command that chooses rows from one or more tables according to specified criteria.

Self-*join*   command that *join*s a table to itself; used, for example, in finding pairs of rows that meet a specified condition.

SMALLINT   data type indicating that a column may contain small whole numbers, that is, those without decimal points. Correct use saves space with some SQL implementations.

SOME   operator found in nested queries that determines whether a condition is satisfied by *any* values generated by the subquery. Equivalent to the ANY operator.

Statement   single SQL instruction; also called *command*.

Structured Query Language (SQL)   computer language designed to process relational databases.

Subquery   in a nested query the query within parentheses; also called *inner query*.

SUM   aggregate function that calculates the sum of all selected values for a given column.

Syntax error   error that occurs when SQL's syntax or grammar rules have not been followed.

System catalog   collection of system tables.

Table   two-dimensional collection of rows and columns that forms part of a relational database.

Transaction   one or more SQL statements handled as a unit.

Transaction processing   SQL processing mode in which the system recognizes transactions, accepting or rejecting one or more SQL statements as a unit.

UNION ALL operator   command that combines the output of two or more separate SELECT statements, generating duplicates.

UNION query operator   command that combines the output of two or more separate SELECT statements, suppressing duplicates.

UPDATE command   statement used to modify the contents of a table.

User-defined words   words chosen by individuals to refer to objects such as column names and table names.

View   peoples' perception of base tables. A single base table may serve as the foundation of several views; several tables may be combined to form one view.

WHERE clause   part of a SELECT statement that generates only those rows meeting the selection criteria.

Index

Administration of database
  data integrity, 165–167
  issues related to, 152
  locking tables, 162–165
  roles in, 154
  security, 153–160
  system catalog, 167–169
  transaction processing, 160–162
Aggregate functions, 53–55
  AVG, 54
  COUNT, 54–55
  and GROUP BY clause, 58
  MAX, 54
  MIN, 54
  SUM, 54
Alias, 70
  misuse of, 123
ALL operator, and nested queries, 80,
  81–82, 85–86
ALTER TABLE, 5, 101, 103, 106
ALTER TABLE MODIFY, 103
AND operator, 36–37, 38, 48, 124
  combined with OR, 37–40
  and nested queries, 80, 81–82, 85–86
Arithmetic operators, 51–53, 63–64
  and dates, 62–63
  types of, 53
Authorization identification, 153–154
AVG, 54, 136

Base table, 131
BETWEEN operator, 44–45, 48

CHARACTER, 6, 7, 8, 24, 26
Character strings, 45
COBOL
  divisions of, 182–183

  See also Embedded SQL, in COBOL
Columns
  and commas, 22
  common errors related to, 73–74
  and data types, 6
  designation of, 21–22
  and keys, 91
  names of, 11
  naming conventions, 90
Commas
  and columns, 22
  separating table names, 73
COMMIT, 161–162, 164, 169
Comparisons, types in SQL, 26, 31
CONNECT, 161
Continuation character, 20
Correlated subquery, 119–122, 126
  incorrect coding of, 124–125
COUNT, 54–55
CREATE, 13–14, 176, 179
CREATE INDEX, 143
CREATE TABLE, 5, 12–13, 89, 92,
  101, 131, 147, 165
CREATE UNIQUE INDEX, 165
CREATE VIEW, 132, 147
Cursor and COBOL, 186–189
  closing cursor, 188–189
  declaring cursor, 187
  fetching records, 187–188
  opening cursor, 187

Data
  loading into tables, 95–96
  validation of, 30–31
Database case study, 193–211
  column descriptions, 194–196
  creating Smlworks table, 208–209

Database case study *(continued)*
    creating Works table, 204–208
    entering data into tables, 197–199,
        202–204
    entering date into tables, 209–211
    full version of database, 193–196
    modification of tables, 200–202
    small version of database, 196–199
Database management systems,
        relational database, 3–4
Databases, nature of, 3
Data control statements, 6
Data definition statements, 5
Data integrity, 131, 137–139, 165–167
    primary key integrity, 165
    referential integrity, 165–167
    WITH CHECK OPTION, 138
Data manipulation statements, 5
Data query statements, 5
Data security, increasing, 132–133
Data types, 6
    listing of, 7
DATE, 6, 7, 10
Dates
    and arithmetic operations, 62–63
    processing of, 27–28
DBA, 161
dBASE IV-SQL, 173–177
    creating central tables, 213–216
    and data-entry errors, 175–176
    entry problems, 174
    report formatting, 177
    start-up steps, 212–213
    terminology, 174
Deadlock, locking tables, 164
DECIMAL, 7, 9, 26
DELETE, 99, 100, 140, 158, 160, 161
Deleting
    indexes, 146
    rows, 99–100
    tables, 95
    views, 141
Delimiting a character string, 24
DESC, 29, 31, 143
DISTINCT, 22–24, 31, 55, 70, 76
DROP TABLE, 95, 100

Embedded SQL
    in COBOL, 182–186
    cursor structure, 186–189
    data entry, 181
    nature of, 180

output, 182
processing, 181–182
Equijoin, 71–72
Errors
    common errors, 56–57, 72–74
    common errors in SQL, 36, 42, 46
    common to SQL, 26–27
EXCLUSIVE MODE, 164
EXISTS operator, 116–118, 122, 126
    misuse of, 123–124
    use of, 117–118

Flexibility, increasing, 135–137
FLOAT, 7
Foreign key, keys, 165
FROM, 84

GRANT, 6, 153–159, 156, 159, 160, 161,
    167–169
GROUP BY, 57–59, 74, 110
    combining with other clauses, 61–62

HAVING, 60–61, 61
    combining with other clauses, 61–62
Host language, 180

Indexes, 143–146
    creating indexes, 143–146
    deleting indexes, 146
    purpose of, 143, 144
    unique index, 145
IN operator, 42–44, 48
    combined with NOT, 43–44
    and nested queries, 80, 81–82, 85–86
INSERT, 98, 99, 100, 140, 161, 176
INSERT INTO, 5, 12, 48, 95–96, 98, 100
INSERT INTO VALUES, 175, 179
INTEGER, 6, 7, 8, 9, 10, 26
Interface with other systems
    embedded SQL, 180–190
    SQL-dBASE IV interface, 173–177
    SQL-R:BASE interface, 178–180

Join operation, 67–74, 108–114
    combined with nested queries, 115–116
    common errors related to, 72–74
    equijoin, 71–72
    example of use, 68–70
    and nested queries, 83–84

self-join, 113–114
three-table join, 110–113
Keys
and columns, 91
foreign key, 165
primary key integrity, 165
Keystrokes, productivity tip, 64

LIKE operator, 45–46, 48
LOCK, 164–165, 169
Locking tables, 162–165
deadlock, 164
statements for, 163–165
LOCK TABLE, 163–164
Logic errors, 42, 56
Lookup table, 118–119
use of, 118–119

Math
aggregate functions, 53–55
arithmetic operators, 51–53
combining clauses, 61–62
GROUP BY clause, 57–59
HAVING clause, 60–61
MAX, 54
MIN, 54
MS-DOS symbols, error message, 46

Naming conventions, tables and
columns, 90
Nested queries, 78–84, 114–116
combined with join operation, 83–84,
115–116
common errors related to, 80–83
IN/AND/SOME/ALL operators in, 80,
81–82, 85–86
inner query/subquery, 78, 81
and several values, 80
NOT, 40–41, 48
combined with IN, 43–44
NOT NULL, 48, 90–91, 105
NULL, 54, 169
NULL value, 47
NUMERIC, 7

Operations, hierarchy of, 39
Operators
AND operator, 36–37
BETWEEN operator, 44–45
IN operator, 42–44

LIKE operator, 45–46
NOT operator, 40–41
OR and AND combined, 37–40
OR operator, 34–36
Oracle SQL, 217–221
creating central tables, 218–220
report formatting, 220–221
saving queries, 220
start-up steps, 217–218
ORDER BY, 28–30, 76
combining with other clauses, 61–62
OR operator, 34–36, 38, 48
combined with AND, 37–40

Parenthesis, and nested queries, 80–81
PRIMARY KEY, 48
Primary key integrity, 165

Queries
correlated subquery, 119–122
nested queries, 78–84
and simplicity, 133–134
UNION query operator, 75–78
writing queries, 18–21

R:BASE interface, 178–180
changing data structure, 179
data-entry errors, 179
and output, 180
Read-only views, 140–142
examples of, 140
updating view, 142
REAL, 6, 9, 26
Referential integrity, 165–167
Relational database, 3–4
setup, example of, 6–17
terms related to, 11
Report formatting, 177
SQL/DS, 226–227
Reserved words, 19, 31
RESOURCE, 161
REVOKE, 6, 159–160, 160, 167–169
ROLLBACK, 161, 161–162, 164, 169
Rows, 11–12
deleting, 99
designation of, 24–25

Security, 130, 153–160
authorization identification, 153–154
data security, increasing, 132–133
GRANT statement, 153–159

Security *(continued)*
  password, selection of, 169–170
  REVOKE statement, 159–160
SELECT, 5, 18–22, 32, 35, 46, 47, 52, 61, 74, 75, 84, 98, 99, 100, 103, 110, 115, 126, 132, 137, 147, 156, 157
  writing of, 18–21
SELECTed columns, 59
SELECT...FOR UPDATE OF, 164, 165
Self-join, 113–114, 125–126
SHARE MODE, 164
SMALLINT, 6, 7, 8, 9, 10, 26
SOME, and nested queries, 80, 81–82, 85–86
Spelling errors, 26–27
SQL/DS
  creating central tables, 223–225
  report formatting, 226–227
  saving queries, 225
  start-up steps, 222–223
Statements
  coding on several lines, 20
  types of, 5–6
Structured Query Language (SQL)
  development of, 5
  interface with other systems, 173–190
  types of statements, 5–6
SUM, 54, 136
Syntax
  formal SQL syntax, 155–156
  syntax errors, 27
System catalog, 167–169
  contents of, 167
  system tables, 168

Tables
  base table, 131
  common errors related to, 100
  creating customer table, 89–92
  creating product table, 94–95

creating purchase table, 92–94
deleting rows, 99–100
deleting tables, 95
loading data from, 95–96
naming conventions, 90
purpose of, 2–3
in SQL, 5
  system tables, 168
  updating structure of, 100–102, 104–105
  updating table values, 97–99
Transaction processing, 160–162
  COMMIT statement, 161–162
  ROLLBACK statement, 161–162

UNION, 75–78, 76, 160
  errors related to, 76
UNION ALL, 76
UNIQUE, 90–91, 105, 147
Unique index, 145
UNIQUE INDEX OPTION, 145
UNIQUE NOT NULL, 165, 169
UPDATE, 5, 97, 100, 101, 140, 156, 158, 161, 164, 175, 177, 180, 181
User-defined words, 19

VALUES, 95–96
VARCHAR, 7
View
  common errors related to, 141–142
  deleting view, 141
  disadvantages of, 142–143
  modifying view, 141
  read-only views, 140–142

WHERE, 24–25, 46, 48, 58, 59, 60, 61, 69, 72, 84, 126, 147, 175, 178, 179
WITH CHECK OPTION, 138, 147, 165
WITH GRANT OPTION, 159